DARK COMPANIONS

DARK COMPANIONS

The African contribution to the
European exploration of
East Africa

DONALD SIMPSON

BARNES & NOBLE BOOKS
10 East 53d St., New York 10022
(a division of Harper & Row Publishers, Inc.)

Published in the U.S.A. 1976 by
Harper & Row Publications, Inc.,
Barnes & Noble Import Division

First published 1976 by
Paul Elek Limited, London

ISBN 0-06-496273-3

Printed in Great Britain

CONTENTS

LIST OF PLATES

between pages 100 and 101

Plates 1 and 12 are reproduced by permission of the Royal Geographical Society; plates 2 and 3, 8 to 11, 13 to 15, 18 and 19 by permission of the Royal Commonwealth Society; plates 4 to 7 by permission of the Livingstone Memorial, Blantyre; plates 16 and 17 by permission of the Commonwealth Institute.

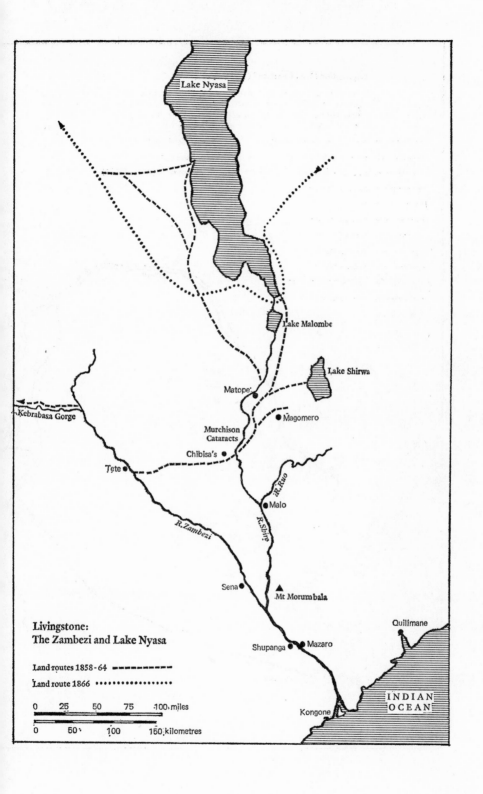

Lake Nyasa

Lake Malombe

Lake Shirwa

Matope

Magomero

Kebrabasa Gorge

Murchison
Cataracts

Chibisa's

Tete

R. Ruo

Malo

R. Shire

R. Zambezi

Sena

Mt Morumbala

Livingstone:
The Zambezi and Lake Nyasa

Land routes 1858-64 ▬▬▬▬▬

Land route 1866 ●●●●●●●●●●

Quillmane

Shupanga   Mazaro

INDIAN
OCEAN

Kongone

| 0 | 25 | 50 | 75 | 100 miles |

| 0 | 50 | 100 | 150 kilometres |

Exploration Map of East and Central Africa

Approximate routes only are shown, e.g. minor deviations on the journey to Unyanyembe are omitted, and only Livingstone's route from Lake Tanganyika to Nyangwe is indicated; those of Cameron and Stanley were similar but slightly more direct

—— —— ——	Main route, coast to Unyanyembe	Towns Mombasa Kitui
••••••••••	Burton & Speke 1857-59	Rivers Zambezi
—+—+—+—	Speke & Grant 1860-63	Races, areas and kingdoms MASAI
—·—·—·—	Livingstone 1866-73	
+··+··+	Stanley 1871	
—··—··—	Cameron 1873-75	
—·—·—··	Stanley 1874-77	
××××××××	Thomson 1879-80	
—×—×—×—	Thomson 1883-4	
×·×·×·×·×	Teleki & Hohnel 1887-88	
··×··×··×··×	Stanley 1887-89	

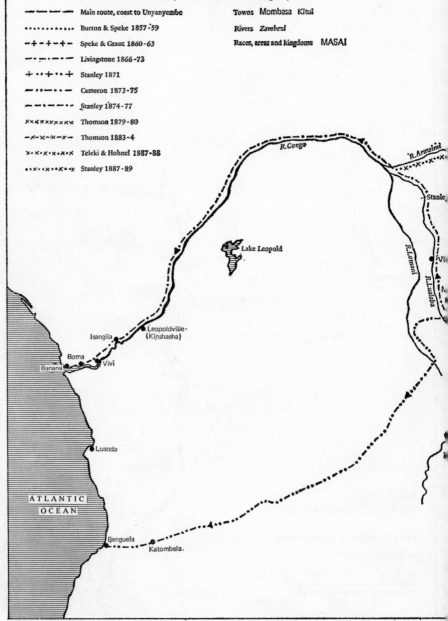

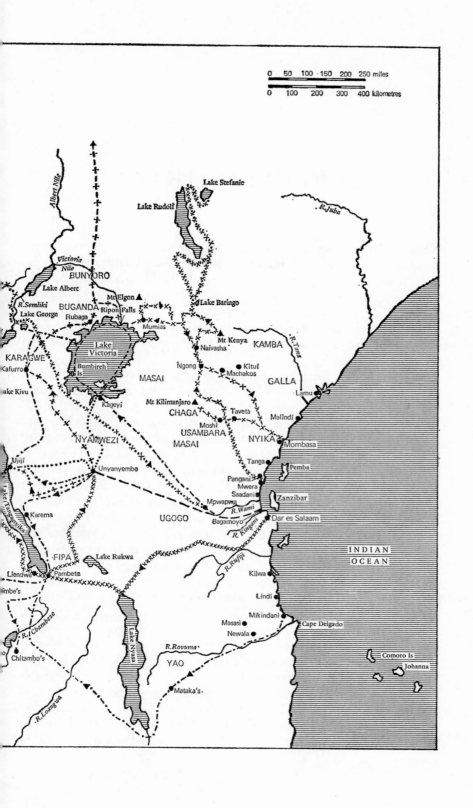

0 50 100 150 200 250 miles
0 100 200 300 400 kilometres

Albert Nile
Lake Stefanie
Lake Rudolf
R.Juba
Victoria Nile
BUNYORO
Lake Albert
R.Semliki
Mt Elgon
Lake George
BUGANDA
Ripon Falls
Rubaga
Mumias
Lake Baringo
Mt Kenya
KAMBA
KARAGWE
Lake Victoria
Naivasha
R.Tana
Kafurro
Bumbireh Is
Ngong
Kitui
Machakos
GALLA
Lake Kivu
MASAI
Lamu
Kageyi
Mt Kilimanjaro
CHAGA
Taveta
Malindi
NYAMWEZI
Moshi
USAMBARA
NYIKA
Mombasa
MASAI
Ujiji
Tanga
Pemba
Unyanyembe
Pangani
Mwera
Saadani
Karema
Mpwapwa
Zanzibar
R.Wami
UGOGO
Bagamoyo
Dar es Salaam
R.Kingani
FIPA
Lake Rukwa
R.Rufiji
INDIAN OCEAN
Liendwe
Pambete
Kilwa
imbe's
Lindi
R.Chambeze
Mikindani
Masasi
Newala
Cape Delgado
Lake Nyasa
Chitambo's
R.Rovuma
YAO
Comoro Is
Johanna
R.Loangwa
Mataka's

FOREWORD

When H. M. Stanley gave the title *My dark companions and their strange stories* to a book, he was referring to legends and fables told by his African followers. Their own lives, however, could have furnished even stranger stories, for the personnel of the caravans which explored east Africa in the nineteenth century included many men whose careers spanned twenty or more years, and whose courage, versatility, and endurance were essential to the successes of the European explorers of the era.

Apart from Dr Edwin Smith's unpublished *An African Odyssey*, no book has been written on the lives and work of such Africans, but in a number of articles and notes contributed to the *Uganda Journal* and *Tanganyika Notes and Records* from 1949 onwards, Sir John Gray and H. B. Thomas demonstrated that evidence could be gathered to trace the careers of Majwara and other followers of David Livingstone. It was my privilege to know and work with these two great amateur pioneers of the study of African history, and to benefit from their encyclopaedic knowledge of sources, and their unpublished memoranda, in the first stages of this book. Its aim is to trace the careers of the most significant Africans involved in the European exploration of a wide area of Africa extending inland from the coast between Somaliland and the Zambezi River. It does not attempt to give a comprehensive account of the exploration as such, but to outline its course as the setting in which the Africans worked and the reason for their engagement.

First-hand African sources are regrettably meagre. The longest account from the African viewpoint is the notebook compiled by Horace Waller from the conversations of Chuma and Susi about Livingstone's last days and their journey to the coast with his body; in using this material for *The Last Journals of David Livingstone*, he amended and polished it a good deal, and it is here quoted in its original form. Shorter accounts by Carus Farrar and Matthew Wellington have also been drawn on. All these sources, however, were recorded by Europeans, and there is no document comparable with Tippu Tip's autobiography to give us the African's opinion of his employer. An attempt has, however, been made to assemble scattered references in published and unpublished works by explorers, missionaries and administrators, which depict the most significant African caravan leaders, interpreters, and others in European service, and to present as honest a picture as possible of the virtues and faults, the successes and failures, of their characters and careers. In some cases the understanding reached between Europeans and Africans gives such records a considerable insight.

In general the spelling of African names follows the usage of the International African Institute's bibliographies, and of the *Oxford History of East Africa*. Geographical names have been given in their contemporary rather than their modern form, so that Lake Malawi and the river Zaire, for example, appear as Lake Nyasa and the Congo. A glossary of African words has been included.

I have been fortunate in the generous cooperation of many friends and colleagues. A. T. Matson has assisted not only from his far-reaching knowledge of east African history but by his constructive and stimulating criticisms. Among many to whom I am indebted in diverse ways I would also like to thank Roy Bridges, Dick Cashmore, William Cunningham, Ian Cunningham, Richard Hall, Dorothy Helly, Brenda Hough, Margaret Hughes, Rosemary Keen, A. J. Keevill, Christine Kelly, Dorothy Middleton, George Shepperson, Kenneth Timings, Rozina Visram and Jean Woods. As Librarian of the Royal Commonwealth Society, I have been enabled to make use of its extensive resources in published and unpublished material of African exploration.

I am grateful for the permission to quote from original material which has been given by Richard Stanley, the Controller of Her Majesty's Stationery Office (for documents in the Public Record Office) and the governing bodies of the other institutions listed in the bibliography, and for their ready assistance in my research. Quotations from the Pocock diaries are from the transcript made by Nicola Harris, by permission of Richard Hall and Rhodes House.

My wife Patricia has given me invaluable help by her typing of successive drafts of this book, and by her perceptive and constructive comments on it.

I

THE BACKGROUND TO EXPLORATION

At the beginning of the nineteenth century the map of Africa showed a few settlements and trading posts along the coasts; the interior was filled in with speculative and semi-legendary geographical features and countries, but virtually no reliable information existed. A century later only comparatively small areas were still unexplored; the physical pattern of mountain ranges, the flow of the great waterways, including the solution to the ancient mystery of the source of the Nile, and the routes into the interior were recorded and mapped. A growing mass of written records described the peoples and natural history of the continent. The completion of the map of Africa was the work of men of diverse backgrounds and motives—explorers and scientists, missionaries and philanthropists, traders and settlers, and, eventually, as European rule was established in Africa, administrators and soldiers.

The different areas of the continent presented their individual problems to the traveller, but there were some general features common to all. To the natural hazards of terrain and climate were added the hostility—real or imagined—of Africans and wild animals. Unknown diseases afflicted men and beasts; food supplies had to be taken or bartered for on the journey; scientific instruments, camping equipment, and weapons had to be carried; and the traveller had to try to make himself understood in strange languages, and to elicit information from people to whom his purposes might seem baffling, even if they comprehended his words.

The solution of these difficulties depended largely on two related factors—manpower and transport. In west Africa some rivers were at least partially navigable; camels were used in travel southward from the Mediterranean coast, and in south Africa the ox-waggon covered great distances.

Such methods were not possible on the east of the continent. Though various attempts were made to penetrate the interior by rivers, these

I

met with very little success. Tsetse, diseases and wild animals killed off most of the various beasts of burden tried. The basic method of transport was therefore by manpower, which was organised in caravans, made up principally of porters (*pagazi*) but with a sprinkling of specialists—*askari* or soldiers to provide protection; cooks and personal servants; interpreters and guides who were often engaged temporarily for their local knowledge; and men to handle animals and boats. The success of an expedition depended to a large extent on the choice of Africans or Asians as NCOs, who helped to control the main caravan, which might consist of several hundred men, sometimes with women and children, or took command of temporarily detached parties. Individuals of this kind might be valuable helpers to one explorer but prove disappointing to another, who in his turn would find among subordinates the men on whom he could particularly rely.

The leader of an expedition could in some cases earn the respect, loyalty and often affection of his followers, so that men from a variety of tribes with different backgrounds, languages, customs and religions worked harmoniously together. His followers, on their part, had not only to adapt themselves to living in close association with comrades, some of whose customs could be strange or even abhorrent, but also to obey a leader whose orders, whims, outbursts of temper, and standards of judgment were inexplicable to them.

It was upon such men as these that explorers had to rely for sustenance and support in journeys which succeeded, during a span of some fifty years, in recording topographical and other information on the vast area extending inland from the Indian Ocean seaboard, reaching Somaliland in the north and the Portuguese territories in the south.

The European explorers were not, at least in their early days, breaking new ground in their journeys. Archaeological evidence has established that during the early iron age, in the first millenium AD, Africans travelled hundreds of miles in order to barter their local products in exchange for the wares of other races. Among the major trading peoples were the Nyamwezi, who occupied the tableland extending south of Lake Victoria. Trade developed chiefly in the valued but localised commodities of iron and salt, and donkeys were bred as transport animals. By the early nineteenth century the Nyamwezi, who had built up a tradition of caravan organisation, with skill in the carrying of heavy loads and specialised duties, were trading with the coast. Nyamwezi elephant hunters also travelled outside their own area in quest of ivory and built up a considerable trade in this commodity.[1]

Along the coast farther to the north the Swahili, of mixed Asian and African blood, initiated commercial links with the interior. Caravans were sent to the Chaga people of Mount Kilimanjaro, but more important was the trade conducted with the hinterland through the

2

Nyika people, inland from Mombasa. Beyond them, in the direction of the Tana River, were the Kamba who engaged in ivory hunting and general trading, and acted as middlemen between the coast and inland tribes such as the Kikuyu of Mount Kenya.

These existing trade routes into the interior were given greater importance early in the nineteenth century by the increased demand for ivory in the world market and the growing Arab involvement with east Africa. Muslim settlement on the coast probably began in the thirteenth century, but did not become a significant factor in Indian Ocean trade until after the Portuguese had been driven out at the end of the seventeenth century. The real establishment of Arab rule dates from Seyyid Said bin Sultan, who became ruler of Oman, claiming authority over Zanzibar and the adjoining coast, in 1804. He steadily consolidated his power in his Asian and African dominions, which he ruled from Zanzibar after 1840, with virtual control of the coast from the Juba River to Cape Delgado, though his authority did not extend far inland. Having a keen eye for commercial development, he encouraged the growing Arab trade with the interior.

Arab merchants began to use the established African routes in the 1820s and 1830s, and engaged Nyamwezi carriers for this purpose. In the 1840s Unyanyembe, an area in the heart of Nyamwezi country, became increasingly important, and an Arab settlement, which soon became the centre of an entrepôt trade, was established in a locality known as Kazeh or Tabora. Another base for the Arab trade was Ujiji, on Lake Tanganyika, and in the early 1840s the merchant Ahmed bin Ibrahim penetrated north of Lake Victoria to the kingdom of Buganda, whose prosperity was based on settled agriculture. Other Arabs established routes south to Lake Nyasa.

As a result, coastal towns developed as ports for the inland trade, among them Bagamoyo which, situated opposite Zanzibar, became a major point of departure for caravans, Tanga and Pangani. Mombasa served the Swahili-based trade farther north and, to the south, Kilwa was the main outlet for the slave trade which drew on the Yaos and other races of the area towards Lake Nyasa.

Zanzibar, the centre through which commerce flowed, developed as a cosmopolitan island; Said encouraged European and Asian merchants to settle there. Among these were Indians, who provided much of the capital for inland trading centres and facilities for the disposal of ivory and other commodities brought back by caravans. They also took over the lucrative customs administration. The Maria Theresa dollar, with a value equivalent to an American dollar or 4 English shillings, became the standard currency in areas where coinage rather than barter was used, though Indian coinage, with a rupee worth about 2 shillings, was also used in Zanzibar.[2]

3

The maritime trade was partly with Asia and with the islands of the Indian Ocean, but Said encouraged shipping from farther afield. American merchants from Salem took to visiting Zanzibar, and the first Consul appointed there, in 1836, was the United States representative. A British Consul, Atkins Hamerton, who was also Agent of the British East India Company, arrived at Zanzibar in 1841, and in later years French, German and other diplomatic representatives followed.

Zanzibar was thus the gateway to east Africa for the Europeans who, in diverse ways, opened the interior of the continent.

2

THE FIRST EUROPEAN EXPLORERS IN EAST AFRICA

At the close of 1843 Johann Ludwig Krapf, who had already spent five years in Ethiopia, arrived in east Africa to establish a base for the Church Missionary Society. Although he was above all a dedicated missionary, he found throughout his career that, in pursuing his evangelical objectives, he was undertaking other tasks. He first employed his linguistic skills in learning Swahili, then extended his studies to other east African languages. He recorded details of the people and country and, visualising a chain of mission stations eventually stretching across the continent, sought to discover all he could of the unknown interior.[1]

Initially he settled at Mombasa, hoping that he could develop friendly relations with the neighbouring Nyika and the widely travelled Kamba, and he was aided in this by Abdalla ben Pisila, a man of some local influence whom he had been able to help. It was through Abdalla's good offices that Krapf, with his newly arrived colleague Johannes Rebmann, was able in 1846 to establish a mission at Rabai, not far from Mombasa.

A year later, Krapf and Rebmann began a series of ventures into what was then unexplored territory. They experienced some difficulties in recruiting followers, and, with the support of a letter of recommendation which Krapf had obtained from Said bin Sultan before settling on the mainland, sought the help of the Arab Governor of Mombasa. On his advice, they engaged Bana Kheri, a widely travelled Swahili trader of the town, as a guide and interpreter, and undertook several journeys with small bodies of Nyika or Swahili carriers under his leadership in the ensuing eighteen months. Bana Kheri told Krapf of his travels in the interior, and of sailing for eight days 'on the waters of the great inland sea Uniamesi'. Krapf also heard of Lakes Tanganyika and Nyasa, but could not be sure whether they were separate lakes, or parts of one vast sheet of water.

5

Rebmann first went with Bana Kheri to the Taita people of Kadiaro, a mountain visible from Rabai, then undertook a longer expedition to the Chaga country. On 11 May 1848 he became the first white man to see the peak of Kilimanjaro, though he was ridiculed by armchair geographers when he described it as snow-capped. Krapf explored to the south and south-west of Mombasa, and was well received by Kimweri, the ruler of Usambara. Rebmann paid a second successful visit to Chaga but when, encouraged by the friendly attitude of the ruler Mamkinga, he went there a third time in April 1849, hoping to find a route to Unyamwezi, he suffered from illness and from the hostility of Mamkinga who plundered him and his thirty followers. Krapf and Rebmann attributed this change of attitude to the influence of Bana Kheri, who for some unexplained reason had become hostile to the missionaries.[2] Soon after, the Swahili trader was killed by the Masai while returning from Chaga to Mombasa.

Krapf took a Nyika, Mana Zahu, as guide when he set out with Nyika and Swahili carriers to visit the Kamba the following November. His men proved troublesome; they were disheartened by rumours of the hostility of Galla and Masai, and by the lack of water, and eventually demanded more pay. They had been given an advance of 3 dollars, and a promise of 5 more, but now declared that the advance pay had already been spent on their families, and the remaining 5 dollars should be doubled. In addition they demanded any ivory that Krapf might be given by the Kamba chief Kivoi. Faced with the threat of desertion, and even of attack, Krapf let their fury exhaust itself and then agreed to pay 10 dollars, or even 13, 'if the demand were recognised as a just one by the authorities at the coast'. At the next village he found a friendly welcome from Kivoi and though Krapf, who was unwell, declined his offer to escort him farther, Kivoi supplied beads and cloth to exchange for food, and admonished the Nyika to take Krapf back to Rabai in safety 'for he is my friend'. As Krapf left, he caught a distant glimpse of Mount Kenya.

Several missionaries were sent out by the CMS, but the only one to stay for long was J. J. Erhardt, who arrived in June 1849. The following year he accompanied Krapf along the coast from Mombasa to Cape Delgado in a small Swahili vessel, whose captain, a Mwera born in Kilwa, had once journeyed to the Yao country, near Lake Nyasa. Krapf also obtained other information about the interior from Nyamwezi traders and learned of a Swahili who had journeyed from Kilwa to Lake Nyasa and thence to Loango on the west coast. After this voyage, he went to England on leave; the Church Missionary Society endorsed his policy of travelling, particularly aiming towards Unyamwezi, and instructed him to open new stations.[3]

Returning to Africa in April 1851, he resumed his journeys three

6

months later with thirty Nyika under Mana Zahu. His goal was the Kamba area, one of those suggested for a mission station, but the journey went badly; most of his men turned back after an attack by a party of robbers had been beaten off. Kivoi again welcomed Krapf, and offered to escort him to the Tana River, whence he could return to Mombasa to recruit Swahilis to build the proposed station. Krapf accepted, and they set off with a party about fifty strong, but Kivoi was killed and his followers routed when they were ambushed in a forest by a superior force of his enemies. Krapf, left alone, was un-injured but endured hunger, thirst and many hardships in the following days, and later met with hostility from the Kamba, who blamed him for failing to save Kivoi. He was eventually able to return to Rabai with a small party of Nyika. Since the Kamba mission seemed hopeless, Krapf returned to Usambara with a few followers including a Nyika named Abbe Gunja (who was later baptised) and secured Kimweri's formal permission to establish a mission. He himself, however, could not follow this up, for his health suffered and he was unable to under-take further journeys.

The travels of Krapf and Rebmann stimulated European interest in Africa, and though they did not themselves penetrate far into the interior, they experienced many of the problems that were to confront future travellers, considerably magnified when leaders had to control and rely on much larger and more mixed bodies of men for longer periods. The CMS had considered that 'a long and perilous Mis-sionary tour affords to your heathen companions the most affecting sermons which a Missionary can preach. When they see him sharing with them the hardships of a houseless desert, and the dangers of an hostile country, for the sake of making known his message . . . they are receiving instruction in the most persuasive form.' The reality was more complex. Rebmann had deplored the use of 'magic sticks' by his Nyika porters for protection on a journey. On the other hand, Bana Kheri, as an orthodox Muslim, had protested at Krapf's readiness to eat pork and other meat killed by the Nyika, and called him *mkafiri*, or unbeliever. Krapf learned tolerance by experience and on a later journey issued his Swahili followers with beads to buy fowls when they objected to eating food provided by the Kamba.

In September 1853 Krapf left for Europe, leaving Rebmann and Erhardt to carry on the mission work, and reached Cairo in November. Another traveller visiting the city at the same time was Lieutenant Richard Burton, who had just returned from a journey in disguise to Medina and Mecca, and was eager to consider new enterprises. He heard Krapf's accounts of the journeys he and Rebmann had under-taken, and of the stories of the interior obtained from African travellers. Though partly incredulous, Burton turned his thoughts to exploring east Africa and persuaded the Royal Geographical Society to sponsor an expedition to Somaliland, which might possibly be extended as far south as the coast adjoining Zanzibar.[4] Burton, given leave from the army to lead it, arrived in Aden in May 1854 to begin preparations.

The following September, Lt John Hanning Speke arrived in Aden on leave from India, intending to undertake a hunting expedition in Africa, but when objections were raised by local officials owing to the dangers of travel on the mainland, he agreed to join Burton as second-in-command, and the latter welcomed Speke's experience, obtained during hunting and surveying journeys in India and Tibet. It was not possible to begin the main expedition immediately, so it was decided that meanwhile Burton should strike south-west to the mysterious city of Harar, while Speke would explore to the eastward. Burton, with his experience of travel in Arab lands, and his linguistic skills, successfully led a small expedition to Harar, and thence reached Berbera, the proposed starting-point for the major journey in January 1855.[5]

Speke was not at the rendezvous; he had in fact returned to Aden, which he reached on 20 February after a frustrating and largely unsuccessful four-month journey. Somali custom required that a traveller should be provided with an *Abban*, or protector, to be 'broker, escort, agent, and interpreter'. The Abban whom Burton had found for Speke at Aden was Sumunter (or Mohammed Sammattar), a Warsingali Arab; his interpreter, Ahmed, who spoke a little Hindustani, was from the same tribe, an arrangement which was realised in retrospect to be a mistake. Speke engaged a Hindustani butler, Imam, and, as a guard, Farhan, an African who had been kidnapped in infancy by an Arab trader on the Zanzibar coast, and had eventually escaped from slavery. Such Africans were sometimes known in Asia as Seedis, a corruption of the Hindustani 'Sidi' meaning 'My Lord', which had originally been applied to visiting chiefs. Farhan was 'a perfect Hercules in stature, with huge arms and limbs, knit together with largely developed ropy-looking muscles. He had a large head, with small eyes, flabby squat nose, and prominent muzzle filled with sharp-pointed teeth, as if in imitation of a crocodile.'

Burton summed up the hazards of travel in Somaliland: 'It is every man's interest to detain you because he and his friends are devouring your rice and dates. It is every man's interest to mislead you because in some distant village he has an uncle or cousin who wants your cloth. These impositions must be endured with patience.' Speke experienced such frustrations to the full. Six weeks passed between his leaving Aden and his departure from the coastal region on 4 December. Delays over transport animals, pay disputes, the intervention of Sumunter's creditors, and local hostility were all factors, and Speke was dismayed to learn from the local Sultan that the office of Abban gave its holder far-

8

reaching rights over the movements and property of the individual he was 'protecting'.

One comforting aspect was the loyalty of the African Farhan. When he was offered a bribe to desert Speke 'the noble-hearted Seedi disclosed their treachery, and gallantly said that he would share misfortune with me, and fight, if necessary, to the last extremity'. During a skirmish between Speke's escort and some other Somalis who wished to have their share in plundering the Englishman, Farhan 'enjoyed the row in the boisterous characteristic manner of a Seedi'.

On 18 January, after weeks of minimal progress, Speke abandoned his attempt and returned to the coast, and in February he crossed to Aden in company with Sumunter, who had a wife and business interests there. In spite of his exasperation, Speke did not wish to take further action against the unsatisfactory Abban—'I was averse to punishing him, from the simple fact of having brought him over; but my commandant thought otherwise, and that he had better be punished, if for no other reason than to set a good moral example to the others.' Sumunter was therefore tried, and sentenced to two months' imprisonment, and a fine.

Speke now travelled to Berbera, purchasing camels on the way, with a small armed escort, Imam, Farhan, and a new guide and interpreter, Mahmud Goolad, nicknamed al Balyuz, or the envoy, for his skill as a negotiator. He had been engaged on the recommendation of the Assistant Political Agent at Aden and proved to be honest, reliable, and a good Hindustani scholar. 'Travelling in his company, after my experiences with Sumunter and Ahmed, was verily a luxury', wrote Speke.

Camp was pitched outside the town, and Burton, Speke, two fellow-officers, Lt Herne and Lt Stroyan, and their servants and escort made preparations to set off, but on the night of 18–19 April the camp was attacked by a strong force of Somalis. The reason for the attack, and the exact details of a confused and tragic night, are not clear. Thanks largely to the resource and courage of al Balyuz, Burton, despite a javelin-thrust through his face, and Herne reached the safety of the shore, but Stroyan was killed and Speke captured. After being stabbed several times while bound, the latter managed to scramble up, fend off his assailants with his tied fists, and run through his captors to safety. The survivors reached Aden three days later, and as soon as Burton and Speke had recovered from their wounds, they returned to military duties in the Crimean War.[6]

3
THE SEARCH FOR THE NILE SOURCES

While these events were taking place, Rebmann and Erhardt prepared a map of the interior of Africa which was published in Germany in January 1856. They had assumed that all the reports of lakes in the interior referred to one huge body of water, and this appeared on their map in a grotesque shape described as being like a slug.

This stimulated interest in the subject, and the Royal Geographical Society accepted Burton's offer to lead an expedition designed to discover the source of the Nile. In September 1856 he obtained two years' leave from the army. He wished Speke to accompany him, and both men travelled to Bombay where in November Speke was also granted the necessary leave.[1]

They left Bombay on 3 December taking with them two Goanese servants, Valentine Rodrigues and Gaetano Andrade, whom Burton had engaged there, and reached Zanzibar in sixteen days. The powerful Said bin Sultan had recently died, and his son Majid ruled over his African possessions. With the aid of the British Consul, Colonel Hamerton, Burton and Speke were cordially received by the Sultan and, in spite of some local suspicions as to their purpose, began to prepare their expedition.

The experiences of Krapf and Rebmann, the fate of Maizan, a young French explorer killed by the Kamba while inadequately escorted, and Burton and Speke's own journeys in Somaliland, demonstrated the importance both of utilising the protection of such authority as the Sultan of Zanzibar and his officials exercised on the mainland, and of taking a reliable escort into potentially hostile country. As a first step, therefore, a caravan leader was obtained through a cousin of the late Sultan. The man chosen was Said bin Salim el Lamki, a half-caste Arab, born some forty years before in Kilwa where his father was the governor. Burton described him with unloving care—his wiry, woolly hair, scanty mustachios and meagre beard. 'Short,

10

thin and delicate; a kind of man for the pocket; with weak and prominent eyes, the long protruding beak of a young bird, loose lips, and regular teeth dyed by betel to the crimson of chess-men . . .' Although he had commanded Saadani he was an ineffective leader and lacked courage and powers of endurance. He did, however, represent the authority of the Sultan, and could vouch for the purpose of the expedition. He knew the coast well, and in the preliminary journeys proved useful and apparently loyal.

Burton was advised by Hamerton not to travel in the dry season, but to use the intervening time in learning something of the coast and gaining experience of organisation. Accompanied by Said and the Goanese servants, he and Speke therefore left Zanzibar on 6 January 1857 on an Arab vessel, with a scratch crew. After visiting Rebmann at Mombasa, they travelled down the coast, hearing at Tanga and Mombasa some reports of the geography of the interior. At Pangani, Burton decided to attempt a journey to Vuga, the capital village of Usambara, and paid off the dhow. The local officials were uncooperative, but the Jemadar in command of the garrison at Chokwe and Tongwe, about seven miles inland, offered help. Accordingly, Said and Gaetano were left at Pangani and, hiring a canoe and four men, ostensibly for a shooting expedition, Burton, Speke and Valentine set off up the Pangani River.

On 8 February they reached Chokwe, a bleak and unhealthy town with a small hill fort garrisoned by twenty-five Baluchis. These were part of a mercenary force first recruited by Sultan bin Ahmad, father of Said bin Sultan, to provide a body that was unlikely to be involved in the feuds of his Arab subjects and thus be able to help assure his authority. Baluchistan lies along the Asian mainland, across what are now the borders of Iran and Pakistan, and the recruits were drawn from the main towns of Kech and Bampur, or from the Makran coast along its seaboard. Some were able fighting men, but over the years this foreign legion had absorbed mercenaries of many races, becoming 'mixed up with a rabble rout of Arabs and Afghans, of Sidis and Hindostan men. The corps spoke some half-a-dozen different languages, and many of the members have left their country for their country's good . . .' wrote Burton. They were paid 2 or 3 dollars a month, from which they had to provide rations and equipment, and their garrisons were commanded by Jemadars at 4 to 5 dollars, who had considerable scope for peculation and petty extortion.

The Jemadar at Chokwe obtained volunteers for Burton and Speke, who left Tongwe on the 10th with a small force consisting of a Swahili guide and his slave, six soldiers, and four slaves—'idle worthless dogs'. Four of the soldiers were Baluchis and one, Hamdan, an Arab from Muscat. The sixth was not an Asian, but an African, a Yao by birth, from the widespread race whose homeland was in the region of Lake Nyasa. When he was twelve a party of Swahilis had surrounded his village and, claiming payment of debts arising from their trading activities in previous years, seized a number of the inhabitants, of whom he was one, as compensation. From Kilwa the captives were shipped to Zanzibar where they were sold as slaves. He became the property of an Arab merchant who took him to India, where he served until freed by his master's death. His original African name had been lost, and he became known by that of the city where his master had lived, Bombay. Returning to Zanzibar, he had enlisted as a soldier and been posted to Chokwe. Bombay was a small man, with a head 'like a barber's block', in Speke's words, or with 'a high narrow cranium, denoting by arched and rounded crown, fuyant brow and broad base with full development of the moral region, deficiency of the reflectives, fine perceptives, and abundant animality', in Burton's. His projecting mouth displayed pointed teeth, his eyes twinkled when, as was usually the case, he was in a good humour, and he worked hard.

Speke's description of Bombay recalls his account of Farhan (see pp. 8–9), whose loyalty in Somaliland had stood out in contrast to the treachery of Sumunter and his fellow Arabs. Speke had noted that on the march to Berbera 'the Seedis . . . have twice the heart and bottom of the Egyptians', and he perceived the same qualities of endurance and loyalty in Bombay. On the first day of the journey, he found that the surveying compass had been left behind, and decided to return for it; it was a fifteen-mile walk each way, but Bombay volunteered to accompany him. The African proved an untiring walker and a lively companion, for he knew a little Hindustani, and could tell Speke of his former life, and chat about animals. Indeed, Livingstone later commented, 'He lifted Speke out of the disagreeable position of being a silent onlooker in all Burton's conversations . . . Speke naturally felt very grateful to him. Before getting him Speke sat on his bottom only.'[2]

The journey inland was hard going, with heavy rain after a few days which made the tracks muddy. A few extra porters were engaged; at one stage five 'wild men' ate a good meal, then declined to do any work; later three others were enlisted. Vuga was reached on the 15th and Bombay was sent to the Sultan to request an interview. Burton and Speke were duly received by the aged Kimweri (see p. 6), with Hamdan acting as interpreter.

On 16 February the return journey began. The three porters had deserted but Chokwe was reached six days later, and after a pause there they returned to Pangani, Burton by canoe and Speke overland with Bombay. The Jemadar was paid 20 dollars for the services of his two slaves, 5 dollars each to the three satisfactory Baluchis, and 4 and

3 dollars respectively to two 'drones'. Speke had by now 'become much attached to Bombay, for I must say I never saw any black man so thoroughly honest and conscientious as he was, added to which his generosity was unbounded.' He arranged with the Jemadar that if a substitute could be found, Bombay should be released to become his servant at 5 dollars a month as well as his keep. The party returned to Zanzibar by boat.

The rains ended on 5 June and the expedition crossed to the mainland on the *Artemise* on the 16th. Burton and Speke had their Goanese servants, eight Baluchis had been engaged as escort, and Bombay had been joined by his 'brother', a slave named Mabruki for whom Burton paid his owner 5 dollars a month. Speke thought him 'a sulky, dogged, pudding-headed brute, very ugly, but very vain; he always maintained a respectable appearance, to cloak his disrespectful manners.' Local advice had been to avoid the dangers of the direct route from Kilwa and the established Arab caravan route to Unyamyembe was chosen.

Said bin Salim was to act as caravan leader again but was very reluctant to do so until ordered by Majid. Through Hamerton's influence he was advanced 500 dollars from public funds and went to the mainland ahead of the rest with four slave musketeers, a boy and two girls, and accompanied by Ramji, clerk to Ladha Damji, Collector of Customs at Zanzibar, both of whom were Banyans, members of the mercantile Indian community of the Island. Ladha himself came over later to see the expedition on its way. It was necessary to provide transport for a large quantity of material. The basic requirements included arms and ammunition, tents and camping equipment, cooking vessels, scientific instruments and books, stationery, medicine chest, tools, clothes, and many other items. In addition there was the 'currency'—cloth, beads and wire—needed for gifts to local rulers and payment for food and passage, which formed a major part of a caravan's burden. Cloth, *merikani* or unbleached cotton sheeting from America, *kaniki*, an indigo-dyed cloth from India, and various patterned fabrics used for garments, were made up into 'bolsters' about 5 feet long and 18 to 24 inches across, strengthened with branches. Each package weighed about 70 pounds, the customary maximum load for a porter who also carried his own belongings. Beads could be obtained in some 400 varieties, and were packed in long bags which, being inflexible, were limited to about 50 pounds. Brass wire, which was used for making bracelets, was carried in coils at each end of a pole; boxes were also slung on poles—light ones at each end, heavy ones in the centre of a pole, carried by two men. Goods were rarely transported on the head.

It was reckoned that one hundred and seventy men would be needed for the material to be taken, including an iron boat, but Said secured only thirty-six Nyamwezi porters, 'men who usually behave well, but who are uncommonly ready to follow bad example'. This batch was sent ahead; thirty donkeys were purchased to carry other loads, and Burton advanced Ladha 150 dollars to hire twenty-two porters to follow on in ten days with more supplies—these men eventually brought what was left of the stores to Unyanyembe, but the boat never left the coast.

The Baluchis consisted of a Jemadar and seven men who volunteered to serve for a maximum of six months after the Sultan had given his approval. They were to receive 5 dollars a month, with rations and clothing, and advance gifts to equip themselves. Burton wrote that this escort 'was according to popular rumour picked up in the Bazar'. At Kaole there were rumours of great danger in the interior, so five more Baluchis from the garrison were added to the expedition and a temporary escort of thirty-four more under Jemadar Yaruk obtained. Ten slaves of Ramji were engaged at 5 dollars a month—half to them, half to Ramji—six months being paid in advance, to act as 'interpreters, guides, and war-men': they were armed with muskets and sabres. There were also five donkey-men.

Two of Ramji's 'sons' went ahead with the thirty-six *pagazi*. The rest of the expedition finally set off, with about one hundred additional Baluchis to escort it on its first few miles.

The order of progress was based on that of the Arab caravans, which tended to be leisurely, by comparison with the Nyamwezi, which were the most rapid of the trading ventures to and from the interior. Each day began at about 4 a.m. when the crowing of cocks, some of which were normally brought with each caravan, wakened the camp. Fires were lit, and about an hour later the meal was eaten. The porters had then to be assembled and loads allocated, much importance being attached to fairness of distribution. In addition each man carried his own property, including rations, cooking-vessel, sleeping mat, three-legged stool and some weapon. Porters wore their poorest clothing while travelling, but were often gaily ornamented with strips of animal skin or bunches of feathers, and some had bells tied below their knees.

The long file would eventually set off, led by the *kirangozi* or guide, in scarlet robe and flamboyant headdress, carrying the blood-red flag of Zanzibar which was borne on all expeditions within the Sultan's territories. Behind him came a drummer, his beats mingling with the multitude of sounds from a caravan on the march—the jangling of bells, the blowing of the *barghumi* or koodoo horn, the chattering, singing, and imitating of bird and animal calls of the porters. It was customary for the master of the caravan to bring up the rear, to check stragglers or deserters; Burton usually took this station, with Speke ahead. The maximum pace was four miles an hour, and the average was about 2·25. As this was on winding paths the net distance travelled was much less.

A halt would be taken about 8 a.m., and the march ended by mid-day when the heat of the ground had become hard on bare feet. This might be at a friendly village, or in an improvised camp. Tents were erected, firewood gathered and shade sought. While their followers rested, smoked tobacco or *bhang* (Indian hemp), or cooked, the explorers could write up their notes and deal with any administrative and medical matters. Dinner was about 4 p.m. and in the evening, especially if there was a village nearby, the porters, after securing pack animals and stacking loads, would dance and sing or sit round the fire talking. They would go to sleep about 8 p.m., though the women could sometimes be heard talking later.

The first goal of the expedition was Unyanyembe. The route from Bagamoyo led across the coastal plain, through Zungomero, the main caravan centre of the eastern area, and ascending wooded uplands to the central plateau, 3,000 feet above sea level. Next came the wilder, infertile region of Ugogo, and beyond was Unyamwezi. The journey, over a distance of some 500 miles, took from the beginning of July to 7 November; this was slow progress—towards the end the expedition was overtaken by a lightly laden caravan which had left the coast two months and twenty days after it. There were various reasons for this. Burton was following an established caravan route, but at best this consisted of foot-tracks, beaten by human transit in the travelling season, and grown over at other times; they went over treacherous ground, winding round obstacles, crossing rivers by unreliable fords, and with inclines often hazardous for a well-laden man or beast to climb. There were also serious problems to surmount among the personnel. Burton had aimed at some degree of disciplined movement in the caravan but it soon became 'a mere mob'. As was customary, it was several days before it got under way; and morale suffered from rumours of dangers ahead.

Said was a nervous, sickly man who exercised little authority, so that the trade goods under his charge were distributed far too lavishly as casual disbursements by him, or, when he was ill, his slaves, and much material passed to the Baluchis or the 'Sons of Ramji'. His four slaves were nominally porters, but did nothing for anyone but their master. He proved dilatory in chasing deserters and feeble in negotiations. Early in the journey, Burton engaged Muinyi Wazira, nephew of a local *Diwan*, as 'linguist and general assistant' to Said. He proved a mixed blessing—he spoke five dialects, could be useful in negotiations, and was a hard worker when sober, but alternated between apathy and pugnacity when under the influence of drink.

15

The additional Baluchi escort was sent back on 21 July, shortly before reaching Zungomero. They were already reduced by desertion, and Burton thought them 'the refuse of their service' but their Jemadar, Yaruk, was 'a good specimen of the true Baloch mountaineer—a tall, gaunt, and large-boned figure, with dark complexion deeply pitted by small-pox, hard, high, and sun-burnt features of exceeding harshness; an armoury in epitome was stuck in his belt, and his hand seemed never to rest but upon a weapon.' He had stopped other desertions and Burton recommended his appointment to the vacant command at Bagamoyo.

The remaining Baluchis, armed with matchlocks, swords and shields, numbered thirteen. Their leader, the one-eyed Jemadar Mallok, had good features marred by small-pox; his followers included an African, Jelai, and ranged from the greybeard Mohammed to the young tailor-boy, Hudul. Burton thought them little better than Yaruk's men, of dubious military value, insubordinate, quarrelsome and foul-mouthed, disputing with their own colleagues and with the 'Sons of Ramji' over rations, status, and any other cause. When Burton endeavoured to redistribute the loads they broke into open rebellion; they demanded more pay and one, Khudabaksh, 'from first to last my evil genius and the mainspring of all mischief', threatened Burton's life. He and Speke, however, determined if necessary to reduce their loads and press on with any followers who remained loyal, and the threatened desertion, like another one two months later, petered out.

The 'Sons of Ramji' were the other main element in the party. In the early stages they presented no major problem, apart from one attempted desertion, but at Zungomero they caught up with their leader Kidogo. He was a Doe—'a short, thin, coal-black person . . . he has a peaked beard, a bulging brow, close thin lips, a peculiar wall-eyed roll of glance.' He had a wife and children in Unyamwezi, and knew the local languages and customs. In spite of a quiet voice and obsequious manner he was self-assured and determined, and soon asserted the rights of the 'Sons of Ramji'—they were soldiers and should undertake no other duties and were not to be subject to the Jemadar—and Burton had no alternative to accepting the situation. He endeavoured, however, to secure smooth working by instituting a daily conference or *shauri* between Said, Wazira and Kidogo, but the last, though a slave, was so aggressive and self-opinionated that the others gave up expressing their views. His value was uncertain; he and Said cut down the expenditure on presents, not from tenderness towards the expedition's resources but to avoid pushing up the accepted level, which might affect them on future travels.

The two Goanese were unreliable, and often ill through over-eating, but had some redeeming features—Valentine picked up Swahili and was handy at cooking and sewing, while Gaetano was a kindly nurse and, though physically weak, courageous.

The final members were the two Africans, Bombay and Mabruki. Burton, quick to discern and record faults, wrote of Bombay that though he 'did nothing well rarely did anything very badly', and praised his efforts on several occasions; he helped to check fighting and more than once he came back from the advance party to meet the rear-guard—'Towards the end of that long march I saw with pleasure the kindly face of Seedy Bombay, who was returning to me in hot haste, leading an ass and carrying a few scones and hard-boiled eggs.' When Said refused to lend Burton and Speke some of his tentage, their own having been delayed, Bombay admonished him, 'If you are not ashamed of your master, be ashamed of his servant.'

Mabruki was a much more morose and sullen character, and when appointed to lead Burton's donkey, dragged it on carelessly over rough ground, to its rider's discomfort. He nevertheless showed loyalty, and he and Bombay carried the ailing Speke when the rest refused to do so. Burton's opinion was that both had deteriorated—'idleness marked them for her own'—when over-indulged, but at the end 'we parted à l'aimable'.

Francis Galton, in *The Art of Travel*, wrote, 'If some of the natives take their wives, it gives great life to the party . . . They are invaluable in picking up, and retailing information and hear-say gossip, which will give clues to much of importance that, unassisted, you might miss.'[3] Of this expedition, Burton wrote, 'The men were hot, tired and testy, those who had wives beat them, those who had not "let off the steam" by quarrelling with one another.' Although Said had a wife, Halimah, with him, he acquired two women en route from an Arab caravan: Zawada, 'a patient and hard-working woman', whom he eventually added to his harem; and Sikujui, a virago whose wandering affections disordered the caravan, and who was sold at Unyanyembe to a man who soon complained of his bad bargain.

Five Zanzibar asses had been bought for the leading members of the expedition to ride, and twenty-nine half-tamed, stubborn, and un-predictable donkeys were obtained on the mainland for carrying goods. The casualty rate was heavy—some ran off, others were killed by hyenas or died of illness, one was accidentally shot—and by the end of October only one of the original animals was left. This made the need for porters all the greater, but numbers fluctuated considerably. Two men died, two were left sick, and there were numerous desertions as well as recruitments from other caravans or from villages on the route.

There was much small-pox in the country; some of the porters caught it, and there were other illnesses. Help was given on several occasions by Arab caravans, and at one time the expedition travelled in company with one. Speke and Burton were rarely in good health and often had to be carried. Their knowledge of the language was limited, though by the time of the homeward journey Burton claimed to have a vocabulary of 1,500 words. Said's Swahili was poor.

Discipline was not improved when news was received of Consul Hamerton's death, which cast doubts on continued official approval for the undertaking. There was little actual hostility encountered—one threat came to nothing, though a straggler was attacked by robbers. There was, however, the usual exaction of toll (*hongo*) notably by the Gogo chief M'ana Miaha, also known as Maguru Mafupi ('Short-shanks'). However, 'the men seemed to behave best whenever things were palpably at their worst.'

As they approached Unyanyembe, Kidogo, spurred on by the nearness of his wife and children, increased the pace and the Nyamwezi porters also wanted to reach home. Powder was issued for the traditional firing of guns when entering the straggling settlement of Unyanyembe on 7 November. The centre, where the leading Arabs lived, was called Kazeh by Speke and Burton but it is generally known as Tabora.

Burton was relieved to be among Arabs, a 'truly noble race' compared with the 'savage and selfish African', and he particularly appreciated the hospitality of Snay bin Amir, a wealthy ivory- and slave-dealer. There was one Indian merchant, Musa, with whom Speke became particularly friendly. It was more than five weeks before the march was resumed, because of illness and the need, to Burton's chagrin, virtually to renegotiate the terms of engagement. The Nyamwezi porters vanished to their homes and the *kirangozi* went off to visit his family. Kidogo and the 'Sons of Ramji' raised complaints and objections to going on in the belief that Ramji himself might soon arrive on a trading expedition and Said bin Salim deteriorated both in honesty and in obedience. Two of the Baluchis—one dying of dysentery—were left behind.

During early December Speke and Burton, both in poor health, experienced, like many travellers after them, the frustrations of trying to resume the march from the comforts of an established settlement. Burton left on 15 December and by the end of the year the expedition had reached Msene. Matters were at a low ebb; the fresh guide was inadequate; the newly engaged porters were unreliable; the 'Sons of Ramji' would not carry loads; and Mabruki was only dissuaded from deserting by Bombay. Even the latter, 'under the influence of some negroid Neaera', would not leave when the journey was resumed, though he overtook the expedition a few days later. Wazira and the 'Sons of Ramji' were dismissed; in a memorandum, Burton and Speke

18

declared of the latter: 'From the commencement of the march their insolence of manner and their independence of action have been so troublesome to us, and so disastrous to our progress, that we feel no compunction in thus summarily dismissing them.'

From mid-January to mid-February 1858 the depleted caravan made its way westward from Msene, and on 13 February breasted a hill from which Burton, suffering from partial paralysis as a result of fever, and Speke, almost blind from ophthalmia, could make out only a gleam of light below. It was Bombay who told them his belief, 'that is *the* water'—Lake Tanganyika.

The next day they reached the village of Kawele, more familiarly known as Ujiji, the name of the area of which it was the principal settlement. Here the Nyamwezi porters hired at Unyanyembe deserted, and the local chief Kannena and the Jiji were unfriendly. In order to explore the lake a substantial vessel was needed. Hearing that the Sheikh Hamid bin Sulayyam, of Kasenge Island on the western side of the lake, had a dhow, Speke went to negotiate for its hire. When he arrived Hamid, through Bombay as interpreter, told him that he had travelled to the north of the lake where there was a river, the Ruzizi, though there was some confusion in interpreting whether it flowed in or out of the lake. Hamid offered Speke the use of his dhow, but made excuses for not providing a crew, and after twelve days of hospitable non-cooperation, Speke returned to Ujiji.

Burton and Speke now attempted to visit the Ruzizi with the chief Kannena in two canoes, but had to turn back some hours' paddling short of the river, as the Rundi were hostile. Speke decided, however, on local reports and his own observations, that the Ruzizi flowed into the lake, and therefore could not be the source of the Nile.

Supplies were now running low, and they decided to leave Ujiji in May to return to Unyanyembe. The usual problems delayed departure —a squabble in which Bombay and Mabruki showed courage but Valentine's panic shooting led to a man being wounded. The expedition finally left on 26 May, many of the party with extra slaves—at Kasenge, Speke noted with distaste that his Baluchis bought children from their parents for a piece of cloth. Mabruki had a small slave, about six years old, named Nasibu; at first he petted him, but tiring of this he began to beat him, so he was transferred to 'the far less hard-hearted Bombay'.

They completed the 265-mile journey back to Unyanyembe, part of the way in company with an Arab caravan, on 20 June. Wazira and the 'Sons of Ramji' were still there. Burton continued to be unwell, and there were others on the sick list but Speke, having recovered considerably, was anxious to visit the great lake Ukerewe, in the north, which he believed from local information could be the source of the

Nile; Burton preferred to stay, gathering information from the Arabs. In forming his party to seek the lake, Speke wished to include Said as a negotiator, but Burton dissuaded the Arab from agreeing. Speke thought this was because Burton wished to keep Said at Unyanyembe on account of his local knowledge; Burton's explanation was that he considered Said might prove too difficult for the inexperienced Speke to control.[4] The Baluchi Jemadar would come only if given extra pay for himself and his men, on the grounds that the journey was outside the agreed route, and they had already exceeded the six months of their engagement. To Speke's surprise, Bombay also demanded advance pay, but it emerged that 'his motives were of a superior order'. He wished to provide gifts for his 'brother' Mabruki, who had entered Speke's service as Burton had found him so unsatisfactory, for his slave, the tall and lazy Maktubu, and for little Nasibu. Speke commented, 'he would do no wrong to benefit himself—to please anybody else there is nothing he would stick at.'

So Speke set off for the lake on 9 July 1858. His party consisted of a *kirangozi* engaged at Ujiji, twenty locally engaged *pagazi*, ten Baluchis, Bombay with his tiny slave Nasibu carrying his sleeping hide and water gourd, Mabruki, Gaetano, and two donkeys Ted and Jenny. Two days later Speke engaged a second guide as hostilities in the country ahead made it necessary to vary the route.

The early stages were not propitious; the *pagazi* temporarily returned home after the very short initial journey, and the Baluchis grumbled. Once started, however, the atmosphere improved, and the second evening:

> ... was spent by the porters in dancing, and singing a song which had been evidently composed for the occasion, as it embraced everybody's name connected with the caravan, but more especially Mzungu (the wise or white man), and ended with the prevailing word amongst these curly-headed bipeds, 'Grub, Grub, Grub!' It is wonderful to see how long they will, after a long fatiguing march, keep up these festivities, singing the same song over and over again, and dancing and stamping, with their legs and arms flying about like the wings of a semaphore, as they move slowly round and round in the same circle and on the same ground; their heads and bodies lolling to and fro in harmony with the rest of the dance, which is always kept at more even measure when, as on this occasion, there were some village drums beating the measure they were wont to move by.[5]

The following day even the Baluchis broke into 'some native homely ditty', the first time they had sung on the march.

One of the first problems was the unsuitability of Speke's 'currency' for buying extra food. He had only white beads, which were not wanted, whereas coloured would have been eagerly received.

Shortly after leaving, Speke secured the enthusiastic support of the Baluchis by issuing them with cloth in lieu of the unsatisfactory white beads. 'Were time of no consequence, and coloured beads in store, such travelling as this would indeed be pleasant', he wrote, considering the agreeable hilly country, the bracing air, the availability of food, and the friendly people. Bombay proved a shrewd negotiator in keeping delays to a minimum though his limitations as an interpreter led to at least one misunderstanding over the engagement of a local guide. There were delays due to sickness, and to the wish of the *pagazi* to barter their cloth for iron hoes, which were valuable for trade at Unyanyembe. The Jemadar and his men, however, supported Speke in pressing on. The least satisfactory member of the party was Gaetano, ill-tempered, dilatory and 'intermeddling'. In spite of obstacles, however, Speke travelled 226 miles in twenty-five days, and on the morning of 3 August he reached the summit of a hill, where 'the vast expanse of the pale blue waters burst suddenly upon my gaze'. He was convinced that he had found the source of the Nile, and named it Lake Victoria.

He turned south again on the 6th; he would have liked to explore further—'all hands being in first-rate condition and health, and all in the right temper for it'—but time and supplies of beads were running out. His followers were pleased to be returning, and his disappointment 'was much alleviated by seeing the happy, contented, family state to which the whole caravan had at length arrived . . . The Beluchis have long since behaved to admiration, and now even the lazy *pagazi*, since completing their traffic, have lighter hearts, and begin to feel a freshness dawn upon them.'

Bombay was entrusted with further negotiations on the return journey. He also proved an interesting companion, as they improved their Hindustani in swapping hunting yarns or indulging in theological speculations about the origin of black men. Bombay suggested that in trading while travelling it was desirable to spend time bartering—but Speke pointed out that the time taken probably represented a loss in the wages of the waiting porters. Speke lent him his donkey because he had a sore foot; 'Bombay rode much after the fashion of a sailor, trusting more to balance and good-luck than skill in sticking on,' and fell off, breaking Burton's gun which he was carrying.

In Speke's view Bombay 'by long practice . . . has become a great geographer', but when they reached Tabora on 25 August, Burton was sceptical of Speke's claims and particularly of his evidence: 'Bombay, after misunderstanding his master's ill-expressed Hindostani, probably mistranslated the words into Kisawahili to some travelled

African, who in turn passed on the question in a wilder dialect to the barbarian or barbarians under examination. During such a journey to and fro words must be liable to severe accidents.' However, if he thought little of Bombay as an interpreter, Burton valued him for 'his unwearied activity, and especially from his undeviating honesty' and appointed him to take over the future distribution of cloth from Said, though the latter retained the supervision of the porters and their rations. This arrangement had the effect of uniting the once hostile Said, the Jemadar and Kidogo in opposition to Bombay.

The caravan was reorganised for the journey to the coast. To the two Europeans and their servants were added Said, with two wives and nine slaves, Bombay with his two slaves, and a concubine acquired at Tabora, who acted as a cook, Mabruki, Nasir, a half-caste Arab, and Taufiki, a Swahili gun-bearer. The twelve Baluchis had fifteen slaves and eleven porters. The 'Sons of Ramji' asked to be allowed to travel down with the caravan and this was agreed; they, with followers, totalled twenty-four, and there were sixty-nine Nyamwezi porters, one of whom, Twanigana or Gopa-Gopa, was made *kirangozi*—in all a caravan of over one hundred and fifty. During this stage, which began on 26 September, Burton was amused by the attempts of the Baluchi Gul Mohamed to impress the merits of the Muslim faith on Muzungu Mbaya, a particularly cantankerous old porter. In general, the Baluchis despised the Africans as pagans.

Speke and Burton were still unfit and thirteen men were hired to carry them to Rubuga. The former suffered from an attack of the 'little irons', a severe fever, during which he was well cared for by Bombay who had some experience of the complaint. There were some other untoward events—on one occasion a 'Son of Ramji' speared a porter; later one of their slave girls set huts on fire, and claims for compensation had to be met. Zungomero was reached at the end of December, and Burton wished to march south-east to Kilwa, but though Twanigana was agreeable, the rest of the Nyamwezi porters refused and left without being paid, despite attempts to bring them back. With the aid of further porters engaged from Nyamwezi caravans, however, the expedition reached the coast at Konduchi on 3 February. The Baluchis and Kidogo returned to Zanzibar almost immediately; Said and his entourage, and the remaining 'Sons of Ramji', soon followed them.

Burton still wished to visit Kilwa Island, and sent to Zanzibar for a boat. When it arrived it brought a young German traveller, Albrecht Roscher, who soon left for the interior. Burton and Speke sailed on 10 February, but cholera struck them, and four of the crew died. They visited Kilwa, but could not obtain a crew to explore the Rufiji River, and returned to Zanzibar early in March 1859.

Burton and Speke sailed from Zanzibar on 22 March, being seen off by Bombay, whose 'honest face' pleased Burton. They parted at Aden but never met on friendly terms again; Burton disputed Speke's claim to have discovered the source of the Nile and resented the fact that he had asserted this immediately on arrival in England. They also disagreed about the treatment of the members of the expedition.[6]

Burton refused to pay most of them; he considered that Said and the Baluchis had been assigned to the expedition by Sultan Majid, and that the former had been more than adequately remunerated by his advance pay. The 'Sons of Ramji' had in effect been on a trading expedition for their master. In general, none of the men had been satisfactory, and they had received more than enough in advance pay and extra issues from the expedition's stores.

Colonel Rigby, Hamerton's successor at Zanzibar, was not happy with the situation. The Sultan had paid the Baluchis, but Ramji and Said were dissatisfied at their treatment. The failure to pay the seventy Nyamwezi porters had given a bad impression, and would create problems for future travellers. The Government in Bombay, to whom he referred the matter, agreed to reimburse Majid and also authorised the payment of Said and Ramji.

Speke upheld the men's claims, though Burton asserted that he had supported the hard line taken at the time. Burton also wrote that Speke had been involved in fierce disputes with the Baluchis, and that he despised Africans. Other evidence contradicts this. Livingstone found that, among Africans, 'Speke's name is one of generosity'—compared to Burton, the 'stingy white man'. Frank Pocock wrote in 1876 'his name is all the rage in Uganda and Karagwe', and two years later the missionary C. T. Wilson commented that Speke was 'undoubtedly the most popular of all the European explorers in this part of Africa'.[7] He certainly had the limited outlook on other races usual in his age, and lost patience with delays and frustrations on occasion, but he developed greater tolerance, and did not harbour grudges, as his unwillingness to prosecute Sumunter indicates. He believed that promises, even if made under duress, should be honoured—'I had seen Tibet ruined by officers not keeping faith with their porters.' He had agreed with dismissing the 'Sons of Ramji', but noted occasions when they might have been useful and thought that their rejoining gave them some claim—at least Ramji should have had his share. He wanted to pay the porters at Zungomero and though he considered Said's refusal to go to Lake Victoria disqualified him from any extra reward, he thought he should have been given the pay due to him. Some unsatisfactory men, such as the Goans, had been paid—'it was simple justice giving them their pay, for they came through with us to the end and did services for us to the last, and for this we were under obligations to them. The same reasoning is applicable to every man who came through the journey with us.'

The quarrel affected one traveller, the German Roscher, who, after leaving Burton and Speke, made his way with one servant, Rashid, south towards the Rufiji, and was the first European to see the natural harbour of what became Dar-es-Salaam. On a subsequent journey, with Rashid and his brother Omar, he travelled with an Arab caravan since Burton's refusal to pay his men had made it impossible to engage any porters. He reached the northern shore of Lake Nyasa on 19 November 1859, two months after Livingstone had arrived at the southern end, but while resting in an apparently friendly village, he and Omar were murdered. Rashid, though wounded, escaped and invoked the aid of the local ruler to arrest the culprits, and they had been sent to Zanzibar for judgment when Speke returned to the island to resume his explorations.[8]

4

SPEKE, GRANT AND BOMBAY

In 1859 Speke was instructed by the Royal Geographical Society to establish the truth of his claim as to the source of the Nile.[1] He chose as his companion an old friend from India, Captain James Augustus Grant who, he noted, had a 'conciliatory manner with coloured men'. They left England in April 1860 and arrived at the Cape on 4 July. Here the Governor, Sir George Grey, with whom they had travelled out, secured a parliamentary grant of £300, with which a dozen baggage mules were purchased. He also called for volunteers from his bodyguard to accompany the expedition and a corporal and nine men of the Cape Mounted Rifles were selected. They are often referred to as 'Hottentots', but were Cape Coloured men of mixed blood, as Grant's description indicates: 'some look "half-castes"; some English; Dutch; a few black:—a strange medley altogether.'[2]

They arrived at Simon's Bay in two 'open four wheeled vans' looking very smart in their red caps. One, 'April', was assigned to Grant as a servant during the voyage to Zanzibar. April later appeared in 'green velvet shooting-coat, tight jockey-trousers, and neat regimental cap'.

Zanzibar was reached on 17 August. During the next five weeks, while the expedition was being organised, they had a reminder of the hazards of exploration when two of the men condemned for the murder of Roscher were beheaded in Grant's presence.

Speke had intended to set up depots in advance of his expedition, and was gratified to learn from the Consul, Colonel Rigby, that he had sent fifty-six loads to Unyanyembe under two of Ramji's men. He now had to recruit his personnel. Said bin Salim was re-appointed caravan leader, as Speke thought that some of his former shortcomings were due to Burton, and 'though rather a timid man is the best one I could find'. 'Bombay and his brother Mabruki were bound to me of old, and the first to greet me on my arrival.' Grant took a stereoscopic

25

photograph of Bombay, wearing a *kanzu* and white cap and armed with a sword and musket.[3]

The Baluchis were anxious to accompany him again, but the Cape men had taken their place. In retrospect, Speke noted, 'if I ever travel again, I shall trust to none but natives, as the climate of Africa is too trying to foreigners'. Bombay had been a member of the Consul's boat crew, and he recruited from his comrades three former sailors, all with a knowledge of Hindustani—Baraka, Frij and Rahan. They found twenty-four more men, and Said engaged ten others—six of them as his personal servants. As porters, Sultan Majid supplied thirty-six labourers from his gardens. All were paid a year in advance— 500 dollars to Said, 60 dollars each to Bombay, Baraka and Rahan, 25 dollars to the rest of the *Wanguana* (a name applied to Africans freed from slavery and living in Zanzibar or on the coast), and 7 dollars to the gardeners. Ladha Damji recruited about a hundred Nyamwezi porters on the mainland at the inflated rate of $9\frac{1}{4}$ dollars to Unyanyembe, and Majid provided a temporary escort of a Jemadar and twenty-five Baluchis as far as the borders of Usagara.

The expedition crossed to Bagamoyo on 25 September and left a week later, over two hundred strong. The order of march was the *kirangozi*; *pagazi* with cloth and beads; the Wanguana, who had been organised into companies of ten under the command of Baraka, with miscellaneous goods and equipment; the Cape men with mules carrying ammunition; Said and the Baluchis; twenty goats, three or four women, and stragglers.

When camp was pitched, Said, assisted by Bombay, doled out pay; the Cape men, though nominally soldiers, did the cooking and the Baluchis mounted guard. Grant commented that 'nothing can exceed the noise and jollity of an African camp at night. We, the masters, were often unable to hear ourselves talk for the merry song and laughter, the rattle of drums, jingling of bells, beating of old iron, and discordant talk going on round our tents. No Hindoo dare be so rude in your hearing, but an African only wonders that you don't enjoy the fun.' Speke, more critical, commented 'song they have none, being mentally incapacitated for musical composition, though as timists they are not to be surpassed'.

The journey to Unyanyembe, about five hundred miles in seventy-one travelling days of from one to twenty-five miles, took nearly four months, 'struggling against the caprices of our followers, the difficulties of the countries passed through, and the final desertion of our porters'.

The qualities of the men emerged. Said displayed his old timidity, trying to avoid displeasing either Speke or the local chiefs who demanded excessive *hongo* by making secret deals with them. Bombay, 'an old traveller, and always ready-witted', could be relied on to dig for water or forage for food, but unfortunately a dispute arose between him and Baraka. Speke thought the latter 'the smartest and most intelligent negro I ever saw', and wrote to Rigby 'I do not know what we should have done without him. Bombay with all his honesty and kind fellow feeling has not half the power of command that Baraka possesses.' Baraka had served in the Royal Navy at the taking of Multan in 1849, and had been senior to Bombay in the Consul's boat crew. Now he saw his inferior preferred above himself, and the caravan led by Said, a man whose weakness he despised. Quarrelling began and continued intermittently. Baraka was relieved of the privileged but somewhat menial office of Grant's valet (being succeeded by Frij), and Speke endeavoured to mollify the two disputants by comparing their posts to those of the Commander-in-Chief and the Governor-General of India.[4]

Rahan, Speke's valet and captain of ten Wanguana, had been in the navy for a shorter time than Baraka, but had served at the taking of Rangoon in 1852. He was 'very peppery' and accidentally shot off one of his fingers as the result of a quarrel during target practice. Frij was also widely travelled, having served as a soldier under Said, and was a fund of stories and legends.

The Wanguana were quick-witted, lively, loquacious, improvident, both with their own possessions and those of the expedition, and given to giggling at silly things. 'Sometimes they will show great kindness, even bravery amounting to heroism, and proportionate affection,' noted Speke, and Grant commented on their custom of running back with a drink to the rear part of the caravan. The Hindustani speakers were fairly useful as interpreters, picking up local dialects on the basis of their knowledge of Swahili, though they proved unable to do so in Bunyoro until several weeks had passed.

Their shortcomings and virtues were illustrated in the attempts to organise them. They had been drilled while waiting at the coast, and later they were taught sword exercises. The India Office had supplied fifty carbines and they regarded these as useful for firing salutes. They left the 'parade ground' if it rained, but, wrote Grant, 'a negro could be made into a good light-infantry soldier and if he only becomes attached to his officer, there is no more devoted follower in the world.'

It was customary for Muslim slave-owners to have their slaves circumcised and made nominal Muslims so that they could kill animals for food in accordance with the requirements of their religion. Speke thought that the Wanguana's religion was only superficial, but they observed orthodox standards of food, and blamed Frij for having unclean hands when meat went bad. Some of them told Grant that they had previously eaten all animal flesh save hippopotamus, dogs, snakes and cats—rats and frogs were particularly good. However, they had subsequently, as Muslims, given up unorthodox food.

Ritual purity did not, however, make them very satisfactory cooks, a duty they eventually took over from the Cape men. In preparing their own food they were limited to sticking a wooden skewer into a piece of meat and scorching it over ashes, or making 'stirabout', a crude porridge. Mabruki Speke (as he was now known) was table-attendant to Speke and Grant for a time: 'Should he have to clean your plate, a bunch of grass or a leaf is generally within his reach; and, if he has to remove the plate, he seldom returns without wiping his mouth . . . dinner over, you see him eating with your spoons and drinking out of the teapot or the spout of the kettle.'

However, though Speke noted many shortcomings, the key fact was 'it is to these singular negroes acting as hired servants that I have been chiefly indebted for opening this large section of Africa', and, contrasting them with his other followers, wrote to Rigby, 'Would that I had listened to Bombay when at Zanzibar and had engaged double the number of his "free-men" for they do all the work and do it as an enlightened & disciplined people.'[5]

On 22 September Speke wrote, 'The Hottentot Guard have shown themselves a very handy willing set of men after they once settled down to work. They now adapt themselves and wear into the different stages of vicissitude in this vagabond sort of life famously, and if the climate, the great enemy of these regions, only spares them we shall find them of the greatest service . . .'[6] However, they eventually proved a disappointment; the Wanguana treated them like children; they were inefficient as a guard, and suffered from the outset from illness, which lowered their morale and led to grumbling. One, Peters, died on 9 November, and five others were sent back. Corporal Mithalder lost a mule; eventually all the mules disappeared or sickened and died, but three of the five donkeys survived.

Majid's thirty-six gardeners were employed in carrying, and looking after the goats, but ten deserted the first day. Others attempted to steal the goats; eight men ran off with fifteen goats on 9 October and five more followed. In an effort to stop the rot, Speke promoted the best of them to the same wages as the Wanguana, but they remained somewhat isolated from the others.

Grant wrote that the Nyamwezi 'are frank and amiable on first acquaintance, eating or taking anything from your hand, singing the jolliest of songs with deep-toned choruses from their thick necks and throats, but soon trying to get the upper hand, refusing to make the ring-fence round camp, showing sulks, making halts, or going short marches.' Pay disputes and delays marred relations with them and there was a steady trickle of desertions, including that of the *kirangozi*.

By the middle of December, in Ugogo, the situation was desperate, with heavy demands for *hongo*, continual desertions, and a lowering of morale. Speke had to carry his goods on a relay system while waiting for reinforcements which he had requested from Unyanyembe. After one promised batch had failed to arrive, he sent Bombay who, in the first of many independent missions on which Speke despatched him, succeeded in obtaining seventy porters, though their rate of pay, 16 yards of cloth each, was very heavy.

Speke reached Unyanyembe on 23 January 1861. Casualties so far were six of the Cape Mounted Riflemen, one freedman sent back with them, and twenty-five gardeners deserted. One freedman, a persistent trouble-maker, was found to be a murderer and was discharged. Of more than a hundred porters, all but three—who were well rewarded—had deserted. Speke now decided to send back the four remaining Cape men, who like their comrades had been unable to stand the conditions of travel,[7] and he also parted from Said, who had been ill as well as timid, and his six slaves who had proved cowardly when tried out as gun-bearers. Bombay was promoted to lead the caravan.

Apart from the problems of resuming the journey from Unyanyembe such as those Speke had experienced on his former journey, the area was disturbed by a conflict between the Arabs and the Nyamwezi chief Manua Sera. Speke therefore welcomed the suggestion of his old acquaintance Musa that they should travel together for greater security as far as Karagwe, where the Indian merchant was going on a trading journey. After numerous delays, this plan was frustrated by the death of Musa.

Meanwhile the militant Arabs, led by Snay, had rejected Speke's advice against becoming involved in a possible guerilla campaign and had sent out a force which, after initial success, was defeated and Snay killed. The Arab leaders now accepted Speke's offer to mediate with Manua Sera, and he sent Baraka with a party of ten men to open negotiations but though they were well received, there was too much mutual distrust for any agreement to be reached.

Speke thus had great difficulty in gathering enough men to provide an independent escort, and though he left Unyanyembe on 17 March, the farthest point he reached in the next seven months was Mihambo, some 150 miles away. Both he and Grant were ill, and the latter had to be left with a small party at Ukuni for several months. Bombay and Baraka took a pessimistic view of the prospects of advancing till the war was over and they could link up with an Arab trading caravan, but Bombay exhibited a fatalistic staunchness—'a man has but one life, and God is the director of everything'—whereas Baraka was tactless in his dealings with the Arabs, proved unreliable with stores,

29

and showed timidity which provoked Speke to declare 'Bombay would never be frightened in this silly way'. In attempts to solve problems of supplies and man-power, Speke twice journeyed back to Unyanyembe and sent Bombay and Baraka on one occasion each, but the only satisfactory follower engaged through these efforts was 'a steady old traveller' named Nasib who, after one attempt at desertion, proved a useful guide.

One recruit during these months came from Mininga, the first stopping place. A slave of Sirboko, the chief of the area, appealed to Speke, whom he claimed to have seen at Lake Tanganyika when he was still a free man. Speke persuaded Sirboko to emancipate him, and named him Farhan (Joy), which was also the name of the loyal African of the Somali expedition (see pp. 8–9).

Grant was at Ukuni from 27 May to 12 September. It was a demoralising period—Grant himself, and an average of half his followers, were ill during the early part of his stay. Meat was hard to obtain, particularly as supplies of beads grew short and prices rose—Grant shot some birds and the Wanguana caught fish in the pools by raking them with a hurdle of sticks. They passed their time drinking the local *pombe* made from sorghum, sleeping, or consorting with the local women. Bombay, who was with him for a short time, and Rahan, the senior man after his departure, made blood brotherhood with the local leaders.

Early in September Grant set off to rejoin Speke. His porters included two of the tough local women, but most of the carriers were erratic and the caravan moved sluggishly. On 16 September it was attacked by some of Myonga's men. Rahan, who had caused trouble by being drunk when due to set out, now redeemed himself by defending his loads with courage. Myonga promised redress, but the recently hired porters had deserted in panic and the local people were hostile, beating to death the donkey Jenny, which had carried Speke to Lake Victoria three years before.

When Grant reached him Speke prepared to leave. He sent the courageous Rahan back to the coast with letters and specimens. Sangizo, engaged locally as a guide, helped recruit enough porters to get the caravan started. While the expedition was in Usui, in October, the rivalry between Baraka and Bombay reached its climax. It had been simmering for months, and though Speke, torn between his old bonds with Bombay and his original assessment of Baraka's superior abilities, had tried to keep them both satisfied—'they do things turn and turn about, and certainly do them very well,' he wrote[8]—disputes had broken out several times with Bombay protesting that he was always put at a disadvantage by Baraka's readier tongue. The immediate cause of this conflict was a woman. In spite of Speke's prohibition, a

30

number of men, including Baraka, had acquired wives during the journey; Bombay had his eye on a girl at Uthungu and, in order to raise the somewhat extortionate dowry demanded, paid for her with wires which Baraka declared were stolen from the general store. Bombay asserted that they were a perquisite from chiefs who had been paid *hongo* through him; he would not use such goods to buy slaves or for his own enrichment, 'but when it comes to a wife, that's a different thing.' Speke felt that in justice he should praise Baraka for his perspicacity, but Bombay protested that he had been a conscientious steward, and a quick check bore this out. Speke's eventual decision was to give a general exhortation that the goods of the expedition were brought for everyone's advantage, and he tried to reconcile the two men. Bombay sobered down and promised amendment, and took Sangizo's sister on credit instead of paying for the expensive local bride. They had a child in Buganda, but it was stillborn.

On 17 November the expedition entered Karagwe, west of Lake Victoria, a kingdom with a much more stable and centralised government than anything Speke had hitherto encountered. They were accompanied by a friendly *mganga* or magic doctor, Kyengo, who was on a diplomatic mission from Suwarowa, a chief in Usui, to Mutesa, the Kabaka or King of Buganda, farther north.

After establishing contact through Bombay and Nasib, Speke and Grant were cordially received by Rumanika, King of Karagwe. Bombay accompanied them and was later sent to the King with presents. From this time Speke disassociated himself from the Arab regime and accepted the reality of the authority of African rulers; when asked by Rumanika if he would stay with him or with the Arabs at Kafurro, he replied that he did not come to trade and 'therefore the Arabs had no relations with us'. While resting, Speke gave his men beads to buy bark cloth to replace their worn-out clothes.

Baraka, as well as Bombay, was given some responsible tasks, but the generous hospitality of Rumanika led to heavy drinking, and in the course of one bout there was a fight in which Baraka beat one of the women who abused him. Speke intervened and, after Baraka had stormed off, Bombay declared that there was widespread disaffection among those who followed Baraka but that his own associates would follow Speke to the end of the journey. There was another fracas in December, when Baraka accused Bombay of trying to kill him by magic.

It was clear that this situation could not be allowed to continue, and Speke was relieved when an opportunity came of sending Baraka away without disgrace. Before leaving England Speke had arranged with John Petherick, an ivory trader on the White Nile, that he would endeavour to meet the expedition from the north and news was received in January 1862 of a white man who might be Petherick. Baraka was therefore sent off with his friend Uledi to try to find him.

On 10 January Speke left for Buganda; Grant who, in spite of remedies suggested by Bombay and Baraka, was not fit to travel, was left with half a dozen Wanguana. Soon after the journey began Bombay refused to strike camp on the ground that there was no adequate guide available for the road ahead, and when Speke impatiently pulled down the tent over his head, Bombay flew into a rage, 'squared up' to Speke, and the latter struck him so that his nose bled. Bombay declared he would serve no more and went off. Speke ordered Nasib to take charge, but the 'good old man' persuaded Bombay to rejoin the expedition and the former relations were resumed.

They reached Rubaga on 14 February and Speke visited Mutesa, the Kabaka of Buganda, for the first time on the 19th. The *kirangozi*, carrying the Union Jack, was followed by a dozen men with fixed bayonets, wearing uniforms of fez caps and red cloaks, improvised from blankets. The rest of the men, carrying gifts, brought up the rear. Bombay, suitably instructed in Indian ceremonial, was interpreter, though any message had to pass from him to Nasib, to one of Mutesa's men and thence to the Kabaka, as direct communication was not allowed.

Speke spent in all nearly five months in Buganda—a frustrating period during which he was anxious to bring Grant up and advance to the north, but was constantly hampered by the capricious behaviour of Mutesa, who would keep him waiting for long periods, lose patience before the lengthy process of interpreting was complete, or invite him to a hunting expedition to show off the performance of his guns when Speke wished to discuss business.

Though he had by now acquired some knowledge of Swahili, he used Bombay for interpreting and also for some separate negotiations, both with Mutesa himself and with the Queen Mother, whom Speke tried to cultivate in order to acquire influence over Mutesa so that he would agree to the journey continuing. One means of pleasing the Kabaka was by providing him with European-style clothes, and some of the men were assigned to making trousers for him.

While waiting for some action Speke was, after some weeks, allotted a group of huts near the palace. He had Ilmas, one of the men recruited by Bombay, as his cook and valet. Food was supposed to be provided, but was received only intermittently, and Speke had difficulty in stopping his men from plundering—on one occasion they did so after being tricked into involvement in a local feud. Even when meat was forthcoming, some of it was rejected by the Wanguana as being ritually unclean. When Speke spoke slightingly of their faith, Bombay (once described by Burton as 'a noted Agnostic in fine weather')

32

replied with some dignity, 'We could no more throw off the Mussulman faith than you could yours.'

Speke made a page of Lugoi, 'a sharp lad' whom he rigged out with a white and red garb, but Mutesa later took a fancy to him and he became a royal page. Speke had other followers, the women he was offered as part of Mutesa's hospitality. The first of these solved any difficulties by promptly running away but when further offers were made, Bombay urged Speke to accept—'for if *you* don't like her, *we* should.' Accordingly, when given the choice of two girls by the Queen Mother, he accepted the younger, about twelve years old, with 'a snubby nose and everted lips', but the Queen pressed him to take the elder as well, as the younger would be frightened alone. The elder, whom Speke called Meri ('Plantains'), from Nkole, had been in Kabaka Sunna's harem; the younger, Kahala (girl), was a Nyoro. These two enlivened Speke's days by attracting others to gossip, and he sometimes walked round the area attended by Lugoi and Kahala, to whom he gave a red scarf; but Meri was fussy about food, became very lazy, shammed illness and dabbled in magic. Speke therefore passed her over to Uledi, a Ganda chief, and his wife, but the Queen Mother said she would have to be taken with Speke when he left the country but offered a replacement since she had proved unsatisfactory.

Kahala ran away on one occasion, but returned. 'As a punishment, I ordered her to live with Bombay; but my house was so dull again from want of some one to eat dinner with me, that I remitted the punishment, to her great delight,' wrote Speke. Finally, however, her dirty habits caused him to give her back to Bombay as a wife. She ran away again but was brought back and eventually reached Egypt with Bombay.

Grant meanwhile had remained sick in Karagwe. His men included Frij as headman, who entertained his colleagues with a song to his single-stringed guitar:

I am Frij, I am Frij; my brother Grin [meaning Grant], my brother Grin, is very sick, is very sick; we'll get a cow, we'll get a cow, when he gets well, when he gets well,' to which the others would all subscribe in a louder voice, 'Ameen', with the most perfect solemnity.

At last a party of Ganda arrived, and on 14 April Grant left, uncomfortably carried on a litter. Kyengo travelled with him. Food should have been provided en route by Mutesa's orders, but the escort and, under their influence, Grant's men, plundered as they went.

On 26 May a party of Wanguana, sent by Speke with food and a message, greeted Grant, and the next day they were reunited. It was still some weeks before they were able to proceed and when, early in

33

July, they were ready to do so, the men—who, in spite of some disturbances over food and occasional drunkenness, had behaved well—showed reluctance to go on and some returned home. The old guide, Nasib, also wished to leave and in view of his good services he was honourably discharged with a handsome gift and a letter of emancipation.

On 7 July 1862 Speke and Grant left Mutesa's capital for Bunyoro, the kingdom to the north ruled by Kamurasi. They had forty-nine men—twenty-two of the original thirty-three Wanguana, eight of Sultan Majid's gardeners, nineteen porters who had been engaged in the interior, and a few women—they declined a parting gift of more from Mutesa. The expedition was given a Ganda escort under Budja which lived off the country, driving inhabitants from the villages and taking what they wanted. Shortly afterwards Speke and Grant separated, the latter going on with the main body, while Speke with a dozen Wanguana under Bombay, 'himself a host', and a few Ganda made for the Nile outlet of Lake Victoria. When they struck the river on 21 July, Speke euphorically suggested that the men bathed in the 'holy river', but Bombay rejoined, 'We don't look on those things in the same fanciful manner that you do; we are contented with all the commonplaces of life, and look for nothing beyond the present.' A week later they reached what Speke named the Ripon Falls. He could not obtain boats so he sent Bombay and the Ganda officer Kasoro back to Mutesa for food, and authority to hire canoes. They returned on 10 August, and after an unsuccessful attempt to enter Bunyoro, the whole party set off in search of Grant and the main body, whom they met on the 19th.

Grant had been travelling with the Ganda under the handsome and intelligent Budja; his own men were under Mabruki, who kept the tally of the cattle each night on a knotted cord, and chastised the goatboy Ulimengo when he let his charges stray. Though discipline and honesty were breaking down somewhat, Grant took a sympathetic interest in his followers, noting their loyalties, and their superstitions, Frij's fund of anecdotes and tall stories, and the improvised campfire songs of the Nyamwezi. Ulimengo was a particular favourite and he also took an interest in little Manua, a twin, who, though taunted by the Wanguana for being a Nyamwezi, and for his superstitions, was widely travelled and a resourceful cowherd, finding pasture under difficulties. He had first come to Grant's attention at Karagwe, when he ran away after being threatened with punishment, but later he 'became a great friend of mine, as he knew the names and uses of every plant and tree in the country.'

However, it proved impossible to make progress as Kamurasi appeared unwilling to let the party proceed, though Mabruki, sent ahead, was unable to find the reason. Grant therefore reluctantly retreated to the Buganda frontier, and later was reunited with Speke and Bombay.

At this stage Kamurasi, on the basis of Rumanika's favourable reports from Karagwe, agreed to let the party proceed, but Budja was unwilling to go on, and it appeared that Mutesa wanted them to return. Some of the Wanguana had already demanded more ammunition and, on 1 September, twenty-eight of Speke's followers deserted, taking with them twenty-two carbines. Speke was now reduced to twenty men, with fourteen carbines among them, a meagre escort through the territories of the reputedly hostile Nilotic tribes to the north. His indignation was expressed later in his letters to Playfair at Zanzibar, which listed the 'unfaithfuls' and suggested they should be punished. Speke laid considerable blame on Baraka, who, unable to go beyond Bunyoro, had returned to Karagwe, and he thought that this fact persuaded the members of the expedition most under his influence to desert.

The situation is not very clear. Speke recorded Baraka's departure for Karagwe in May, though the mass desertion did not take place until September. On 30 October Speke sent one of his remaining men, Msalima, with Baraka and Uledi's pay which hardly suggests serious wrongdoing on Baraka's part.[9]

Speke attributed the loyalty of his small remnant to Bombay and Mabruki—'had they not [on the first expedition] gained confidence in me I believe I should have been deserted by every man on this occasion.'[10] They had acquired an *esprit de corps* and one who had considered deserting was mercilessly chaffed by his comrades. Manua made blood brotherhood with Kamurasi's officer, Kidgwiga, according to the widespread practice of mingling or drinking blood as a sign of friendship.

Kamurasi proved an awkward man to deal with during the two months the expedition stayed in his capital. Bombay was sent as an intermediary and had to spend much time showing Kamurasi the power of guns. It was 18 September before Speke met Kamurasi, Bombay acting as interpreter. He was called on to demonstrate the use of scissors, part of Speke's gift to Kamurasi, by clipping the beard which he had grown during the journey. When asked if the Queen of England had any children he at once pointed to Speke and Grant.

Following this, Bombay and Mabruki were given an escort to try to contact Petherick. They left on 22 September but it was 1 November before they returned, having reached Faloro, and brought back news of Europeans (actually Maltese traders) who had been there. While they were away, Frij became senior man, piping Kamurasi in and out with his boatswain's whistle when he visited Speke, and acting as envoy and interpreter. When Bombay returned the expedition thankfully bade farewell to Kamurasi and set off on 9 November, now nineteen strong.

The Nile was reached on the 11th, but most of the journey was by land; they were a party of eighty in all, including Nyoro, local porters

35

and Gani guides. There were some minor fights with local people, in which Uledi and Frij showed bravery and resource, but on the whole relations were good, partly as a result of Bombay and Mabruki having passed this way before, and the Wanguana actually restored some goods plundered by the escort.

On 3 December they reached the town of Faloro and entered it to a welcoming fusillade. The garrison, 'Turks' of mixed races who were more traders than soldiers, was reviewed by Speke, accompanied by Bombay, whose disreputable appearance resulted from some heavy drinking. Frij also had been carousing, and rushed about, blowing his boatswain's whistle, and giving his own orders. Speke left early in January and arrived at Gondokoro on 15 February.

Here they were warmly welcomed by another explorer, Samuel Baker, who, accompanied by his wife, was seeking to reach the source of the Nile from the north. Before leaving on 26 February Speke and Grant were able to give Baker first-hand information on the course of their travels. The Bakers continued southward and, despite fever, delays and extortion in Unyoro, and desertions and mutiny by their followers, on 14 March 1864 they reached a lake which Baker named Albert. The White Nile flowed in and out of it. They returned to Khartoum in 1865 with their original armed escort of forty-five 'miserable cut-throats' reduced to about a quarter by death and desertion. Baker singled out two consistently loyal followers for special mention; Saat, a Bari lad educated by the Italian Mission at Gondokoro, who gave unflagging service until his death from plague very near the end of the journey, and Richarn, from Khartoum, who had at first been unreliable owing to drink, but became a stalwart of the expedition, and was left with his Dinka wife at Cairo as a servant to the owner of Shepherd's Hotel.[11]

After leaving Baker, Speke and Grant travelled on to Khartoum, which they reached on 30 March. It was a curious experience to be re-entering civilisation, and the Africans found it difficult to accustom themselves to local use of money instead of barter. At Khartoum the Governor's representative supplied Speke and Grant with new clothes, and Bombay took over their old ones. Once the tension was relaxed, the men, Bombay, Frij and Uledi among them, dropped into bad habits—the two former turning up as tipsy uninvited guests when Speke and Grant visited the Baroness Capellen. They sorted out their matrimonial problems when Bombay handed over one of the women acquired in Buganda to Frij, and the couple were duly married; however, it was agreed that if Frij tired of her, she would revert to Bombay. Bombay's wife (which one is not clear) gave birth to a child, but the infant died. The Wanguana were taken to the Roman Catholic Church where Mabruki was greatly impressed by the crucifix.

They left Khartoum, travelling by water and land.[12] At Abu Ahmed the nineteen were reduced to eighteen by the desertion of Mijaliwa who had been punished for stealing earlier in the journey. While still in Khartoum Speke had written to Rigby of his intention to give these 'faithfuls' extra pay, a gift and a wife each, and asked his advice on providing them with a 'Free-man's Garden'; he suggested paying 1,000 dollars, 'but I should be glad if you would inform me how many acres it would purchase, when I might increase it, if not sufficient to keep them on an equality with free men.'[13]

These eighteen, by now each with his character and qualities well established, comprised five of the original Wanguana: the resourceful Bombay; Frij, the 'Caleb Balderston' of the expedition, full of anec-dotes and yarns; the stolid but courageous Mabruki; Uledi, Grant's intelligent servant, with qualities of 'tact and bravery'; and Ilmas, Speke's servant. Six of Majid's gardeners came back: Mektub and Uledi, close friends; Mkate, a cook-boy, 'ever obliging and good-humoured' who once walked back twelve miles to fetch a cooking vessel; Baruti, who had met his sister in Bunyoro, but found that their languages had become different; Umbari; and the goat-boy Ulimengo. Seven men engaged in the interior also came: Sangoro or Mahoka, Bombay's servant, a half-witted, hot-tempered but hardworking porter; Manua, the resourceful little Nyamwezi traveller, who planned to set up as a trader in his own country; Farhan, freed in Mininga, who had served loyally; Sadiki, Matagiri, Khamsin and Mtamani.

In the latter part of their journey the 'faithfuls' had novel experiences such as riding a camel, witnessing a mirage, and seeing the ruins of ancient temples. At Cairo they were lodged in the public garden, and taken to various entertainments. Speke had his men photographed by a Frenchman, Royer (who also took a group of the four women who had accompanied the expedition—Sikujua, Kahala, M'Essu and Faida, some of whom at least were wives of Bombay). 'They were not well done', he commented, but they sufficed to identify them, and he gave Bombay three copies of each, to be given to the Consuls at Suez, Aden and Zanzibar so that they could be recognised as his 'faithfuls'.[14]

On 1 June Speke said goodbye to his followers. He gave them drafts for an extra year's wages and for a ten-dollar dowry when they married, in addition to the 'freeman's garden' already arranged. It was a moving parting—'they all volunteered to go with me again, should I attempt to cross Africa from east to west,' he wrote. It was intended that they would go to Suez, Aden, the Seychelles and Zanzibar, but the ship did not stop at the Seychelles and they found themselves in Mauritius with a month to wait. Captain Anson, Inspector-General of Police, took charge of them, raised a subscription, took them to a circus and otherwise entertained them. When they left, he divided the remaining money between them, but Bombay claimed all the amounts allotted to the women, on the grounds that they were all his wives. They arrived back at Zanzibar in the *Pleiad* on 26 August 1863.[15]

Speke and Grant sailed for England on 4 June but did not forget the 'faithfuls'; the former wrote to thank Anson, and corresponded regularly with Playfair, who did a great deal to carry out his wishes, including arranging for the Africans to receive shambas at Bububu and Ziwani on the outskirts of the town. He also had Baraka and ten other deserters who returned to Zanzibar imprisoned. Playfair encountered some problems; Speke wrote to him on 7 February 1864 that he was 'extremely sorry to hear that Bombay's head had been turned by his elevation. On the journey I had often occasion to wig him for getting drunk, but always made it up again, as he was the life and success of the expedition.'[16] During the year the Royal Geographical Society awarded a silver medal to Bombay and bronze medals to the other seventeen. Grant sent £100 to be shared among them. One of the 'faithfuls', Matagiri, seems to have disappeared. Neither Grant's gift, nor one from Speke, was given to him. A possible explanation comes from Samuel Baker who, ten years later, had among his soldiers, known as 'the forty thieves', Selim, 'one of Speke's Faithfuls, who, having got drunk at Alexandria, was seized by the police and made a soldier'. Baker sent him with a letter to Mutesa on 13 February 1873, ordering him to remain there after delivering it. Chaillé-Long, one of Gordon's officers, found him at Fatiko in May 1874 and took him on to Buganda as an interpreter. Mutesa wished him to remain, but Long did not accede to this request and in September, when Selim was dilatory in bringing up his horse and some supplies, ordered him fifty stripes. This is the last known of Selim. Sir John Gray suggests that he could well be Matagiri, the only one of the 'faithfuls' to fit the circumstances; since he was engaged in the interior, he was not presumably a Muslim before his forcible enlistment, and renaming would therefore be appropriate.[17]

Speke's continued interest in Africa was evidenced by a 'Scheme for opening Africa', including the abolition of slavery, and he must have had the Wanguana particularly in mind in his idea of using 'educated negroes' as allies, and in establishing depots of freed men round the coast. He had made comparatively little progress in promoting his scheme when, on 15 September 1864, he was accidentally killed while out shooting. His brother wrote to ask Playfair, 'if there is anything you may think he would have wished to have further done with what he called "his faithfuls" '. Bombay is said to have commented, on receiving news of his death, 'Now my father is dead and my right arm is cut off', and he told Livingstone he wished to visit Speke's grave.[18]

38

5

AFRICANS IN THE ZAMBEZI EXPEDITION 1858–1864

While Speke was leading his first expedition to Lake Victoria in June 1858, David Livingstone was disembarking at the mouth of the Zambezi, 1,250 miles to the south. At the close of 1856 he had returned to England after sixteen years in Africa; during the last three of these he had crossed the continent from west to east, and was nationally acclaimed as a heroic missionary-explorer. In the ensuing fifteen months this fame enabled him to promote several schemes for Africa, in which his restless zeal for the future of the continent tended to override practical considerations. Three separate Christian missions were founded, and Livingstone himself was given command of an official expedition to explore the Zambezi, whose potentialities he had described so enthusiastically.[1]

For transport up the river a 75-feet long paddle-wheeled, flat-bottomed boat, the *Ma-Robert*, intended to carry thirty-six men, was taken out to Africa in sections on board HMS *Pearl*. The *Ma-Robert* was to be manned by Krumen, members of a race which lived in Liberia and other parts of the west African grain coast. They had acquired a considerable reputation as sailors in ships of the Royal Navy on the west and south coasts of Africa and in merchant vessels. Krumen had also conducted themselves well, and had kept in good health, during the ill-fated Niger Expedition of 1841–42.

The *Ma-Robert* and her crew were under the charge of Commander Norman Bedingfeld, RN, second in command of the whole expedition. The remaining British members were Livingstone's brother Charles, 'general assistant and moral agent', John Kirk, economic botanist, Richard Thornton, geologist, Thomas Baines, artist and storekeeper, and George Rae, engineer.

The expedition left England on 10 March and a dozen Krumen

39

under Tom Jumbo as headman were enlisted at Sierra Leone and issued with blue 'slops', in the tradition of British naval ratings. After several attempts HMS *Pearl* entered the Zambezi by the Kongone mouth in May.

It soon became clear that the original instructions for the *Pearl* to accompany the expedition as far as the Portuguese settlement of Tete, more than 250 miles from the coast, could not be carried out, for she had too deep a draught for the river and had to leave the men and goods near the mouth. From June to early August the expedition was working in small groups, transporting supplies and equipment in relays. This work soon revealed the shortcomings of the *Ma-Robert*, which proved to be a vast consumer of wood. Livingstone estimated that 150 tons were burned in the first year—'Perpetual wood-cutting: it wears the heart out of us', he wrote.[2] Adding to these difficulties was the smouldering animosity between Livingstone and Bedingfeld, which flamed into open hostility at the end of July and led to the latter's resignation.

These early events revealed three problems which were to recur throughout the next six years. Naval vessels bringing supplies could not travel beyond the Zambezi delta, and consequently the record of the expedition is a confusing one of tedious journeys up and down stream to collect goods and personnel and to receive news, often handicapped by the second adverse factor, the unsatisfactory transport. Not only was the *Ma-Robert* wasteful of fuel, but her hull leaked. The river was difficult to navigate, and delays due to mud-banks and shoals sometimes made it impossible to keep rendezvous with supply ships. Discord among the British members did not end with Bedingfeld's departure; Thornton and Baines were both dismissed during 1859, and relations between the remaining officers were not always harmonious.

The effect on the morale of the African members of the expedition was inevitably adverse. As Livingstone later wrote, 'No doubt the natives are at times as perversely stupid as servants at home can be when they like; but our conduct must often appear to the native mind as a mixture of silliness and insanity.' The Krumen, already discouraged by the shortcomings of their vessel, witnessed at least one angry exchange between Livingstone and Bedingfeld, their nominal commander, and proved less satisfactory with the passage of time. Livingstone, looking back, wrote that eight of the eleven man-of-war's men originally recruited deserted on learning that Bedingfeld was to command them, and their replacements were less experienced; moreover they were Fishmen, not Krumen, 'a very bad lot', but it is not clear why he regarded this sub-tribe of the Kru as inferior. At the time of their engagement, he thought they seemed 'good active men'.

In the delta, they had helped put the *Ma-Robert* together and acted as boatmen and personal servants. Tom Jumbo, their leader, was ignorant of the local language, but the presence of an African helped to reassure the inhabitants as to the benevolent intentions of the expedition. At a later stage he saved one of his colleagues from drowning. Another, Tom Coffee, acted as engineer's mate. The Krumen cut wood, loaded the boat, and carried out miscellaneous duties ashore and afloat.

Livingstone wrote in August that 'The Kroomen all work admirably'. One, however, was found guilty of pilfering and in September he, with another man who had been invalided, was sent on board HMS *Lynx*, and one of the ship's company, Quartermaster John Walker, was assigned to the expedition to take charge of the remaining Krumen. These did good work, particularly when the *Ma-Robert* kept running aground. 'Kroomen going into water willingly', wrote Livingstone. 'Grounded again—then a third and fourth time; very trying to their tempers. I thought I saw evidence of them failing at last. I feel very sorry to exact such work from them.'

To supplement the Krumen, local Africans were engaged as the need arose, usually through the Portuguese residents at Shupanga, Tete, and other riverside settlements. They were required mainly for the interminable task of wood-cutting, but were also hired for supplementary transport as canoe crews.

One man who had a long association with the expedition was an African slave named Joao Tizora who was generally referred to as Jerry or Joe Scissors ('tesouras' is Portuguese for scissors). He was hired as a river pilot, probably at Shupanga in August 1858. His father had sold himself as a slave and with the proceeds had bought further slaves. Scissors himself was a 'colona' or slave living in the country, cultivating land, and paying his master for the use of it. He was sometimes bullied by the Krumen, but Kirk wrote, 'The native pilot . . . has a first rate eye for the water'; he also interpreted, as well as undertaking trading on his own account. References by missionaries, naval officers and members of the expedition indicate that he was a useful man who remained, at least intermittently, with the expedition until 1863.[3] Other local men were hired from time to time as guides.

The Africans most closely linked with the expedition, however, were the Makololo. They were a people of Sotho stock who had migrated to the Barotse Valley, where Livingstone first encountered them in 1851. From November 1853 twenty-seven had accompanied him on his ten-month journey to and from Loanda. He was so impressed by their quality that when he set out for the east coast in November 1853 he took another 114 from Linyanti. They were with him when he discovered the Victoria Falls on 17 November 1855, and were left at

41

Tete in April 1856 when he promised to return and take them back to their own country. He was eager to meet them again; as he wrote later, 'In fairness I must tell you that my judgement may be warped by the very great affection I have to the Makololo. They are a jolly rollicking lot of fellows with a great deal of the soldier in their character. They contrast very favourably with the tribes living under them.'

On arriving at Tete early in September, he was 'at once surrounded by my faithful Makololo', and heard of their misfortunes; six had been murdered, and thirty had died of smallpox. Although the survivors had not received the support from the Portuguese Government that had been promised, they had been helped by Major Sicard, the Commandant, and were settling down. They were now 'anxious to come on service', but for the moment Livingstone could engage only one, Matengo, who became a stoker on the *Ma-Robert*.[4]

In November, however, he took parties of them, with some of his British colleagues, and local guides, on two explorations of the Kebrabasa rapids, upstream from Tete. After clambering over blisteringly hot rocks, he found that the report by one Makololo, from local information, that there was 'a waterfall as high as a tree' was correct, and he had to face the fact that the Zambezi was not navigable beyond this point.

Nevertheless, he had unflagging zeal and an unquenchable belief in a divine purpose supporting his work, and at once turned his energies in seeking other routes into the interior. He took the *Ma-Robert* down the Zambezi and up the Shire River. Near the junction he and Kirk led six Makololo to explore Mount Morumbala, and then continued up the Shire River as far as the cataracts which he named after Sir Roderick Murchison, President of the Royal Geographical Society. He returned to Tete in February 1859 impressed by the possibilities of settlement in the Shire highlands.

He found the Makololo disappointingly deficient in linguistic knowledge and wrote, 'I never was so badly off for means of communicating with the people.' He used them for collecting specimens and, though they never seemed very promising material for evangelism, tried teaching them the Lord's Prayer and the Creed. He wrote that they 'may now almost be considered part of the Expedition'.

In March he left Tete to attempt the second exploration of the Shire, taking fifteen Makololo. By now the Krumen were out of favour. Kirk wrote on 25 March, 'When the Krumen are cutting wood, we prefer the voyage along shore with the Makololo at the helm. This is the first attempt. We shall soon see them the only crew. The signs of the times work that way fast. The Krumen won't be any loss.' There were several reasons for dissatisfaction—though they had done useful work wood-cutting, they had not been well-disciplined. There had been an episode in November when they brought women on board the pinnace and they had flouted Walker's authority in January. They had not shown the hoped-for immunity to fever, were 'useless on land journies' and would overload the boat if Makololo were taken to relieve the Krumen for porterage. Livingstone and Kirk made some allowances for the bad influence of Bedingfeld, but matters came to a head early in June when the Krumen tried to 'work to rule' and refused their food. 'Resolve to send them all on board the first man of war we meet . . .', wrote Livingstone. Kirk thought that unsystematic storekeeping in, for example, their rum ration, was a contributory cause of discontent but considered the Makololo, 'decent fellows for savages and will do some work well', preferable to 'a worthless set of Kroomen'.

The *Ma-Robert* was taken up the Shire as far as Chibisa's, the town of a friendly chief, which was to be used as a base for several inland journeys. Livingstone and Kirk, with local guides and twelve Makololo, then went on overland seeking the large lakes reported to lie farther up the Shire. They reached Lake Shirwa, but not the larger 'Nyinyesi' beyond. The Makololo showed their worth as a bodyguard when a local chief threatened attack, and were also useful in bargaining for goods. On their return they told Livingstone they would journey with him 'to Nyinyesi or wherever else I may wish to go'.

The expedition went down to the coast in July, and on the journey trouble came to a head when the Krumen and Makololo were involved in a quarrel which began as horseplay and ended in a fight, and Kirk's sympathies changed—'If what I saw was a specimen of the Makololo fighting, they are a bloody set of cowards. The Krumen would thrash twice their number.' Livingstone quieted both parties but later in the day, faced with disobedience, laid about the dissidents with a cook's ladle.

At the Kongone mouth the remaining Krumen were sent on board HMS *Penguin*, together with Walker, who was invalided. Livingstone 'rigged out eight Makololo to supply their place'. Though he was aware that they sometimes stole, he wrote, 'the Makololo . . . besides being good travellers, could cut wood, work the ship, and required only native food.' Kirk however wondered if the action had been too drastic; the Makololo were inexperienced—'The handling of a boat is a mystery as yet to them'—and only Livingstone could speak their language. They appeared to be useless as hunters, and in place of a Kru cook who made a cabbage tart, the expedition acquired a Makololo who made coffee with cold water and later used the whole of the mulligatawny paste on one meal. After a few days, however, the Makololo were 'coming into shape' and on 4 August Livingstone wrote 'Makololo steer pretty well'. One problem was that the men were Batoka, and not true Makololo, and did not always understand even Livingstone. This

43

was evident when boats being towed up stream capsized, the men could not understand instructions and one was drowned.

By now forty-six Makololo had joined the expedition for various duties, and at the end of August Livingstone took thirty-six of them when he set out from Chibisa's to seek the great lake to the north. On 17 September he 'traced this river up to its source in the hitherto undiscovered Lake Nyassa or Nyinyesi'—a mighty area of water whose extent no one knew.[5] Impressed by the fertility of the area, he decided that settlement and legitimate commerce could replace the slave trade whose depredations were all too obvious. For the proper exploration of the lake, he needed a vessel which could be taken in sections past the cataracts, and he sent a request to England for a new steam-launch, the *Lady Nyassa*, to be built and to be paid for from the proceeds of his *Missionary Travels*. Early in 1860 Rae returned to England to supervise its construction.

Thornton and Baines had also left under unhappy circumstances, and with his man-power depleted and his ship virtually useless, Livingstone had the opportunity to pause in his main task and fulfil his promise to take the Makololo back to their own country. He paid off those who had served as his crew.

The sojourn at Tete had not improved the Makololo. He noted, 'Makololo learn Portuguese, but as usual always the bad words first', and, 'They have got into the careless improvident slave customs, spending all as fast as it is earned. Had I known the state of society here in 1856 as well as I do now, I would have returned them, though it would have involved another year's separation from my family.' Many had formed connections with slave women and had children, and the fact that most of them were not true Makololo, but subject tribes, who preferred their status at Tete to what they would find at home, made them reluctant to return. A number stayed behind, others deserted on the way, so only twenty-five or thirty reached Linyanti in August.

However, a journey with his favourite Makololo heartened Livingstone, and on his return journey a month later he was accompanied part of the way by an embassy to a local chief, and took back to the Zambezi sixteen men—two young Makololo, Moloka and Ramakukan, who had never travelled before, and fourteen members of subject races. Among these latter were half-a-dozen canoe men under Mobita, who had previously gone with Livingstone to Loanda.

In November Livingstone began to journey downstream from Tete but the *Ma-Robert* sank, and the expedition travelled on in hired canoes, paddled by local men, since the Makololo were not experienced in handling big canoes. In the lower-lying coastal areas they, like their predecessors, suffered in health, particularly from diarrhoea.

44

On 31 January 1861 HMS *Sidon* arrived at the Kongone mouth, bringing the *Pioneer*, a new launch, 115 feet long, provided by the Admiralty, and the first members of a mission sent out to the Zambezi by a new society which had come into being as the result of a stirring speech by Livingstone at Cambridge in December 1857. It was originally known as the Oxford, Cambridge, Dublin and Durham Mission, but later adopted the more familiar name of the Universities Mission to Central Africa (UMCA). The remainder of the party arrived early in February, among them the Bishop who was to lead the Mission.[6]

Charles Frederick Mackenzie was Archdeacon of Natal when, in November 1859, he was appointed Missionary Bishop in central Africa. He was in his mid-thirties, a man of wide sympathies and attractive personality. During 1860 he had gathered his first missionaries and had brought them out via the Cape. There were three clergymen and four laymen—three artisans and a Lay Superintendent, Horace Waller. Waller, twenty-seven years old, had a warm heart and courageous impetuous nature. These were to be placed at the service of Africa for the rest of his life.

Mackenzie brought from England a Jamaican cook, once a slave in America, named Lorenzo Johnson, and at Cape Town he selected five Africans from volunteers at St Paul's Mission, where a young clergyman, T. F. Lightfoot, had built up a congregation from freed slaves who had been landed in south Africa. The men chosen came from the area proposed for the mission and it was hoped their local knowledge and ability as interpreters would be valuable. Four were chosen for the mission itself—Henry Job of Senna, Apollos Le Paul of Tete, and two Makoas, Charles Thomas and William Ruby; the fifth, Joseph Antonie of Senna, was engaged as an interpreter for HMS *Pioneer*.[7]

Livingstone was anxious to find a way of access to the Shire-Nyasa region which avoided territory controlled by the Portuguese whose involvement in the slave trade angered him. This might, he thought, be provided by the Rovuma River, 600 miles north-east of the Zambezi, and he persuaded the Bishop to delay establishing his mission and to accompany him. The whole party therefore sailed to Johanna, in the Comoro Islands, where many were left while Livingstone, the Bishop, Kirk, Charles Livingstone, the Rev. Henry Rowley and a number of naval officers attempted to ascend the Rovuma in March in the *Pioneer*. Joseph acted as interpreter and the Makololo formed part of the crews. They told the sailors that 'they liked the English, because they were the only people besides themselves who were not afraid, and liked fun.' Rowley enjoyed their traditional chants, and 'grew to be very fond of the Makololo'. Though regretting their use of *bhang*, he thought they had redeeming qualities, particularly Moloko, 'for there seemed in him capacities for good which none of the others had'.[8]

45

Wood-cutting proved a problem with the *Pioneer* as with the *Ma-Robert*, but the main difficulty was the shallowness of the river, which forced the expedition to turn back after thirty miles. About a third of its members were sick when the *Pioneer* returned to the Comoro Islands, and in April six men from Johanna were engaged to replace members of the *Pioneer*'s crew who had been invalided. Apollos and Joseph were left at Johanna to return to the Cape, and Johnson and the other three Africans accompanied the mission back to the mainland and up the Zambezi. The Makololo had by now 'turned quite obstinate and worse than useless . . . This trouble seems to come principally from the two true Makololo who have influence over those of the subject tribes and while doing nothing themselves, have instigated the others,' commented Kirk, who therefore recruited thirteen men from Senna. Rowley noted that the older men seemed degraded by long slavery, but the younger ones 'were quickwitted, and readily attached themselves to you, and were anxious, when once you had their confidence, to be of service to you'. The *Pioneer* journeyed laboriously up the Shire, with groundings, fever, and crew shortcomings. Chibisa's was reached on 8 July and preparations made to establish the mission.

On 15 July most of the missionaries, with several of the expedition led by Livingstone, the Makololo, twelve men from Senna, and numerous locally engaged porters, set off inland. Two days later the sound of trumpets was heard and a slave caravan, consisting of a small armed party escorting a column of fettered men, women and children came into sight. When the slavers saw a substantial body approaching, they fled, leaving their eighty-four captives. The women and children were cut loose, and a saw was used to free the men from the forked wooden 'slave sticks', which were then used for a fire to cook a meal for the liberated Africans. The Bishop wrote in his diary, 'one little boy looked up at the Doctor—said they starved us, you bid us cook food, where do you come from.'[9]

'Our men . . . behaved admirably', wrote Kirk, and they also gave support when, a few days later, Livingstone and the Bishop were engaged in a skirmish with slave-holding Yao. The eighty-four were joined by other freed slaves in the next few days, and became the responsibility of the mission, which established its first station at Magomero. After this Livingstone returned to Chibisa's.

In the months that followed, the mission developed its activities at Magomero, and Johnson and the three Africans had an important part to play since they were the link between the missionaries and the local chiefs, as well as the released slaves. Charles Thomas, who took his name from a retired merchant captain in Cape Town who had befriended him when he was released from slavery, was the senior man. A leading member of Lightfoot's congregation, he had acquired fluent English

46

during twenty years in Cape Town. His native tongue was Makoa, but his Manganja was poor. William Ruby, 'an intelligent fellow' spoke Manganja but his English was not good. Henry Job was a practical helper, working particularly well with Waller; and Johnson the Jamaican cook was a genial man with some musical ability, a quick ear for languages, and a kindly attitude to the freed slave children. Their linguistic shortcomings made it difficult for the missionaries to give satisfactory religious instruction, so they had to concentrate instead on trying to build up the practical aspect of the settlement. The Cape Africans assisted in this; Charles trained one lad, Wekotani, as a page. They were also helpful in obtaining provisions, hiring porters, and assisting in journeys.

Kirk and Livingstone, with Charles Livingstone and Neil, a seaman, had gone to explore Lake Nyasa, carrying the *Pioneer*'s gig. They left five Makololo at Chibisa's and took the remainder, as well as ten Senna men. For porterage past the Murchison cataracts, fifty Manganja men were engaged for a cubit of cloth a day. Livingstone found them 'difficult to get on with, but payment will improve them'. Lake Nyasa was reached on 2 September, and though not achieving all he had hoped, Livingstone added much to his knowledge of the area. He accompanied the shore party much of the way, and later went on the lake. 'Our Makololo acknowledged that, in handling canoes, the Lake men beat them; they were unwilling to cross the Zambesi even, when the wind blew fresh.'

There were other causes of dissatisfaction with the Makololo. Kirk thought them as cowardly as the Senna men, and little use for protection against local thieves. They seemed restive at not having been sent home and in October, on the journey back, broke into open mutiny and went off to hunt elephants. Livingstone and his comrades, with one Batoka and two Senna men, reached the lowest navigable point of the Shire on 1 November and left the gig in a tree. Six days later the Makololo returned. 'They thought that we had been put to vast inconvenience for want of them and began to act the independent gentlemen deluded individuals,' wrote Kirk. Even Livingstone was exasperated with his favourites and they were left at Chibisa's, where they rejoined their fellow-countrymen.

A few days after his return Livingstone heard that his wife Mary was arriving on board HMS *Gorgon*. The *Pioneer* set off downstream with a crew of Johanna men and others hired en route, but owing to grounding on shoals, it was late January 1862 before she reached the Luabo mouth. On the 31st HMS *Gorgon* arrived. On board were not only Mrs Livingstone, but Miss Mackenzie, the Bishop's sister, other mission reinforcements, and the Rev. James Stewart, a young Scot inspired by Livingstone's writings to come out to assess missionary prospects. The ship

47

also carried George Rae, and the new launch, the *Lady Nyassa*, in sections.

Stewart noted the appearance of the Johanna men 'in red and blue velvet coats', but however smart, they were ill-disciplined. The presence of the naval contingent was a welcome reinforcement; Gunner Edward Young of HMS *Gorgon* was assigned to help with the assembly of the *Lady Nyassa* and, being a down-to-earth man, began to make order out of the chaos which to the naval eye was all too prevalent in the expedition.[10]

Bishop Mackenzie was to have joined Livingstone on the downward journey, but there was no news of him, and Captain Wilson of HMS *Gorgon* went up-river to investigate. The story he learned was a tragic one. After an unsuccessful attempt to travel overland, Mackenzie had essayed the journey by canoe from Chibisa's, accompanied by three Makololo and a young missionary, Henry Burrup. The canoe overturned and equipment, including medicine, was lost. The Bishop was attacked by fever and died on Malo Island on 31 January. The Makololo, who had given loyal service, buried him on the banks of the Shire and helped Burrup back to Magomero, where he too died. Captain Wilson himself returned to the *Gorgon* and sailed for the Cape in April, but left Young with the expedition. This was not the end of the tragic losses, for Mary Livingstone contracted fever, and on 27 April she died at Shupanga.

The *Lady Nyassa* was assembled, and launched on 23 June, but it was too late in the year to use her. Livingstone therefore decided to explore the Rovuma again, but for this he needed a fresh crew. Kirk wrote that the Johanna men were 'very steady and useful fellows, little subject to fever or disease which incapacitate Europeans and not so difficult to manage as Krumen', but their term of service had expired. Livingstone therefore took them back to Johanna in August in the *Pioneer* and recruited a fresh crew with the aid of William Sunley, the British Consul. He had also engaged some men from Shupanga or Mazaro, a few miles away.

Remembering his earlier problems, Livingstone used two boats for the second Rovuma journey, which began on 9 September. He was accompanied for two days by the galley and cutter of HMS *Orestes*, under Captain Gardner. The *Pioneer*, which had been towed to the mainland by the *Orestes*, was left in charge of Gunner Young. Captain Gardner commented that Livingstone's crews were 'made up of Zambesi and other black natives, one of the former a very fine specimen of a man'. The lifeboat had David and Charles Livingstone, two seamen and five Zambezians; the whaler, Kirk, a seaman, three Zambezians and one Johanna man. 'The Zambesi men thoroughly understood the characteristic marks of deep or shallow water, and showed great skill in finding out the proper channel,' wrote Livingstone. They used the traditional method of a Molimo or steersman at the helm, and the Mokadamo, or headman, standing in the bows with a pole. The rest of the crew preferred punting to rowing, as they were unaccustomed to the long oars, compared with canoe paddles. After the party had escaped from an attack, one of the Zambezi men named Chiko commented that 'His fear was not the kind which makes a man jump overboard and run away; but that which brings the heart up to the mouth, and renders the man powerless, and no more able to fight than a woman.'

The expedition reached a point 156 miles up the river and arrived back at the coast on 9 October. Gunner Young, who had a poor opinion of the Johanna men left with him, kept them at work by crude but effective methods.[11] On Livingstone's return they 'complained of having been brutally treated by Mr. Young—knocked down & put in terror of their lives.' Livingstone and Young had already had one dispute but this appears to have passed over. Livingstone thought that his difficulties in recruiting another crew were due to Young's methods, but Devereux believed the cause was the King of Johanna's annoyance that some of his slaves had been included in the previous batch. However, Livingstone was able to engage six men—five at 7 dollars a month and a headman at 10—in October. Before leaving early in November, he issued an order 'that no man should strike any native without my orders'. After a tedious return journey Shupanga was reached on 17 December, and the local men paid off. In four and a half months they had 'become good sailors and very attentive servants'; they received 16 yards of cloth, the equivalent of 10 shillings a month, as well as gifts of clothes. Stewart found the Zambezi natives 'perfectly quiet and peaceful . . . anxious to trade and to cultivate friendly relations with white men', and the missionaries grew familiar with 'the well-known Shupanga boat-song'.

Livingstone was therefore glad to engage ten more Shupanga men, friends of his former crew, who were willing to take half pay until experienced. He left in his two vessels on 9 January 1863; among those with him was Thornton, who, after travelling in east Africa, had returned to the expedition. In mid March Livingstone reached Chibisa's, and in response to an urgent request went up to the mission to find that Dr Dickinson had died, and other members were ill. After treating the sick, he gave his attention to the complaints which Waller and others had made about the activities of the Makololo.

Though few in number, they had, by virtue of their superior organisation and arms, established their own rule, and gathered wives and slaves around them with scant regard for the rights of their neighbours. Rowley wrote of them, 'The Makololo were the admiration of the Chibisian women. They possessed just those qualities most calculated

49

to lead women astray, and astray many of them went.' Similar problems arose with the mission protégées, but Rowley 'liked these Makololo, notwithstanding the trouble they gave us. They were a brave set of men, and had we needed assistance at any time when on the Shire, they would have given it unhesitatingly.'[12] Livingstone thought that there were faults on both sides, and particularly blamed the Cape Africans, three of whom had been sent home for moral lapses—indeed, he could find no good word for the latter, and used 'Job and William sort of fellows' as a term of reproach. In this he was less than just, for, in spite of their faults, they had served the mission under extremely difficult circumstances to the best of their ability. Kirk was not convinced that the Makololo were blameless, and even though Livingstone upheld them, he later apologised to Waller for the way in which he had reacted to the latter's complaints.

Livingstone went on to the Murchison cataracts, where he established a base camp, with huts built by the Johanna men. The *Lady Nyassa* was taken to pieces and a road commenced along which she could be taken in carts drawn by oxen brought from Johanna. The expedition was, however, disintegrating; Thornton, after assisting the mission to obtain much-needed food, died of fever. In May Charles Livingstone and Kirk were invalided, and some of the Shupanga men wished to return home. Livingstone asked Kirk to try to recruit some of their former employees for another six months.

In mid June he found that the gig left in a tree had been destroyed in a bush fire, and at the beginning of July came the news that the expedition was to be recalled. The despatch was brought by Bishop Tozer, Mackenzie's successor, who had arrived with his colleague, Edward Steere, almost a month earlier.

The *Lady Nyassa* now had to be reassembled to return to the coast, and was never to sail on the lake after which she was named. Livingstone, however, determined to make a last attempt to explore the eastern and northern shore of the lake, and set off with his Johanna men bringing a boat on the ox-cart, five Zambezi boatmen, and Makololo making his strength up to twenty. Waller recruited Yao men to take the boat beyond the cataracts when the ox-waggon reached the end of the track. At the top of the cataracts the Zambezi men—Kanyai, Peoso, Arimasau, Ropa and Mandzu, a slave, tried to show that they were better boatmen than the Makololo, but their experience was with heavy canoes, and the boat was overturned and lost down the cataracts. 'Sic gloria sailing on Nyassa transit'[13] commented Livingstone and, undaunted, continued his explorations by land. Guides were engaged locally and the lake reached at the end of August. The high altitude had one bad effect—'The Shupanga men, who are malaria-proof in the Delta, succumbed on the heights—and one of them actually died from change of air.' Despite the difficulties, this journey enabled Livingstone to add still more to his information on the region. He arrived back at the *Pioneer* on 1 November.

On 27 November a Johanna man was seized by a crocodile, but his colleagues, one of whom, Musa, was the victim's brother-in-law, did nothing to rescue him.[14] To Livingstone, this callousness was in great contrast to the mutual loyalty usually shown by the Makololo. He also contrasted the Johanna men's low standard of cleanliness unfavourably with the Shupanga men, who 'wash every evening'.

Meanwhile the Mission's problems had grown acute; the survivors of the original party, notably Waller, had resented Tozer's removal of the mission from Chibisa's to Mount Morumbala, since the latter was in the territory of the slave-owning Portuguese. It seemed to them, also, that Tozer was betraying the ideals of Mackenzie by vacillating about taking with him the African protégées of the Mission, though the Bishop pointed out that not all of these wished to move. Tozer did take some boys with him, and Waller resigned from the Mission in order to be free to look after the women and girls.

In mid November Tozer decided that Mount Morumbala was unhealthy, and that the Mission should be withdrawn altogether, taking such boys as wished to go, but sending back up the Shire those who did not—among them Katapolo, the eldest, and Wekotani, Bishop Mackenzie's favourite boy. Waller commended him to Livingstone—he 'would make a first rate servant on board ship, is a good little tailor and can wait on table.'[15] Livingstone was indignant; he took charge of the six boys sent back, and demanded custody of all the rest from Tozer; the Bishop welcomed this as a solution of a complex problem. At Chibisa's, in January 1864, Livingstone said goodbye to the Makololo for the last time, and travelled downstream on the *Pioneer*, collecting Waller, his colleague Alington, and the rest of the Africans on 2 February. Livingstone told Young to 'pitch into the water' any Portuguese who tried to stop his progress. The various elements gathered at Mozambique and Waller wrote in his diary:

The Dr thinks of taking Wekotani home and Rae of taking Juma. How I wish I was in a position to take Chinsoro [his servant] and Chasika with me. I shall hardly be able to part from them. They are not married yet. I promise them this at the Cape. They would do well in England I think Chinsoro as a gardner and his wife as servant in some other capacity. Since she got well she has filled out into the woman and for beauty of form and artless prettiness it would take a very pretty English girl to beat her . . . I never can keep cross 10 minutes with her even when the most flagrant deviation from my code of European requirements call for it.[16]

51

Eventually forty-two Africans went to the Cape, and Waller saw that all of them were apprenticed or otherwise provided for before he left. Lightfoot undertook their general oversight.

The two boys, Wekotani and Chuma (Juma), remained with Livingstone and sailed with him to India on the *Lady Nyassa*, which he would not sell in Zanzibar as it might be used by a slaver. He had three white men—Pennell, Collyer and John Reid, and seven Zambezians, 'quite raw fellows', Chiko, Susi, Amoda, Bizenti, Safuri, Nyampinga and Bachoro: 'They were not picked men, but, on paying a dozen whom we had in our employment for fifteen months, they were taken at random from several hundreds who offered to accompany us. Their wages were ten shillings per mensem.'

The epic voyage of the *Lady Nyassa*, about 110 feet long, across 2,500 miles of ocean, lasted from 30 April to 13 June.[17] Steam could be used only in emergencies, since the coal stock was limited to fourteen tons. For many days the vessel was becalmed or made little progress; nearing India she was battered by gales and one of the sails ripped to shreds. The Africans had a significant part to play, for some of the white men were ill or unsatisfactory, and three of the Zambezi men learned to steer. Livingstone noted, 'so eager were they to do their duty that only one of them lay down from sea-sickness during the whole voyage. They took in and set sail very cleverly in a short time, and would climb out along a boom, reeve a rope through the block, and come back with the rope in their teeth, though at each lurch the performer was dipped in the sea.'[18] He paid them off at Bombay on 22 June, and left Chuma and Wekotani in a school run by Dr Wilson before returning to England.

The Zambezi expedition and the missions associated with it were in many ways disastrous ventures. However, Livingstone himself and many of those involved were to return to Africa. Kirk, with Livingstone's support, was appointed Agency Surgeon at Zanzibar in 1866, and for twenty-one years, as Vice-Consul, Consul and Consul-General, played a major role in east African affairs and the campaign against the slave trade. Edward Young and James Stewart had further work to do in Africa; members of the crew of the *Lady Nyassa*, as well as some of the freed slaves sent to the Cape, also had their part to play. Of the missionaries, Tozer and Steere, notwithstanding Livingstone's strictures on their actions, had their own concept of responsibility and purpose; they determined to re-establish the mission, and sailed to Zanzibar to make it a base from which, in due course, they could return to the mainland. Waller, who was ordained in 1867, never revisited Africa, but for the rest of his life he was deeply concerned in the welfare and future of the continent and its people.

52

6

LIVINGSTONE'S JOURNEY TO UJIJI

When Livingstone returned to England from the Zambezi the source of the Nile was the subject of heated debate. He had hoped to meet Speke but was able only to attend his funeral. There was discussion as to the validity of Speke's claims, and the news of Baker's discovery of Lake Albert raised further questions—was this Lake the true source or was it perhaps fed by a stream from Lake Tanganyika? Livingstone welcomed the invitation of the Royal Geographical Society to return to Africa and attempt to solve the problems.[1]

In the spring of 1865 he began to organise his expedition and considered the choice of personnel. As he would have to return to India where he had left the *Lady Nyassa* and her African crew, the recruitment of Indians was discussed. Sir Bartle Frere, Governor of Bombay, whom he had met the previous year, recommended Baluchis, but Colonel Rigby, who had retired from Zanzibar, dissuaded him, and he was undecided as to the best course to adopt. Recalling his old associates, he thought he might 'go down to the lake to get Makololo, if the Indians don't answer'. He was anxious not to have untried men— 'It does not seem feasible to go into Mombasa and hand oneself and goods over to people of whom we know next to nothing and on whom we have no hold'—and on 2 June he wrote to Sunley, the British Consul in the Comoro Islands:

Can you give me an encouragement to hope for 20 or 25 men if I come to Johanna? I want them as carriers chiefly . . . I liked the first lot I had from you very much, and blamed the headman most for the second party turning out dishonest . . . If you give me hope in a letter to Bombay . . . I should ask the man-of-war to put me down at Johanna instead of on the coast . . . I would like them all Johanna men, if I could have two trustworthy headmen and a cook . . .

C

This optimistic approach is in strange contrast to his comment only a few weeks before that Johanna men 'are a poor lot to trust to'.[2]

He sailed for India in August 1865 and arrived at Bombay on 11 September. He made enquiries about the Africans whom he had left in Bombay. Chuma and Wekotani, who had been boarded with a Christian family, had made good progress in Dr Wilson's school and had kept in good health, but four of the seven Shupanga men had died, leaving Chiko, Amoda and Susi.[3]

On 20 September Livingstone went to Poona where he saw Major Clarke about the engagement of some sepoys. He had decided to attempt to use buffaloes—'I am thinking it will be an experiment worth making in reference to the tsetse—they make good beasts of burden and the cows *give milk*—so if we cant get the worth of our money out of their bulk, its a pity,' he wrote to Waller.[4] Sepoys could look after the animals and also act as hunters. Those selected eventually were a havildar and twelve men from the Marine battalion 'who having served as Marines in the old East Indian Navy in the Persian Gulph and on the coast of Africa are prepared to undergo hardship.' 'The Marines are intelligent men,' he wrote, 'and will pick up some native tongue—a few words of Hindustani picked out of a book in Roman characters helps me along with them.' Two of them were assigned to him as orderlies during his stay.

Livingstone recruited Africans from the Nasik school, which originated in 1854 when the Rev. W. S. Price founded the Christian village of Sharanpur (city of refuge) near Nasik, about 100 miles north-east of Bombay, and built schools and workshops there. In 1860 the Rev. C. W. Isenberg took charge. He had originally been a missionary in Ethiopia, and in Bombay he had cared for some of the former slaves from Africa who had been released there but for whose welfare there had been no adequate arrangements. He therefore took twenty-nine boys to Sharanpur and initiated the policy of training Africans as well as Indians. In 1864 two pupils, Ishmael Semler and William Jones, returned to Africa to assist the veteran missionary Johann Rebmann. At the time of Livingstone's visit there were 108 pupils of varied races at Sharanpur.[5]

His arrival there on 15 September coincided with the examination of the school by the Bishop of Calcutta. Livingstone was impressed by the beautiful singing, and noted 'An African composes tunes and has made about 25 with songs in his own language—the tongue of Londa.' He spoke to the pupils, warning them 'it was not play they were going to but work', and in the course of the next few weeks he enlisted nine young men, to be paid 5 rupees a month. Their names were Simon Price, Abraham Pereira (both Gallas), Edward Gardner, Andrew Powell, James Rutton, Richard Isenberg, Reuben Smith, Albert

54

Baraka and Nathaniel Cumba, usually referred to as Mabruki. Several of the names were derived from missionaries; Isenberg and Price were the founders of the institution; the Rev. S. Powell and the Rev. W. Smith were CMS missionaries in Ceylon and Northwest India respectively; Captain Allen Gardiner was famous for his heroic work in South America; and Ruttonji Nowroji was a noted Parsee Christian whom Price had baptised.[6]

Livingstone wrote that some 'have a knowledge of carpentry and smith work, and they may be useful if we try to build up a canoe for navigating Tanganyika,' and he also appears to have had hopes of their teaching technical skills to African villagers. W. S. Price, reporting to the CMS, commented, 'most of these had completed—or nearly so—their term of apprenticeship in the Ind. Inst.' Livingstone does not seem to have realised that some of their training was incomplete, although he did express some reservations as to their quality. 'I am not very sure about the African Boys from Nassick,' he wrote to Waller. 'I fear that they may turn out Job and William sort of fellows [see p. 50]. I have more hope in the buffaloes than in them.' His doubts were increased by the receipt of an anonymous complaint about the school but Price made no attempt to identify the writer.[7]

Livingstone had higher hopes of the two freed slaves: 'Juma & Wikatani have given much satisfaction to Dr Wilson and as they wish to be baptised the Dr consulted me and as they have a general knowledge of our faith and desire it, I see no reason to object,' he wrote to Waller. 'They read in the second book which contains fables like Aesop's little tales of that kind—speak it too but not very well are quite willing to go back to Africa and have invested in a suit of greys with your money and Wiko a coat and blanket and they are to write to you by next mail.' A letter from Wekotani to Waller written in a phonetic version of Yao survives, as well as a later one written in English for him by an Indian. Chuma wrote to Waller in English on 21 September, 'I bought of that money coat and trowser and wescoat and shirt for six rupees.'[8]

Wekotani—the spelling varies, but Livingstone wrote to Waller, 'Wekotani—not the Cockney Wakatane. The e is as in met'—was originally rescued from slavery by Bishop Mackenzie's Mission in 1861 when he was about eleven. His father had been a chief but he had been sold into slavery during tribal wars. He had become Bishop Mackenzie's servant and appears to have been an attractive lad— when he visited the *Pioneer* to fetch stores, one of the sailors made a straw hat for him with 'Pioneer' in gold letters on the band. He was highly regarded by the missionaries as truthful and reliable and was used as a guard against thieves. He continued as a waiter after the Bishop's death and was eventually given blue livery instead of his

55

'ever dirty shirt'. A minor drawback was that 'having to be spoken to in the native language, there was great risk of his bringing beer in a teacup instead of tea.'[9]

Chuma (sometimes referred to as Juma) was about the same age as Wekotani, though shorter. He was a Yao, the son of Chimilengo, a skilled fisherman, and Chinjeriapi, who lived in Kusogwe. He had two younger sisters. The peace of the area was disturbed by tribal conflict, and in the ensuing confusion Chuma was taken as a slave; though he escaped once, he was eventually sold to a Portuguese slave-trader. He had been rescued with Wekotani, and his name appears in one of Bishop Mackenzie's class lists. In the mission he had been Rowley's servant, and had unsuccessfully urged on him the palatable qualities of rats fried whole. Livingstone wrote 'Chuma is a very sharp fellow. Never got into any quarrel at school—I suspect his appearance put the fear of death into the Hindoos but Dr Wilson thinks it is his goodness. He lost his cap the other day and as it was given by poor Col. Stewart and had gold lace his grief is great.' He acted as Living-stone's servant, and a picture of them together was taken by a Parsee photographer at Poona, though no copy is known to survive. On 10 December the two boys were baptised by Dr Wilson in the presence of Livingstone as John Wekotani and James Chuma.[10]

Livingstone had retained the Shupanga men on his payroll, but Chiko—who from references to him in letters was probably the leader—apparently wished to return home. The other two survivors, Amoda and Susi, agreed to accompany Livingstone. He took no Europeans.[11]

He sailed from Bombay in the *Thule*, sent as a gift to the Sultan from the Bombay Government, on 5 January 1866. On 17 January he wrote in his journal, 'Issued flannel to all the boys from Nassick; the marines have theirs from Government. The boys sing a couple of hymns every evening, and repeat the Lord's Prayer. I mean to keep up this, and make this a Christian expedition, telling a little about Christ wherever we go.' He also noted 'Most of the marine-sepoys were sick.'[12]

Zanzibar was reached on 28th. The Sultan provided accommodation and board for Livingstone and his men and formally received the expedition on 18 February; 'The sepoys came in and did obeisance; and I pointed out the Nassick lads as those who had been rescued from slavery, educated, and sent back to their own country by the Governor. Surely he must see that some people in the world act from other than selfish motives.'

Chiko, with his colleague Dungudza, was given twelve days' pro-visions and put on board a trading vessel for Quilimane on 11 February and eventually reached his home at Shupanga, where E. D. Young met him some months later.[13]

56

Livingstone disliked 'Stinkibar' for its adverse effect on health—six of his men were ill there—and for its slavery, and he was relieved when HMS *Penguin*, under Lt Garforth, arrived on 13 March with the long-awaited Johanna men. Sunley had engaged them on 9 March 'to accompany Dr Livingstone into the interior of Africa and to serve him as porters, boatmen or in any other capacity for a period of twenty months for the sum of Seven (7) dollars each per month,' and they were given two months' advance pay. Their leader, to receive 10 dollars, was Musa, who had been with Livingstone on the Zambezi (see p. 51). Lt Garforth agreed to take Livingstone to the mainland, and on 19 March he embarked on HMS *Penguin*. In tow was a dhow with the animals—three buffaloes and a calf, the survivors of twelve brought from India, six camels, two mules and four donkeys. There were two dogs, one belonging to Wekotani which was killed by a leopard, and Livingstone's poodle Chitane, drowned crossing the Chimbwe River. His human followers were the havildar (sergeant), naik (corporal) and eleven sepoys; ten Johanna men (rigged out with blue jumpers); nine Nasik boys; Chuma, Wekotani, Susi and Amoda. He was put ashore at Mikindani Bay on 24 March.[14] Here his last journey began.

While preparing for this journey, Livingstone wrote in a notebook:

Genuine sympathy with human beings obliterates the distinction of race & clime rank & religion & even of intellect. It is evidence of brutal vulgarity of mind to treat all natives as 'niggers'. Avoid this unhappy form of slang & without falling into unreal sentiment endeavour to return to that chivalry which regards with especial forbearance & consideration the inferior & helpless.[15]

These precepts were to be tested to the utmost in the problems of personnel that emerged in the first few months of the journey.

The party set out on 6 April. For the first 200 miles they had as guide 'a good looking coast Arab', Ben Ali,[16] who led them by a roundabout way so that he could visit his Makonde wife, but otherwise he seems to have been a reliable guide and, on occasion, interpreter and forager. The route was at first through jungle, so woodcutters were required to enable the camels to pass. Though a Banyan at Mikindani had told him 'no carriers could be hired' and he had left some goods, Livingstone found that the local Makonde were 'glad to engage themselves by the day either as woodcutters or carriers'. For one yard of calico a day the 'jolly young Makondé . . . went at the work with a will.' Livingstone was in good spirits and praised their efforts. Even when one carrier stole a shirt, his companions tracked him down and he was fined by the local headman—'this was the only case of theft

57

we had noticed, and the treatment showed a natural sense of justice.' However, they would serve for only brief spells and pages of Livingstone's notebooks are filled with lists of names—over 200 were temporarily employed between April and early June. Inevitably this rapidly reduced his supplies of cloth. At the beginning of June the expedition had left the wooded area and was going through drought-stricken country in which the carriers were weak from lack of food. One of their number, Chikungu, attempted to gain a rest by sending others off in what he knew was the wrong direction for food, but Livingstone refused to pay when no work was done.

On 20 May Livingstone halted at Ngomano and paid off Ali, giving him an extra two and a half dollars and a musket 'for his great services', and entrusted him with despatches to take to the coast.[17] Livingstone remained there for more than a fortnight, trying to build up his food supply and solve his personnel problems, which were becoming acute. There had been some illness among his men but the major handicap was the attitude of the sepoys. On the second day out he noted their overloading of the camels. A few days later he wrote, 'when these animals fall down under them, they assure me with so much positiveness that they are not overloaded, that I have to be silent, or only, as I have several times done before, express the opinion that they will kill these animals.' The journals record a depressing story of the deterioration of the animals, which had suffered from their sea journey and were now exposed to tsetse and brutal treatment by the sepoys.

This was not the only problem with the sepoys. They were dishonest, lazy, malingerers and unclean—'The Makondé villages are remarkably clean, but no sooner do we pass a night in one than the fellows make it filthy. The climate does give a sharp appetite, but these sepoys indulge it till relieved by vomiting and purging.' They disagreed with their fellow Muslims, the Johanna men, about the correct way to kill a goat, and called them 'Caffirs, &c'. They also tried to bribe Ali to take them back to the coast. One sepoy persuaded a woman to carry his musket, bayonet and belts—and Livingstone had to pay her.[18]

Worst of all, their influence had a corrupting effect on the Nasik boys; they urged them to go slow and threatened those loyal to Livingstone. He even asserted that their 'scheme seems to have been to detach the Nassick boys from me first, then, when the animals were all killed, the Johanna men, afterwards they could rule me as they liked, or go back and leave me to perish.'

These problems became apparent at an early stage—on 7 May he wrote, 'Sepoys are a mistake'—but his attitude was curiously detached and irresolute. He shouted at one sepoy, Pando, for belabouring a camel but more typical are the comments 'if I remain behind to keep the sepoys on the move, it deprives me of all the pleasure of travelling'

58

and 'I went on with the Johanna men and twenty-four carriers, for it was a pleasure to get away from the sepoys and Nassick boys . . . I gave up annoying myself by seeing matters, though I felt certain that the animals would all be killed.'

The Nasik boys had in any case proved inadequate interpreters and unsatisfactory workers. Soon after landing he noted that a few of them 'have the slave spirit pretty strongly . . . some look on work with indifference when others are the actors.' On 9 May Baraka refused to work 'and growled out in addition something about the crime I had been guilty of in bringing them into this wild country. I applied a stick vigorously to a part of his body where no bones are likely to be broken till he came to his senses. On the first gentle application he said "you may take your gun and shoot me I'll do nothing." This shewed me that a gentle chastisement would not do and I gave it him in earnest till he was satisfied he had made a mistake in ringleading.' About this time, too, he noted 'to annoy me they reiterated perpetually "Mr Price told us lies"—they knew that I could not relish a clergyman being called a liar—on demanding an explanation they replied that he said that they were just to go to Mozambique and then return & get wives at Nassick—this was so evidently false I let them rave to each other about their benefactor unnoticed.'19

By the time of the halt at Ngomano the sepoys and some of the Nasik boys were well behind. On 20 May the sepoys sent Abraham forward to tell Livingstone that they would not come on. He sent back a stern note, threatening to order them to the coast 'as soon as I received the havildar's formal evidence'. This did bring up the havildar who 'says that all I said in my note was true, and when it was read to the sepoys they bewailed their folly . . . I may give them another trial, but at present they are a sad incumbrance.' He summed up his dilemma in his diary for 3 June: 'I have sometimes thought of going back disarming half & sending them back . . . on the other hand in going back armed they may use their arms among the Makonde and bring disgrace on the English name. If I had known their language it might have been different but there they have stood and hindered my progress some twelve days.'20

He next turned to the Nasik boys and on 4 June told them that 'they must either work or return, it was absurd to have them eating up our goods, and not even carrying their own things, and I would submit to it no more.' He therefore ordered them to carry loads, but raised their wages to 10 rupees a month. The march was resumed, with nineteen carriers engaged at Ngomano but a week later they refused to go farther 'because they say that they fear being captured here on their return' and they were paid off.

Meanwhile, news came from the rearguard that Richard, a Nasik

59

boy, was ill; Livingstone sent back 'the only cordials we could muster'. Ten days later, six sepoys came up with Simon, and the news that Richard had died at Liponde. 'I am told now that he never consented to the sepoy temptation: he said to Abraham that he wished he was dead, he was so much troubled. The people where he died were not very civil to Simon.' This did stir Livingstone to action. He reprimanded the sepoys, disrated the naik, and sentenced the others to carry loads—'they carried willingly so long as the fright was on them, but when the fear of immediate punishment wore off they began their skulking again' and one threw away most of the stock of tea. A few weeks later the same man and a colleague gave away their loads and Livingstone 'gave Perim and the other some smart cuts with a cane, but I felt that I was degrading myself, and resolved not to do the punishment myself again.'

By mid June Livingstone was 'as much dependent on carriers as if I had never bought a beast but in time our goods will diminish so we can carry all ourselves—the carriers are not unwilling but they dawdle',[21] and the availability of recruits varied. In the middle of July he arrived at the substantial town, on an established slave-trading route, ruled by the prominent Yao chief Mataka. There was abundant food, and he stopped for a couple of weeks to reorganise. At this stage the last of the animals died—the sepoys killed and ate the buffalo calf and claimed it had been the victim of a tiger. This settled the issue; on 15 July he paid off the sepoys with 18 yards of calico, keeping on the havildar, whose discipline had been hopeless but who professed loyalty and 'will count in any difficulty'. 'They have neither spirit nor pluck as compared with the Africans', he wrote, and in a later letter, 'the Sepoys were morally unfit for travel.' Their bad influence remained after they had been dismissed. The day after leaving the town, Reuben, 'feeling that his character was gone resolved to return & stay with Mataka . . . a happy release.' He joined up with the sepoys and reached Zanzibar with eight of them in October—the fate of the other four is not known.[22]

Livingstone nearly lost another follower at Mataka's: 'Abraham recognised his uncle among the crowds who came to see us. On making himself known he found that his mother and two sisters had been sold to the Arabs after he had been enslaved.' His uncle asked him to remain; Livingstone would not have objected if he had possessed practical agricultural knowledge but 'He is a smith, or rather a nothing, for unless he could smelt iron he would be entirely without materials to work with.' He wrote to Lord Clarendon, 'I promised to endeavour to get some lads from the same school; who had acquired a knowledge of Indian agriculture to show [Mataka] how to make and use ploughs.'[23]

On 28 July, with guides provided by Mataka, the depleted party left and with occasional temporary help reached Lake Nyasa on 8 August and followed it southward. Livingstone lost another Nasik boy on 4 September; 'Andrew sulked because he got a blanket & bag only a few pounds more to his load than he liked. As it was a second offence—gave him twelve cuts with a ratan and told him that he might leave us and go to his own people as he had come to do but if he remained he must do what he was told. He preferred to go and I was glad to get rid of him. Mataka's place has great attractions for them as they get plenty to eat there & had nothing to do.'[24]

The next major halt was on 19 September at Mponda's, at the south end of the lake. Here Wekotani met a brother, and heard of other members of his family in the neighbourhood. His father, who had sold him into slavery, was dead. Livingstone had mixed feelings when Wekotani wished to remain. 'Chuma and Wikatani are very good boys', he wrote to Waller, 'but still boys utterly.' They had been his personal servants and cooks, but had not been satisfactory. In an excess of zeal, Wekotani had attempted to take rice for Livingstone from the havildar's stock, and the Indian had seized him by the throat, placing Livingstone in the dilemma that he wished to uphold the havildar's authority but would not punish Wekotani further. In August he replaced Chuma and Wekotani as cooks by Simon. 'I had them about me personally till I was reduced to the last fork and spoon,' he wrote. 'They shewed an inveterate tendency to lose my things & preserve their own. If I did not shout for breakfast I got it sometime between eleven and two o'clock. I had to relieve them of all charge of my domestic affairs. Wikatani was at that stage when civilized boys assume tailed coats. He *would* wear a night shirt I gave him Arab fashion, and if not engaged in an everlasting giggle or smoking in which he screamed in a most disagreeable fashion, was sure to be singing Dididey dididey or Weeweewee.' He also noted their irresponsibility at Chimsaka's—'thieves . . . kept up a succession of jokes with Chuma and Wikatani and when the latter was enjoying them, gaping to the sky, they were busy putting the things of which he had charge under their clothes.' They had, however, been useful as interpreters.[25] Livingstone wrote to Waller about Wekotani's future:

His excessive levity will probably be cooled by marriage—& I think he may do good by telling some of what he has seen & heard. I asked him if he would obey an order of his chief to hunt the Manganja he said no—and I hope he wont. In the event of any mission coming into the country of Mataka he will go there. I gave him some cloth—a flint gun instead of a percussion one, paper to write to you and, commending him to the chief, bade the poor boy farewell. I was sorry to part with him, but Arabs tell the Waiyau chiefs that our object in liberating slaves is to make them our own and turn them to our religion. I had declared to them through Wikatani as interpreter that they never became our slaves & were at liberty to go back to their relations if they liked, and now could not object to Wikatani without stultifying my own statements.

'A blessing go with him,' he added in his diary. Stanley was very much less tolerant in his comments and suggested that Wekotani wanted Chuma to join him in order to make him his slave.[26]

Livingstone left, with a couple of Yao as guides and carriers, on 21 September, and at the first stop, Pima's village, the havildar 're-mained behind'. He had 'never been of the smallest use.' According to Musa he died of dysentery.

The Johanna men were still with the party. Musa had taken some degree of responsibility during the early stages but the men had not been very satisfactory. When the party reached Marenga's, to the west of the lake, an Arab told Musa that the country ahead was full of Mazitu (also known as Maviti or Ngoni), who had killed a party of which he was the sole survivor. 'Musa's eyes *stood out* with terror' and the Johanna men refused to go on. 'They have been such in-veterate thieves that I am not sorry to get rid of them,' Livingstone commented, and went on with his depleted following.

Musa and eight of his comrades reached Zanzibar in December, and, to cover up their desertion and in the hope of receiving their pay, reported the murder of Livingstone and the rest of his men by Mazitu.[27] Kirk found their account plausible, but doubts remained, and in May 1867 the Royal Geographical Society accepted the offer of Gunner Edward Young, who knew and distrusted Musa, to lead an expedition to discover the truth.[28] He landed at the Kongone mouth of the Zam-bezi on 27 July from HMS *Petrel*, taking three boats, one of which, the *Search*, had been made to his specification in steel sections. After consultation with Waller he had decided on a small expedition, and took Henry Faulkner, a former army officer, as second-in-command, John Reid, carpenter of the *Pioneer* on Livingstone's earlier expedition (see p. 52), and two seamen. At the Cape on the outward journey he enlisted two of the mission boys left there by Waller in 1864, Chin-soro who had married Chasika (see p. 51), and Sinjeri, once an in-telligent and resourceful assistant to Dr Dickinson.[29] Two Krumen, Antonio, who knew Portuguese, and John Brown, were assigned to him from the *Petrel*'s crew.

Local recruits, some of them former employees of Livingstone's Zambezi expedition, took the boats upstream. Young was a staunch evangelical Christian, and held daily services for his European and African followers, at which Faulkner accompanied the hymns on his cornet-à-piston. On reaching Chibisa's, Young asked the Makololo for help. Though expressing some concern about the safety of their settlement, twelve, led by Moloka, volunteered to join him, and they enlisted some two hundred porters who, after the customary bargaining for pay, showed great endurance in the hard ascent round the Murchison cataracts and brought their burdens, which included thirty-six sections of the *Search* and twenty-one other loads comprising the mast, sails, anchor and sundry items, safely to the top by 28 August.

The Makololo again spoke of returning, saying that there was no one to protect their families. Young 'told them their lives were not of more value than his own. They thought they were. He asked them why. They said, "If you are killed, there are plenty of Englishmen to protect your wife." He told them if their wives were killed they could get more, and perhaps he could not.' Moloka declared his willingness to go on, and after a long conference the rest agreed.

Young had left the Krumen and one seaman behind, and now had three Britons, two Africans from the Cape, twelve Makololo, and their three Yao servants. The *Search* was assembled under Reid's direction and Lake Nyasa reached on 6 September. The following day, landing on the eastern shore, Young met a solitary African who told of a friendly Englishman who had passed that way, and farther along the lake another African described the white man's appearance and clothing, his 'artificial horizon', the names and relative heights of Chuma and Wekotani, Musa and the Johanna men, the havildar, and even Livingstone's pet dog. Further news was gathered in this area and by a small party sent towards Mataka's.

Crossing to the western shore, Young then traced Livingstone's route backwards through several villages, establishing that he had gone on after Musa had turned back; at Mponda's there was news of Wekotani, though he himself was temporarily absent.[30] The *Search* was taken apart and transported to the foot of the cataracts by 150 Yaos early in October.

At Chibisa's Young parted from the Makololo. At times both he and Faulkner had been disappointed by their faint-heartedness and lack of skill as boatmen, but they had nevertheless been essential to the expedition's success. Moloka—'Tall, active and daring . . . one of nature's gentlemen' in Young's words, and a 'faithful and plucky' hunting companion to Faulkner—had justified their hopes, and Faulkner also praised Chippootoolah 'a hard-working man, but a great ruffian'.

Of the other Africans, Chinsoro and Sinjeri 'had been invaluable to us during our travels,' wrote Young. 'The intelligence of the one could hardly be placed before the untiring zeal and hard work of the other.' Their lively chaff made them popular with the other Africans, they were

63

useful interpreters, and Chinsoro helped Faulkner in his many hunting expeditions, as did the Kruman, Antonio. The Shupanga boatmen gave good service, and Young wrote of one, 'there was sorrow, the true test of our common humanity, in the leaving him and his companions, for when should we meet again?'

Young returned to England, having led an outstandingly successful expedition, in which no life was lost, and the objective was achieved in less than the anticipated time; he wrote a brisk account of it which was edited for publication by Waller, and of which a copy eventually reached Livingstone in the heart of Africa.

It was, however, a long time before he learned of the alarm at his supposed murder. At the end of September 1866, after Musa's desertion, he surveyed his handful of men and commented laconically, 'my party is now inconveniently small'. Of the thirty-six men and sixteen beasts of burden with which he had left the coast less than six months before, nine men were left—Abraham, Gardner, Simon, James, Baraka and Mabruki of the Nasik boys; Susi and Amoda, and young Chuma.

In a letter to Waller, Livingstone described Chuma:

. . . he has most character, and is likely to turn out the most influential man of all the *Libertos*. He [is] now a boisterous roaring laughter-provoking boy—some modesty and reads frequently. Wikatani never opened a book spontaneously. Chuma has forgotten all about the Magomero affairs—thinks seriously that the Manganja are the aggressive slavers & not the Waiyau. I found this out by Wikatani saying I had only been the length of Mbame's. He was relating the affair quite seriously to the other boys & Chuma put it that the Manganja caught & sold the Waiyau to the Portuguese. I struck in & asked if the Waiyau did not sell their own people as well as Manganja. He maintained that Waiyau never sold their subjects—not perversely but evidently believing what he said. The elder Nassick boys said that, when taken very young as Chuma was they forgot all about the state from which they had been rescued. This seems to be the case & is one of the reasons why I think that the boys and girls of the O.C.M. may disappoint expectations. I overheard Chuma telling with great glee how he & other Waiyau boys stole from the Manganja & then bamboozled the missionaries. This I knew before. It is just what boys will do. If I had the means of educating him I would prefer him to all the others.[31]

Early in October a woman persuaded Chuma that she was his aunt, and he wished to give her cloth and beads, to be deducted from his pay. Livingstone doubted the genuineness of the relationship and

64

persuaded him to give a few beads only—'It shows a most forgiving disposition on the part of these boys to make presents to those who, if genuine relations, actually sold them.'

At this stage porters were hard to find, and one chief, Kissusa, 'an old friend', brought his six 'strapping wives' to carry loads and shame the young men into doing so. 'The men he at last provided were very faithful and easily satisfied.' He pressed on with his reduced company, at times so fast that he had to stop to rest his men, and made reasonably good progress away from Lake Nyasa and towards the Loangwa. Porters were hired, chiefly for short stages and local guides of very varied quality were engaged. Where possible Livingstone persuaded the local headman to escort him to the next village and vouch for him. The loads were evidently considerably reduced, as five or six extra carriers were adequate. Problems sometimes arose—cloth was not acceptable at one village, but beads 'pleased them perfectly'; elsewhere high wages were demanded in advance. He later summed it up: 'I got carriers from village to village, and got on nicely with people who had never engaged in the slave-trade.'[32]

Rain fell towards the end of October and progress became more difficult. When porters could not be found, the loads were carried on a relay system, with a couple of men left to guard the stocks. On 21 November the loads were redistributed and reduced to twelve, three more than the available men, or 'four just now, Simon being sick again'. Early in December Livingstone recruited two Yao ex-slaves, Chimolose and Akaheka—'these two seem good men, and we want them to fill up our complement.' Another volunteer was employed at Chipeta to look after the four goats, bartered for with gunpowder, which were intended to supplement the food supply, but these were stolen on Christmas Day and the goatherd presumably became redundant.

The Loangwa was crossed on 16 December, but progress became more difficult and reliable guides were harder to obtain. References appear to the 'lazies' in the party and one of the chronometers was damaged when the boy carrying it fell. The year 1867 opened in food shortage and heavy rain. It was particularly galling to Livingstone when Simon Price, who had twice given up food to him, 'called my attention to Chuma having 2 bags of meal—I went into the hut assigned & found my boy munching cakes he had made and his bag of powder (about 5 lb) placed on the ashes about one foot of the live coals'. Livingstone, who had given Chuma favoured treatment 'as a sort of member of my family', expressed himself forcefully, and the African 'blushed if a black man can blush'.[33]

On 20 January there was a disastrous loss. Baraka, who was carrying the medicine chest, exchanged his load with one of the Yao carriers and both Yaos deserted. 'It felt like sentence of death by fever',[34]

65

wrote Livingstone, but he went on to excuse the runaways. 'These Waiyau had few advantages . . . they behaved well for a long time; but, having had hard and scanty fare in Lobisa, wet and misery in passing through dripping forests, hungry nights and fatiguing days, their patience must have been worn out . . .'

On 28 January they reached the Chambezé, the ferryman keeping one of the party on the south bank as surety for his pay, and on the 31st reached Chitapangwa's. Here they found a party of Arab slave traders led by Maguru Mafupi ('Shortshanks'), also known as Bundouky ('Gun'). One of Bundouky's men, Janja, 'who could imitate a trumpet by blowing into the palm of his hand', had been a member of the expedition of Burton and Speke, but this was no advantage, for Livingstone suspected that he was responsible for the local chief's demand for *hongo* by telling him that his former employers had paid up readily. Livingstone entrusted letters to Bundouky, which reached the coast safely and were the first confirmation of Young's report.[35]

Abraham and Simon were used as interpreters, but Livingstone thought them unsatisfactory—they were afraid of Chitapangwa and 'They assume a chirping, piping tone of voice in speaking to him and do not say what at last has to be said, because in their cringing souls they believe they know what should be said better than I do.' 'Though I have these 9 boys, they are so thoroughly useless except for running away I feel quite alone,' he wrote.[36]

He left Chitapangwa's on 20 February. Before long Simon caught fever. Livingstone himself struggled on against illness and by the end of March Chuma was also sick. Lake Tanganyika was reached at the beginning of April but Livingstone was unable to go on and for some weeks could not write his journal. He was still unwell when he eventually left, moving west towards Lake Mweru.

On 18 May the party left Mokambola's village on the way to Chitimba's where a large party of Arabs made Livingstone welcome. This was the beginning of a curious and morally ambiguous association with Arab slave-traders; he travelled in their company in order to pass through areas in which it would be unsafe for his small party to venture. In this case, he sought an Arab escort to Lake Mweru because the region was disturbed. At a neighbouring village he met Hamed bin Muhammad, better known as Tippu Tip. Tippu was then about twenty-seven, and in the early stages of a remarkable career as a trader in which he was to achieve great wealth and power. The caravan eventually left on 30 August; two days later Baraka, who had tried to desert before, ran away to join Tippu Tip—'He has only one complaint and that is dislike to work . . . he will probably return to Zanzibar, and be a slave to the Arab slaves after being a perpetual nuisance to us for upwards of a year.'

66

The problem of finding guides now fell upon the Arabs. Soon after the journey began, Livingstone learned that some of his much-needed supplies had reached Ujiji, but he decided to continue southward. The customary pace of Arab caravans was painfully slow—'Nothing can be more tedious than the Arab way of travelling', wrote Livingstone, but he admitted that the Arabs 'have been extremely kind'. On 7 November he was near enough to Lake Mweru to set off with his eight followers, and from the lake he continued south to Casembe's, where he met two more Arab traders, Muhammad bin Saleh and Muhammad bin Gharib or Bogharib. The former was proposing to travel to Ujiji, and Livingstone decided to accompany him; much as he would have liked to explore Lake Bangweolo, still farther south, it was reported to be unhealthy and he had no medicine. The caravan set off on 22 December, and Livingstone was able to visit Lake Mweru again in January 1868. Travel became increasingly difficult; it was the wet season, and Livingstone suffered from fever. Late in March they reached Kabwabwata, a little to the north of Lake Mweru, and Livingstone learned that the flooded state of the country to the north made it impossible to go on. He decided to strike out on his own again, south to Lake Bangweolo.

Livingstone and his party had now been travelling in company with Arabs for nearly a year, and their way of life was proving a corrupting influence; references in his diaries to malingering, theft, cowardice and other shortcomings of his followers are frequent. Now, in a sudden burst of energy, he proposed to take them from this leisurely life to march back through the country to the south which they had traversed during the previous five months. On the morning of 13 April, when he was ready to start, his men refused to go:

Susi for no confessed reason but he has a black woman who feeds him. Chuma for the same reason but he pretends fear of Cazembe— came with his eyes shot out by Bange and insisted on telling me what Cazembe said and did at an interview where I was present and he was not—'Cazembe would kill us'. This to me, to others 'he could not leave Susi'—and I had 'cut his pay at Bombay'. The only work I know of at Bombay was going to school and it never occurred to me to pay for that. Susi had made some statement equally false, and Abraham had brought up some old grievance as a justification for his absconding. James said 'he would go to Ujiji but not backwards. He was tired of working.' Abraham apologised and was forgiven—Susi stood like a mule. I put my hand on his arm & said 'take up your bundle & let us go'—he seized my hand & refused to let it go. When he did I fired a pistol at him but missed. There being no law nor magistrate higher than myself I would not

67

be thwarted if I could help it. The fact is they are all tired and Muhamad's opposition encourages them to give themselves over to *Bange* and black concubines, they would like me to remain here & pay them for smoking the *bange*; and deck their prostitutes with the beads which I gave them regularly for their food.[37]

This was the nadir of the expedition's morale. Chuma, in spite of his shortcomings, had been a particular protégé of Livingstone's, and Susi, the more able of the two survivors of the Zambezians from the *Lady Nyassa*, had begun to show his capabilities—trading for food and giving a good account of himself in a dispute. Livingstone was determined to go on, however, and the next day recorded 'Started off with five attendants . . .' One of the five, Amoda, 'tired of carrying', went back to the Arab camp. In this desperate situation, Livingstone wrote of the 'runaways': 'I did not blame them very severely in my own mind for absconding: they were tired of tramping, and so verily am I . . . Consciousness of my own defects makes me lenient.'

The four who accompanied him were Abraham, who was sent ahead as a messenger to Casembe on 1 May, Simon, Gardner and Mabruki. Casembe was friendly, but Livingstone was detained in his village until June, when he resumed his journey south, with a Nyamwezi guide to help him. The way lay through hostile country—at one time the three goats which Livingstone had were stolen, but restored. On 18 July they reached Lake Bangweolo. To mark the occasion, he allowed each of his companions ten rupees worth of cloth, and also awarded them an extra five rupees for each of the three months of the journey—all this was carefully noted in the book in which he recorded the bonuses and deductions of his followers.[38] He hired canoes and explored the lake before setting off north again, with local guides, on 30 July.

The diary entries are sketchy in the next few weeks—the country was unsettled owing to Mazitu incursions as well as conflicts between Arabs and local chiefs. In late September he joined up with a party of Arabs, with which he reached Kabwabwata on 1 November. Here he received a deputation from his 'runaways' asking to be allowed to rejoin him. 'I resolved to reinstate two. I reject the thief Suzi for he is quite inveterate, and Chuma who ran away "to be with Suzi" and I who rescued him from slavery, and had been at the expense of feeding and clothing him for years was nobody in his eyes. "Bange" and black women overcame him, and I feel no inclination to be at further expense & trouble for him.' Though he did, for the moment, reject the two men whose names are now imperishably linked with his, he softened, and on the 13th wrote: 'I have taken all the runaways back again—after trying the independent life they will behave better. Much of their

68

ill conduct may be ascribed to seeing that after the flight of the Johanna men, I was entirely dependent on them—More enlightened people often take advantage of men in similar circumstances, though I have seen pure Africans come out generously to aid one abandoned to their care. Have faults myself.' As he later told Stanley, Susi and Chuma 'soon repented, and returned to their allegiance'.[39]

He was intending to go on in company with Muhammad Bogharib to Ujiji, but hostilities which flared up between the Arabs and the local villagers during the latter part of November prevented the party from leaving until 11 December. At the crossing of the Lofunso River on 22nd the Zambezian Susi was among those who saved two men from drowning.

January 1869 found Livingstone seriously ill, and he was carried for the first time in his life. Muhammad the slave trader treated him with great care, and on 14 February they reached Lake Tanganyika. Syde bin Habib helped him with canoes and he arrived at Ujiji on 14 March. The stores he had hoped to find there were almost non-existent. He had arranged for the first batch to be sent there in March 1866, and two more consignments had been despatched, but of the material sent some was inferior, some had been stolen, and some was left at Unyanyembe. A few more items were later brought from Unyanyembe in poor condition and at extortionate charges. To continue his explorations on any adequate basis, Livingstone needed more men—he had only eight of his own—and goods for trade, as well as medicines. While recovering his health at Ujiji, he wrote forty-two letters—among them one sent to Zanzibar asking for reinforcements. Livingstone had already sent an earlier letter to Zanzibar which did not apparently arrive, asking for 'fifteen good boatmen to act as carriers if required', and had also sent to the Sultan, thanking him for his letter of recommendation to local potentates and asking his help in preventing future loss of his goods 'If one or two guards of good character could be sent by you, no one would plunder the pagazi next time. I wish also to hire twelve or fifteen good free-men to act as canoe-men or porters, or in any other capacity that may be required. I shall be greatly obliged if you will appoint one of your gentlemen who knows the country to select that number, and give them and their headman a charge as to their behaviour.'[40]

Livingstone hated Ujiji—'This is a den of the worst kind of slave-traders; those whom I met in Urungu and Itawa were gentlemen slavers: the Ujiji slavers, like the Kilwa and Portuguese, are the vilest of the vile.' He was anxious to do what he could while waiting, and proposed to go into the Manyema country in the hope of striking the Lualaba again and perhaps proving it was the Nile. The area had a reputation for cannibalism, but 'I may have to go there first and down

Tanganyika, if I come out uneaten and find my new squad from Zanzibar.' As soon as the rains slackened he set off, with hired canoes, on 12 July; part of the way he travelled with Muhammad Bogharib, and had a hired guide and some carriers. He reached Bambarre, a place of some importance which was to become all too familiar, on 21 September. Attacks of fever, heavy rain, and disturbed conditions hampered his explorations. On 26 June 1870 he tried to reach the Lualaba but only Susi, Chuma and Gardner would accompany him and he had to abandon the attempt. On 6 July he was back at Bambarre.

Before we reached this, Mohammad made a forced march, and Moenemokaia's people came out drunk: the Arabs assaulted them, and they ran off. Gardner uninvited went too and brought a woman he captured into the Arab camp—and Chuma came back caricolling in front of the party like a spaniel running 20 yards or so on one side & then making as if discharging his gun—then off to the other side and there mimicking shooting which he is too cowardly to do actually anywhere. Ibram went against orders and captured two fowls & some tobacco! I did not order them not to go at first because I thought that Christian boys from Nassick who had been trained for years there and were confirmed by Bishop Harding did not need to be told not to murder. I said to Chuma 'What a fool you make yourself—What would Waller & Dr Wilson think if they saw you capering there as I have?' He said, 'Well the English went to fight . . . from Bishop Mackenzie's station'—'Yes to make slaves free but you want to make free people slaves.'[41]

Livingstone had to stay at Bambarre for eight months, suffering ill-health, and from July to October he was confined to his hut by ulcerated feet, while rain made travel impossible and a cholera epidemic swept along the trade route from Zanzibar. The five followers who had deserted him in June—Amoda, Mabruki, James, Simon and Abraham—had also apparently made their way to Bambarre but they resisted his efforts to re-engage them. This was more serious than a mere defection, particularly on the part of the two ring-leaders, Simon and Abraham. They

. . . refused duty in order to be fed and lodged by slave women in the camp whose husbands were away on the ivory trade. They thought that Muhammad Bogharib would receive them as Muhammad Saleh had done my deserters before when I was about to start for Bangweolo, but M. Bogharib had been unwearied in his kindness to me on all occasions and refused them, though they asked wives from him, a way of becoming his slaves. Price begged ammunition from Arabs in Kabuire and, when quite safe, fired at and killed, he said, two of the men who had been most kind to us. He reported it to me himself. Then, on my denouncing the murders, justified himself, then tried to deny them. From that point he became an incorrigible thief and awful liar.[42]

The other three, James, Mabruki and Amoda, eventually rejoined him. The last-named had deserted him for a slave woman, Halima, (later a faithful cook); her master, wrote Livingstone, 'gave me the slave and he followed her not me.'

In many letters he wrote of his bitter disappointment at the inadequate training as well as the backsliding of the Nasik boys. 'I am greviously tired of living here', he wrote in November, 'yet am forced to remain by want of people.' The traders he met could not spare men from their ivory collecting, the Manyema would not travel outside their own country[43] and in view of the disturbed state of the area, his only way of making a third attempt to explore the region to the west was to wait for an armed Arab caravan from Ujiji to afford him some protection.

On 27 January 1871 came news that the men and goods he had asked for were at Ujiji and on 4 February ten men arrived. The same day James Rutton was killed by an arrow from a man hiding in the forest. To add to this tragic event, the new men were a sad disappointment. There were seven of the original party, mostly slaves, and with them were three alleged freemen. These porters had been sent by Kirk at Livingstone's request for reinforcements with the help of Ladha Damji. Fifteen men, who declared themselves to be freed slaves, though still in the service of their old masters, had been engaged and before the end of October 1869 they left Zanzibar under the leadership of Sherif Basheikh bin Ahmed. In November 1870 Sherif wrote reassuringly to Kirk: 'We have sent off twelve of our men with American cloth, kaniki, beads, sugar, coffee, salt, two pairs of shoes, shot, powder, and soap, and a small bottle of medicine (quinine). All that he was in need of we have sent to him, and I remain at Ujiji awaiting his orders.'[44]

Behind these reassuring but untrue statements lay an intrigue the details of which only emerged when Livingstone reached Ujiji, when they helped to sour his feelings towards Kirk and provided a grievance to which he referred again and again in his last letters. Sherif had used the expedition for a speculation of his own, transporting his goods for trade in the interior by the porters hired for Livingstone's stores and making free with the stores. He had then established himself at Ujiji, with his own three slaves and with the other headman, Awathe,

71

and had sent on his porters with a few supplies to Bambarre. The men who arrived there in February 1871 soon showed their quality by refusing to accompany Livingstone 'influenced probably by Shereef, and my two ringleaders, who try this means to compel me to take them'. After demanding, and receiving, a pay increase to 6 dollars a month, they declared that their instructions were to bring Livingstone back, not accompany him on fresh journeys. When he confirmed from Kirk's written orders that they 'were to follow me as porters, boatmen, woodmen and in any other capacity', they complained about lack of percussion caps for firearms, and made other excuses. The matter was resolved by the Arab slaver, Muhammad Bogharib, who threatened to shoot them if they did not go on with Livingstone. Under these bitter circumstances he prepared to set off on 13 February, but was detained by the illness of Mabruki. There was no way back for the two ring-leaders, however; 'Simon and Ibram were bundled out of the camp, and impudently followed me: when they came up, I told them to be off.' These two were not apparently welcomed by the Arabs: 'Mohamad would not allow the deserters to remain among his people, nor would I. It would only be to imbue the minds of my men with their want of respect for all English, and total disregard of honesty and honour: they came after me with inimitable effrontery, believing that though I said I would not take them, they were so valuable, I was only saying what I knew to be false.' About eighteen months later Carus Farrar noted that Simon Price was trading between the coast and the interior, and Abraham was living at Unyanyembe.[45]

The party finally set off on 16 February for the west and reached the Lualaba at Nyangwé on 29 March. Here Livingstone was to pass nearly four months of frustration and tragedy. He was prevented from obtaining canoes by false rumours as to his true intentions spread by his new followers. They preferred to dabble in the local quarrels, in which their firearms gave them power. At last, on 18 May, he decided to disarm his men and drive them away, but 'they relented, and professed to be willing to go anywhere; so, being eager to finish my geographical work, I said I would run the risk of their desertion . . .' An Arab slaver, Dugumbe, showed Livingstone kindness, and though unwilling to provide carriers himself, tried to persuade Livingstone's men to go on beyond the River Lomani, but without success.

Only a couple of days after this conversation, on 15 July, the Arabs opened fire on the Africans in Nyangwé market and many were killed. Although Dugumbe was only marginally involved, the main culprit being his colleague Tagamoio, Livingstone was 'sick at heart' and wrote 'Who could accompany the people of Dugumbé and Tagamoio to Lomamé and be free from blood-guiltiness?'

He decided to return to Ujiji, though the prospect there was bleak—

'if I do not trust to the riffraff of Ujiji, I must wait for other men at least ten months there.' He left on 20 July with his unsatisfactory followers—'One of the slaves was sick, and the rest falsely reported him to be seriously ill, to give them time to negotiate for the women with whom they had cohabited: Dugumbé saw through the fraud, and said 'leave him to me: if he lives, I will feed him; if he dies, we will bury him: do not delay for any one, but travel in a compact body, as stragglers now are sure to be cut off.'

Livingstone reached Mamohela on 11 August, and, though ill, travelled on. Four days later, 'scarcely able to crawl', he 'sat under a tree and Susi came back with coffee and a bit of fowl which revived me'. At the end of the month he arrived at Lake Tanganyika. After two weeks' further delay he crossed, and reached Ujiji on 23 October. Sherif was still there, and Livingstone learned through Chuma and Susi of the full extent of his depredations, but he 'was evidently a moral idiot, for he came without shame to shake hands with me, and when I refused, assumed an air of displeasure, as having been badly treated.' The men sent by Sherif had accompanied Livingstone back to Ujiji but then went off with their guns.[46]

With no goods of his own, his state was desperate. 'I had made up my mind, if I could not get people at Ujiji, to wait till men should come from the coast, but to wait in beggary was what I never contemplated.' Some of the Arabs offered to help him but he was reluctant to accept any more aid from such sources. 'But when my spirits were at their lowest ebb, the good Samaritan was close at hand.'

7

THE BIG MASTER AND THE LITTLE MASTER

Speke's 'faithfuls' returned to Zanzibar in 1863; some settled there, others went to the mainland. One at least, however, took service with another explorer. In November 1864 Baron von der Decken, who had revisited Germany after undertaking three journeys based on Zanzibar (see pp. 164–65), returned to the island, bringing with him a number of German colleagues and two boats in sections—the *Welf*, a paddle-steamer, and the *Passepartout*, a steam-launch—with which he hoped to penetrate the interior of Africa by river. Both were assembled by June 1865, and the Baron set off for the Somali coast. He had nine German colleagues and thirty other followers. These included Abdio ben Nur, a Somali from Brava, as Abban; Kero, an interpreter; Baraka, a Galla, as pilot; a Malabar Indian as personal servant; and a crew of Yaos, Gallas, Makuas, Nyamwezi and others recruited at Zanzibar. Among them, described as one of his most trusted men, was Mabruki Speke as second helmsman.

The *Passepartout* was sunk at the entrance to the Juba River in July, and twenty miles beyond Bardera, up the river, the *Welf* was wrecked in rapids. Von der Decken left most of the expedition in camp by the river and returned to Bardera in a gig to try to organise transport animals and supplies; he had with him his colleague Dr Link, Abdio, Kero, Baraka, Mabruki Speke and three other men. On 1 October, while they were absent, the camp was attacked by Somalis and two Germans and a number of crew members killed; the survivors reached Zanzibar after a hazardous journey of three weeks by land and water. On 15 November Mabruki Speke arrived at Lamu with the news that the Baron and Dr Link had been killed at Bardera, but that most of the men had escaped, and several of these later arrived at Zanzibar.

Mabruki now settled in Zanzibar on the *shamba* he had received from Speke and married a freed slave named Hadeeya. He was employed by Captain Fraser, a retired Indian Marine officer, to command

74

a coasting schooner plying between Zanzibar town and Fraser's sugar plantations in the north of the island. Later, he fell on evil days. He had a feud with a neighbour, who was one of Sultan Majid's soldiers, and this man and some of his comrades hung him from a tree by his wrists. After two days he was found and rescued, but though Dr Kirk was able to heal one hand to some extent, the other remained useless.[2]

This episode had only recently taken place when, on 6 January 1871, a journalist named Henry Stanley arrived in Zanzibar with instructions from his employer, James Gordon Bennett, junior, of the *New York Herald*, to find Livingstone, though he did not reveal the purpose of his journey to anyone except the American Consul, Captain F. R. Webb. He brought with him Selim Heshmy, a Christian Arab boy from Jerusalem, who had been in his service since January 1870, and W. L. Farquhar, a Scottish seaman. Stanley had no personal experience of African travel, save for the very different conditions of the British expedition to Abyssinia in 1867 and, though he had read the works of explorers, he found them deficient in the practical details of organising caravans. He obtained assistance from Sheikh Hashid in dealing with problems of types of beads, cloth and wire, and methods of packing, and spent 8,000 dollars.[3]

Stanley decided that he needed a corps of twenty men as soldiers, guides and servants. Learning from Johari, dragoman of the United States Consulate, that some of Speke's 'faithfuls' were still about, he was able to engage Mabruki Speke, Ulimengo, Baruti, Umbari, and Grant's former servant Uledi. Others were dead or away from the island, but Uledi knew that Bombay was in Pemba and felt sure that he would wish to join the expedition, so a message was sent to him. When he appeared, Stanley saw 'a slender short man of fifty or thereabouts, with a grizzled head, an uncommonly high, narrow forehead, with a very large mouth, showing teeth very irregular, and wide apart . . . at his first appearance, I was favourably impressed with Bombay.' He later noted that Bombay spoke 'broken English'. Bombay was engaged, and recruited eighteen free men to serve as *askari*. 'They were an exceedingly fine-looking body of men, far more intelligent in appearance than I could ever have believed African barbarians could be. They hailed principally from Uhiyow, others from Unyamwezi, some came from Useguhha and Ugindo.' These were to be paid 36 dollars per annum and given a flintlock musket and equipment each. Bombay was to have 80 dollars and the other five 'faithfuls' 40 dollars a year. An English sailor, John Shaw, was also recruited. On 4 February Stanley and his men sailed for the mainland, though somewhat inauspiciously, as Farquhar, Shaw, Bombay and several other Africans had to be dragged from the local liquor shops.

Stanley's first task at Bagamoyo was to engage enough *pagazi* for

75

his journey to the interior: he estimated a hundred were needed, but also provided himself with twenty-five donkeys. He had bought two boats in Zanzibar. There was some delay since the Nyamwezi porters were frightened off by a recent epidemic of cholera at the coast. Ali bin Salim, brother of Said bin Salim, promised to help, but he delayed action. Eventually Mabruki Speke declared his belief that Ali would never supply the men, so Stanley sent Selim back to Zanzibar specifically to obtain the help of Sewa Haji Paloo, who though only nineteen, showed a shrewd skill in extracting the maximum payment. Men were engaged, and sent off in caravans, the first of which left on 6 February.[4]

While this was proceeding, Stanley learned that another party organised by Consul Churchill intended to relieve Livingstone was at Bagamoyo. There were seven men—Johannese and Yao, four of them slaves, who were instructed to place themselves at Livingstone's disposal; they had letters, trade goods, provisions and clothes which would need thirty-five carriers. Churchill commented to Livingstone, 'they were not perfect, but had expressed willingness to go'. They left for Bagamoyo on 1 November 1870, with the intention of reaching Ujiji by February; when Kirk learned that they had not even started by that date, he crossed to the mainland and the expedition was sent on its way.[5]

Stanley's caravans, totalling 192 men, left during February and March. The second was led by Uledi Manua Sera, who is probably the Uledi sent by Speke with Baraka to find Petherick. He could well have been one of Baraka's colleagues in his embassy to Manua Sera in 1861 (see p. 29) and have added the Nyamwezi leader's name to his own.[6] Farquhar was in command of the third caravan, and the fourth was under Maganga, who proved a dilatory leader. Stanley, leading the last caravan, twice overtook 'procrastinating Maganga and his laggard people'. Stanley's caravan, with Shaw as rearguard, included a *kirangozi* (Hamadi) and twenty-seven *pagazi* with the boats; Bombay in command of twelve soldiers, among them Uledi as sergeant, Mabruki Speke as tentguard, and Ferrajji, described as 'a runaway of Speke's'.[7] Selim was interpreter and there were two men from Malabar, Bunder Salaam (cook) and Abdul Kader (tailor). Another Indian, Jako, from Goa, was cook to the third caravan. Most of the donkeys were with Stanley's caravan. On 22 March, the day after leaving Bagamoyo, a start was made from the camp on the banks of the Kingani River. ' "Sofari, Sofari, leo—a journey, a journey to-day", shouted the Kirangozi as he prepared to blow his kudu horn—the usual signal for a march. "Set out, set out," rang the cheery voice of Captain Bombay, echoed by that of my drum major, servant, general help and interpreter, Selim.'

Stanley's attitude to Africans has been much discussed and often condemned. He himself wrote, 'I had met in the United States black men, whom I was proud to call friends. I was thus prepared to admit any black man, possessing the attributes of true manhood or any good qualities, to my friendship, even to a brotherhood with myself; and to respect him for such, as much as if he were of my own colour and race.' It may also be noted that, in 1867, when reporting on the American Indian question, he dissented from the extreme views of some white Americans.[8]

During the early stages of the journey he had the opportunity of studying his African followers at first hand. 'The soldiers' points of character leaked out just a little', he wrote. 'Bombay turned out to be honest and trusty, but slightly disposed to be dilatory. Uledi did more talking than work; while the runaway Ferajji and the useless-handed Mabruki turned out to be true men and staunch.' Deserters were pursued by Stanley's two detectives, Uledi and Sarmean.

There was an unpleasant episode in April when Bunder Salaam, the cook, was flogged for stealing and driven out of the camp. Stanley later asserted that this was not intended to be permanent, but the Indian ran off and was almost certainly murdered. Bombay lost the fine uniform he had been given and other items through leaving them on the ground while he helped push the expedition's cart out of a quagmire in the desolate and swampy Makata Valley. This provoked Stanley to a fierce denunciation of Bombay's various failings, at the end of which he degraded Bombay and Uledi and promoted Mabruki Speke to be captain. Though his account of this episode is circumstantial, Stanley originally wrote in his despatch to the *Herald* on 4 July of Bombay and the men he had recruited 'all these men are with me to-day. I could not have been better served by any set of men than I have by these faithful people.' There are certainly numerous references to Bombay still having a position of authority as well as approving mentions of Mabruki. Stanley later wrote 'My ideas respecting my Zanzibari and Unyamwezi followers were modified after a few weeks' observation and trials of them. Certain vices and follies, which clung to their uneducated natures, were the source of great trouble; though there were brave virtues in most of them, which atoned for much that appeared incorrigible . . . no quality was so conspicuous and unvarying as good-temper.'[9]

On 5 May, hearing disquieting news of the third column under Farquhar, Stanley overtook it at Kionga and the two caravans went on together. Farquhar had mismanaged his men and stores and was ill; Shaw had also proved a broken reed. By the time he reached Mpwapwa, Farquhar was too ill to go on, and Jako, the cook from Goa who also spoke English, was left to look after him. Farquhar died a few days later, and Jako after a few weeks. Stanley was able to engage twelve *pagazi* at Mpwapwa and on 23 June he reached Unyanyembe where he was greeted by Said bin Salim. His other caravans had arrived safely with only minor mishaps and the leaders were rewarded with cloth. His casualties totalled two soldiers, eight *pagazi*, and all the horses and donkeys dead, and a number of desertions, and after paying off his carriers he had twenty-five men left.

At Tabora Stanley found the other Livingstone relief column which had arrived in May. There had been thirty-three *pagazi* with the seven men sent by Churchill. The man in charge, Thani Kati-Kati, died of dysentery before he could engage carriers for the next stage; his successor, a Johannese, died of smallpox soon after, and the headman was now Asmani. They still had the letter bag prepared for Livingstone the previous November, but had been delayed by the hostilities between the Arabs based on Tabora and the Nyamwezi leader Mirambo. The remnants of this expedition accepted Stanley's invitation to take quarters with him.

He lived in a large mud-built house with one storey and a flat roof, assigned to him by Said bin Salim, at Kwihara, about three miles from Tabora. His and Livingstone's goods were stored in a strong-room, and the adjoining hall was guarded day and night, 'bull-headed Mabrouki, who acts as my porter or policeman' being in command by day. The room across the hall was used for receiving visitors. Round a courtyard at the back were granary, kitchen, stables, barracks for the soldiers and their wives, and Shaw's quarters. Stanley had rooms in the house itself, with a lock-up for 'incorrigibles' adjoining.

His main staff were Bombay, in command of the remaining men, Ferrajji, his cook, and Selim. Towards the end of his stay in Unyanyembe, Stanley was presented by an Arab named Mohammed with a small slave-boy, about seven years old, called Ndugu M'hali ('My brother's wealth'). Various names were proposed for him, but Ulimengo's suggestion of 'Kalulu'—a young antelope—was accepted because he was slim and swift moving. He soon became a zealous and valued servant and 'ousted Selim from the post of chief butler by sheer diligence and smartness'. Selim however proved a devoted nurse when Stanley had a severe attack of fever.

On recovering, he was anxious to set off again, but the disturbed state of the country due to the successes of Mirambo's forces against the Arabs made this impossible, so Stanley agreed to assist the Arabs in their fight. He mustered fifty men and set off on 29 July. Bombay had to be dragged from 'his Dulcinea of Tabora'. Ulimengo, one of Speke's 'faithfuls' and 'the maddest and most hare-brained of my party' led the way carrying the Stars and Stripes and chanting an improvised war-song. It was a disastrous enterprise; while Stanley was ill some of his men, against his orders, joined an Arab attack on Mirambo, in which more than half the Arabs were killed; five of Stanley's followers, including Uledi, once Grant's servant, died with them.[10] Stanley was wakened from a feverish sleep by the sound of the Arabs in flight, most of his own men, with the boastful Ulimengo outpacing the rest, joining them. Bombay, though in a panic, stayed with Stanley as did Mabruki Speke, Sarmean and the cool Selim, and a couple of others were kept at pistol point. Stanley and his men followed the Arabs back to Unyanyembe and when, shortly after, Mirambo carried the fighting to Tabora, Stanley fortified his house and gathered a garrison of Wanguana and other refugees, but the hostilities did not extend to Kwihara.

Stanley would have nothing more to do with the Arabs' problems, and decided to go to Ujiji by a more circuitous route to the south. The survivors of the expedition against Mirambo were disinclined to continue and he was reduced to thirteen men; the Nyamwezi carriers would not enlist during the fighting and yet he had a hundred loads in store, apart from Livingstone's supplies. News came of the deaths of Farquhar and Jako; several of his remaining men were ill, including Shaw and Selim, and the Speke 'faithful' Baruti 'one of my best soldiers' died of smallpox and was given a ceremonial Muslim funeral.

In late August and early September Stanley reorganised his goods, leaving many behind and reducing loads from 70 to 50 pounds. He wanted to bring his strength up to fifty men; he had about a dozen of his own, including Selim and Bombay, as a basis, and engaged some thirty 'Wangwana renegades' at 30 doti for the journey to Ujiji instead of the customary 5 to 10, and also ten Jiji *pagazi*. Two guides were Asmani 'considerably over six feet without shoes, and has shoulders broad enough for two ordinary men', and Mabruki. He also took Kaif Halleck ('How d'you do'), a member of the earlier relief party who had the letter bag for Livingstone. Kalulu accompanied Stanley; another boy was Majwara, a Ganda, whose father, the chief Namujulirwa, had been murdered after falling into disfavour with Mutesa; the lad had been sold as a slave to Njara from whom Stanley redeemed him.[11] Bilali, a Uemba boy, was gunbearer.

On 20 September Stanley led fifty-four 'braves whom I had enlisted for a rapid march' out of Unyanyembe, though Bombay had to be separated from 'his Delilah' and helped on his way with a whip. Once travelling, he recovered his good humour and assured Stanley of the success of their mission. However, the party was soon reduced by illness and death, including that of Shaw, to less than forty, some of whom were very experienced travellers.[12] Bombay had been 'a stumbling block' and was a disappointment to Stanley, though he still used him for negotiations, but Mabruki Speke was proving courageous and

79

faithful—a valuable watchman or bringer up of stragglers. Chowpereh was 'the strongest, the healthiest, the amiablest, the faithfullest of all'. Umbari, one of Speke's 'faithfuls', was lazy but useful in small responsibilities, and Ulimengo, another, was a humorous man, a good worker and hunter, if cowardly. Ferrajji, reputedly a supporter of Baraka against Bombay in Speke's expedition (though the evidence is not clear), was weak on hygiene but a useful rough and ready cook. Maganga, unlike his dilatory namesake (p. 76), was an excellent *pagazi*, leading the marching chant of the Nyamwezi porters. 'The most important member of the Expedition, next to myself . . . honest and faithful . . . without fear, and without reproach', was Selim.

Early in October the caravan paused for two or three days by the Gombe River to hunt and prepare food for the next stage of the journey. When Stanley was ready to go on, Bombay, on behalf of the men, asked for a further day's rest. This was refused, the *kirangozi* ordered to sound the horn, and the march was resumed; but soon Stanley, bringing up the rear, found it had halted. As he reached the main body, he saw that Asmani and Mabruki, the guides, were awaiting him with muskets in their hands. Stanley levelled his own gun and for a moment he and Asmani faced each other with loaded weapons at the ready, until Mabruki Speke swept Asmani's gun aside and asked Stanley to forgive the rebels. This he did, but blaming Bombay for the breakdown in discipline, put him and another senior man, Umbari, in chains. However, they were soon released, and Bombay restored 'to his full honors as captain'. Happier relations were achieved as the expedition neared Lake Tanganyika and Asmani and Bombay were shortly after engaged in successful bargaining as to the amount of *hongo*.

At the beginning of November they met a caravan whose members told them a white man had just arrived at Ujiji. As they pressed on, demands for tribute became even more exorbitant. Stanley was prepared to fight his way ahead, but Bombay, Asmani, Chowpereh and Mabruki dissuaded him. The situation grew worse, however, and Stanley obtained a guide who would lead him by night. They set off on 7 November, creeping out in small batches. On the first night the wife of one of the party began screaming hysterically and Stanley had to strike her several times to stop her cries from endangering the whole party. On the morning of the 10th they descended the slope to the lakeside town of Ujiji. The caravan was led by the giant Asmani carrying the Stars and Stripes, followed by Stanley in his new flannel suit, and Bombay who had seen the same scene with Speke and Burton at his side. Fusillades of shots announced their approach to Ujiji. Susi heard the sound and saw the approaching column—'An Englishman— I see him' he called to Livingstone and dashed off. As Stanley neared the town he suddenly became aware of an African at his elbow, asking in English, 'How do you do, sir?'

'Hullo! Who the deuce are you?'

'I am the servant of Dr Livingstone' cried Susi and hurried off again.[13]

The people of the town, Arab and African, turned out in large numbers to watch the meeting. As soon as the greetings were over, Stanley gave orders to Bombay and Asmani for the provisioning of the men, and summoned the errant letter-carrier Kaif Halleck to hand over Livingstone's correspondence. This was however put aside for later reading and the two men settled down for a long interchange of news, drinking each other's health in the champagne served in silver goblets by Selim, while Halima, 'a stout, buxom woman of thirty',[14] dashed about in the kitchen, preparing food and chattering to the bystanders who had gathered. The next morning, Ferrajji served breakfast—'excellent tea, and a dish of smoking cakes', or dampers, which were necessary for Livingstone's inadequate teeth. Halima, who 'never can tell the difference between tea and coffee' was not called on to help prepare this meal.

Future plans were discussed. Livingstone could not travel independently, so it was agreed that he would accompany Stanley to Unyanyembe where, if no more men could be recruited, Livingstone would wait while Stanley went back to the coast and sent up reinforcements. First, however, they decided to explore Lake Tanganyika, in order to settle whether the Ruzizi flowed in or out, and set off in a borrowed canoe on 16 November with Selim, Ferrajji, two Jiji guides, and sixteen rowers including Bombay, Chuma and Susi. Mabruki Speke was left in charge of the rest. The circuit of the lake, which took until 12 December, established that the Ruzizi was an influent, and therefore not a source of the Nile. During a halt on shore there was an encounter with drunken and hostile villagers, which the timely arrival of Livingstone, who had been out of the camp with Susi and Chuma, prevented from developing into serious hostilities. On another occasion Bombay and Susi drank too much palm toddy and failed to wake up when items were pilfered from the canoe which they were supposed to be guarding. 'This was the third time that my reliance in Bombay's trustworthiness resulted in a great loss to me, and for the ninety-ninth time I had to regret bitterly having placed such entire confidence in Speke's and Grant's loud commendation of him,' wrote Stanley. He retained a higher opinion of Susi, however, even though he records an episode when he, having got drunk on *pombe*, climbed into bed with Livingstone and took all his blankets. He described him as 'the invaluable adjunct of Dr Livingstone' and thought he 'would have been worth his weight in silver if he were not an incorrigible thief.' On returning to Ujiji they found that Mabruki Speke 'had done most excellently', and had preserved discipline by effective strong-arm methods.

Plans now went ahead for the journey to Unyanyembe, and Stanley sent a party of armed men under Susi to reclaim the Enfield rifles still held by Livingstone's deserters. Christmas Day was disappointing— Stanley was suffering from fever, and though ample supplies had been obtained 'Ferajji spoiled the roast, and our custard was burned—the dinner was a failure. That the fat-brained rascal escaped a thrashing was due only to my inability to lift my hands for punishment; but my looks were dreadful and alarming, and capable of annihilating any one except Ferajji. The stupid, hard-headed cook only chuckled, and I believe he had the subsequent gratification of eating the pies, custards and roast that his carelessness had spoiled for European palates.' Some of Stanley's men commented to Livingstone's on the two leaders: 'Your master is a good man—a very good man; he does not beat you, for he has a kind heart; but ours—oh! he is sharp—hot as fire—mkali sana, kana moto.'

On 27 December the party, forty strong, left, some in two canoes, the land party under Bombay and Asmani. They were reunited on 7 January and struck inland, arriving at Unyanyembe after six weeks. During the journey they suffered from shortage of food and from illness.

Asmani the guide was baffled by the superior abilities of the compass in finding the right direction. He and his colleague, Mabruki Kisesa, proved somewhat ineffective as hunters and Stanley himself, accompanied by Kalulu, Bilali, or Khamisi, went hunting several times with greater success. On one occasion he left Khamisi to look after the carcase of a giraffe, but he climbed a tree for fear of lions and the vultures had first pick. Diet became monotonous, though Halima could be relied on to make *ugali*, or porridge, and had a sack of fine flour specially prepared for Livingstone.

Livingstone was interested in Bombay and made a tiny sketch of him, little more than an inch square, in one of his notebooks. It shows Bombay's face fringed with a beard, and he wears a white cap. By it, Livingstone wrote 'square head of Bombay top depressed in centre'. He also added 'Bombay says his greatest desire is to visit Speke's grave ere he dies.'

Livingstone appears to have accepted Stanley's unfavourable view of Bombay without question and the drinking bout with Susi may also have rankled. In another notebook he wrote,

Bombay has M'Yao peculiarities exaggerated very timid & very apt in making excuses however false. He volunteered to go with me but

Grant said he is such a fine fellow for humbugging the natives—this was enough as I felt sure he was Do Do for his employers. He seemed ashamed that I did not jump at the offer of his company and to smooth the disappointment I said that I had men enough already. He turned this rebuff to his own advantage by telling Mr. Stanley that I asked him to go but though he refused me he would go with Stanley not for pay but to be respectably employed. When he laughs it is only with his mouth. His small somewhat deformed eyes look serious & scan you as they move from side to side. When in difficulty or in fear the mouth takes on the grin it does in feigned laughing.

In Livingstone's view it was due to Bombay's rescuing Speke from the 'mute chagrin' of hearing Burton converse with the Arabs while he was excluded that made Speke favour Bombay '. . . and his gratitude spoiled him for anyone else'. In Stanley's service he 'was perpetually making difficulties in order to have the credit of smoothing them away and became a sore nuisance to Mr. Stanley in consequence.' To his tally of criticisms of Bombay, Livingstone added that he had sold the medal for the Speke and Grant expedition 'to some Arab and it was of course melted down' and tried to pass off as his own the medals belonging to two Speke 'faithfuls' who died at Unyanyembe. Echoing Stanley's view, he wrote: 'Mabruki Speke—Burton's "Bull-headed Mabruki" was a much better man in his own place (but not as a valet) for honest carefulness of all his master's goods in his charge he was invaluable'. Finally, with sublime self-assurance, he wrote 'The previous travellers were no judges of character.'[15]

On 7 February Stanley sent Ferrajji and Chowpereh ahead to Unyanyembe to bring back letters and medicine. It was probably at this stage that Ulimengo was temporarily appointed cook in place of Ferrajji. Stanley,

. . . being half-mad with the huge doses of quinine I had taken, and distressingly weak . . . sharply scolded him for not cleaning his coffee-pots, and said that I tasted the verdigris in every article of food, and I violently asked if he meant to poison us. I showed him the kettle and the pots, and the loathsome green on the rims. He turned to me with astounding insolence, and sneeringly asked if I was any better than 'the big master', and said that what was good for him was good for me—the 'little master'. I clouted him at once . . . Ulimengo stood up and laid hold on me . . .

At this stage Livingstone appeared on the scene, reprimanded Ulimengo, and made peace between the two.[16]

83

Unyanyembe was reached on 18 February, but hopes of ample supplies there were dashed when it was found that Asmani (Othman), the headman of the last Livingstone relief party, had helped himself not only to Livingstone's stores, but to some of Stanley's also. The culprit was dismissed and it was some days before Said bin Salim, who had signally failed to protect Livingstone's property, showed himself. Eventually, Livingstone recorded on 28 February, 'Syde bin Salem called a china looking man tried to be civil to us.' In spite of losses, Stanley was able to assign goods to Livingstone making up seventy loads, and as no Nyamwezi recruits were available owing to the unsettled state of the area, Stanley agreed to send up reinforcements. In a memorandum of his requirements Livingstone asked for 'Fifty freemen at twenty-five to thirty dollars a year to be engaged to go with me till I finish my work and do all kind of service—additional pay for carriage and they may invest their wages in ivory as our goods decrease. Half a years advance.' They were to have muskets and other equipment. He also asked for two strong donkeys and various items of food and equipment including a chain for punishment. With his recent experiences in mind, he wrote to Kirk 'No slaves must be sent' and asked for 'an able headman to lead them quickly here, and continue with me until I have finished what I have still to do'. He also wrote to Barghash, Majid's successor, asking his help in finding a reliable man.[17]

On 12 March a farewell dance was given by the *pagazi* of a Ganda caravan which had halted at Unyanyembe. Stanley's men—and at one stage even Stanley himself—joined in:

Bombay, as ever comical, never so much at home as when in the dance of the Mrima, has my water-bucket on his head; Chowpereh—the sturdy, the nimble, sure-footed Chowpereh—has an axe in his hand, and wears a goatskin on his head; Baraka has my bearskin, and handles a spear; Mabruki, the 'Bull-headed', has entered into the spirit of the thing, and steps up and down like a solemn elephant; Ulimengo has a gun, and is a fierce Drawcansir, and you would imagine he was about to do battle to a hundred thousand, so ferocious is he in appearance; Khamisi and Kamna are before the drummers, back to back, kicking up ambitiously at the stars; Asmani,—the embodiment of giant strength,—a towering Titan,—has also a gun, with which he is dealing blows in the air, as if he were Thor, slaying myriads with his hammer.

Two days later Stanley left:

We wrung each other's hands, and I had to tear myself away before I unmanned myself; but Susi, and Chumah, and Hamoydah—the

Doctor's faithful fellows—they must all shake and kiss my hands before I could quite turn away. I betrayed myself!

'Good-bye, Doctor—dear friend!'

'Good-bye!'

'MARCH! Why do you stop? Go on! Are you not going home?'

This was not quite the final farewell. Uledi Manua Sera and another man stayed to take some last letters to Stanley, and when they left on the 16th, Susi and Amoda went with them, returning to Livingstone with Stanley's last letter. Stanley now acquired some reinforcements in a number of Wanguana who were afraid to go on unaccompanied. He set off on the 21st. The march to the coast was rapid—Bombay was in charge of negotiations over *hongo* which went reasonably well.

On 13 April Rojab, a young *pagazi*, was wading across a river with Livingstone's journals on his head when he stumbled into a hole. Stanley pointed his revolver at him with the challenge: 'Drop that box, and I'll shoot you.' Not for the last time, Stanley's drastic shock tactics worked; Rojab brought the box to safety, whereupon it was entrusted to the 'sure-footed and perfect pagazi' Maganga.

On 7 May the expedition reached Zanzibar and the following day Stanley paid 'my dusky friends and faithful soldiers'. Bombay, despite his failings, received a bonus of 50 dollars, and the others from 20 to 50 dollars. 'They, poor people, had only acted according to their nature, and I remembered that from Ujiji to the coast they had all behaved admirably,' he wrote. 'Though they give plenty of trouble an Expedition of white men would give 50 times more.'

He still had to fulfil his promise to Livingstone to send up reinforcements, a task which was complicated by the presence of a new relief expedition.

In November 1871 the Royal Geographical Society decided to sponsor a Livingstone Relief Expedition, for which over £5,000 was raised by public subscription. The command was given to a naval officer, Lt L. S. Dawson, with Lt Henn as his second-in-command. Oswell Livingstone, the explorer's younger son, was the third member.

As it was thought that the Nasik boys had proved useful to Livingstone, the Rev. W. Salter Price was asked to obtain further volunteers; in February 1872 he chose six—Jacob Wainwright, John Wainwright, Richard Rutton, Benjamin Rutton, Matthew Wellington and Carus Farrar (named after the Rev. C. P. Farrar, a CMS missionary in India), who wrote an account of his experiences. Jacob was leader; Price wrote that he 'was occupying a useful position at Saharunpoor, and I was scarcely willing to part with him, but his heart was so set upon the enterprise that I was obliged to let him go.' They left Bombay in the sailing ship *Livinia* and Carus wrote:

D

85

We had pleasant wind which made our ship to glide rapidly over the mighty foaming ocean. But it did not continue so for many days. One day a heavy storm made our little ship to reel fearfully, so much so that we and other passengers on board had entirely despaired of our lives. But God in whose hands the powers of the sea are, was with us. The raging of the water soon ceased and our hearts began again to look on the blue sea with less fear.[18]

The *Livinia* reached Zanzibar on 13 March and four days later the expedition leaders arrived; they were joined by the Rev. Charles New, a Methodist missionary and experienced traveller who, Kirk wrote, 'has shown a general aptitude for observing, and a facility in dealing with natives, that promise to be invaluable.' Early in April New crossed to Mombasa to recruit men, including some who had accompanied him to Kilimanjaro. 'By enlisting men from Mombasa as well as Zanzibar, with the Nasik boys, we shall have three distinct parties in the camp, strangers to each other's interests, and the probabilities of any approach to conspiracy will be lessened,' wrote Dawson. It was also proposed to engage about two hundred Nyamwezi porters, but the day after the expedition crossed to Bagamoyo three Africans led by Umbari arrived with the news that Stanley had found Livingstone and was on the way to the coast. There was a period of some confusion which eventually resulted in all the leaders of the relief expedition resigning.[19]

Stanley eventually enrolled fifty men, including twenty of his own followers who recruited more men; he was offered twenty men engaged by New and the six Nasik boys, and added the latter to his party. Stanley found, on the eve of departure, that he had paid an advance to three slaves who had been engaged in the belief that they were free men. He therefore signed a contract that their master had a claim on their pay—a curious action for a man who was to make so much of Livingstone's strictures on Kirk for sending slaves in relief caravans.[20]

The senior member was Uledi Manua Sera. He and the Nasik boys were to receive 5 dollars a month, and the porters half that amount (At this time Bishop Steere reckoned that 2 dollars a month was the minimum subsistence wage.)[21] There were Speke veterans such as Ulimengo and Mabruki Speke; Farjallah Christie who took his name from having been a servant to Dr James Christie, Physician to the Sultan of Zanzibar; and the freed Ganda slave Majwara who was engaged at no fixed wage as a servant for Livingstone who had cured him of illness when he was with Stanley's expedition. They had fifty carbines and carried a diverse collection of supplies and equipment. A number of wives accompanied the men. Though the majority of this body was to remain together to Livingstone's death and beyond, i

86

was Sir Bartle Frere's view that the actual quality of the men recruited by Kirk and sent into the interior was about the same as those engaged by Stanley; the difference could be attributed to the effects of Stanley's leadership on the initial expedition.[22]

When Oswell Livingstone resigned, Stanley, on the recommendation of Sheikh Hashid, engaged as leader a young Arab, Mohamed bin Galfin, who 'though not remarkably bright, seemed honest and able'. He was to have 500 dollars a year if Livingstone decided to engage him. As Stanley was due to leave for the Seychelles on 28 May, and Kirk would not accept responsibility for the despatch of the party, Johari, Chief Dragoman of the US Consulate, took them to the mainland in a dhow at 4 p.m. on Monday the 27th, after Stanley had addressed them on their responsibilities, urged them to follow 'the Great Master' faithfully, and said goodbye to 'my dark friends'. They left Bagamoyo on the 30th and Johari saw them over the Kingani on their way to Livingstone.

Stanley sailed with Selim, whom he paid off at Suez, and Kalulu, who accompanied him to Europe. News of the finding of Livingstone had preceded them, and in Paris Stanley attended a banquet with Kalulu in European clothes topped by an officer's kepi. In London they were photographed together, and Kalulu was modelled for the group in Madame Tussaud's representing the meeting of Stanley and Livingstone. After his stay in England, during which controversy as to the credibility of his account and the justice of his attacks on Kirk made a somewhat sour postscript to the expedition, Stanley crossed to America in November where Kalulu entertained newspaper men with Swahili songs and mimes, and appeared on the platform at Stanley's first New York lecture on 3 December. Stanley brought him back to England in April, and entered him at the Rev. J. Conder's Holbrake school at Wandsworth. He also took him to Newstead Abbey, once the home of Lord Byron, and purchased a few years earlier by W. F. Webb, the soldier and traveller whom Livingstone had met in south Africa. Augusta Webb remembered Kalulu's 'excellent manners and general intelligence', his fund of African legends, and his facility for picking up live coals without injury, but was not impressed by his alleged fleetness of foot since her sister Geraldine easily outran him. Stanley named his one venture into fiction after him—*My Kalulu* (1873), is a romance of Africa embodying background from his travels and stories and legends told by Kalulu and others.[23]

In May 1873 Stanley again took up his newspaper work, covering first of all the Carlist War in Spain, then the Ashanti Campaign in west Africa. On his return he heard that Livingstone was dead.

8

'DEEDS OF FAITH-FULNESS AND HEROISM'

Assured of reinforcements, Livingstone could settle down to await them at Unyanyembe. He had time to write up his records, talk to the local Arabs, and plan for the future. His diary records a great variety of facts and ideas; one theory that increasingly dominated his thoughts was that the story told by Herodotus of four fountains rising in the heart of Africa was a fragment of correct geography, and that it described the origin of the Lufira, Lualaba, Zambezi and Lunga rivers.[1]

He also considered the future development of Africa, and wrote a long note suggesting the organisation of mission caravans to set up stations in the interior. These could be conducted by a 'respectable Arab' with free porters, in order to develop trade in legitimate commodities. His experience with Nasik boys obviously coloured some of his remarks, such as:

Educated free blacks from a distance are to be avoided: they are expensive, and are too much of gentlemen for your work. You may in a few months raise natives who will teach reading to others better than they can, and teach you also much that the liberated never know. A cloth and some beads occasionally will satisfy them, while neither the food, the wages, nor the work will please those who, being brought from a distance, naturally consider themselves missionaries. Slaves also have undergone a process which has spoiled them for life; though liberated young, everything of childhood and opening life possesses an indescribable charm . . . Some of my liberados eagerly bought green calabashes and tasteless squash . . because this trash was their early food; and an ounce of meat never entered their mouths.

Looking back on his long career, he wrote to his daughter, Agnes 'I have travelled more than most people, and with all sorts of followers

88

The Christians of Kuruman and Kolobeng were out of sight the best I ever had. The Makololo, who were very partially christianised, were next best—honest, truthful and brave. Heathen Africans are much superior to the Mohammedans, who are the most worthless one can have.'[2] He had some problems with his present followers, though of a more domestic nature than earlier disputes. At least three women had attached themselves to the party in Manyema—Halima, from Katombe's country, married to Amoda, Mochosi, Susi's wife and Ntaoéka. On 29 May the women quarrelled and Halima ran away, but soon came back penitent. Livingstone was glad to receive her again. She was '. . . always very attentive & clever—never stole nor would allow her useless husband Amoda to steal. She is the best spoke in the wheel—this her only escapade is easily forgiven and I gave her a warm cloth for the cold by way of assuring her that I had no grudge against her. I shall free her and buy her a house & garden at Zanzibar when we get there.'[3] One cause of the quarrel was perhaps that, with all her merits, 'she has an outrageous tongue'.

There were other problems with the women, however, for in June he wrote:

When Ntaoéka chose to follow us rather than go to the coast I did not like to have a fine looking woman among us on the loose and proposed that she should marry one of my three worthies—Chuma Gardner or Mabruki but she smiled at the idea. Chuma was evidently too lazy ever to get a wife the other two were contemptible in appearance and she has a good presence and is buxom. Chuma promised to reform—'He had been lazy he admitted because he had no wife.' Circumstances led to the other women wishing Ntaoéka married and on my speaking to her again she consented. I have noticed her ever since working hard from morning to night—the first up in the cold mornings making fire & hot water—pounding—carrying water—wood—sweeping cooking and Chuma is still as lazy as ever. If he does not amend he will lose her when my men come.[4]

His reinforcements arrived on 14 August, having been seventy-four days from Bagamoyo. 'I have to give them a rest of a few days, and then start,' he wrote. When he came to organise his expedition he decided that, in spite of his hopes of having a good headman, the Arab had been slipshod in his administration of the caravan and was expecting extra pay for even a short additional term. Livingstone therefore dismissed him and made Manua Sera, Chowpereh and Susi heads of departments at 20 dollars extra if they gave satisfaction. 'This they have tried faithfully to do', he wrote to Stanley some months later, 'and hitherto have been quite a contrast to Bombay, who seemed

89

to think that you ought to please him . . . I give my orders to Manwa Sera, and never need to repeat them . . . I owe a great deal to you for the drilling of the men you sent.'[5] In an unfinished letter early the next year he wrote, 'I have a party of good men . . . [who] have behaved as well as Makololo. I cannot award them higher praise, though they have not the courage of that brave kind-hearted people.'[6]

Before starting, he had to sort out his following. To Stanley's re-inforcements, Livingstone added Kaif Halleck, his 'postman', Ali, and Tofiki, from the 1870 relief expeditions; Safen (Wadi Safeni), one of Muhammad Bogharib's men who volunteered; Asmani, Stanley's guide, and eight or ten other men, to carry the goods stored at Un-yanyembe. He was wary of Nasik boys, and two of the new arrivals had complained of Manua Sera's giving them menial tasks on the journey from the coast. He therefore spoke bluntly to the new half-dozen and in Carus Farrar's words, 'gave us a day for consideration as to whether we would go and be faithful to him in all the trials and enormous difficulties and countless privations while journeying about through countries unknown to finish his work assigned to him, or make our way to the coast again . . . After a little consultation we all made up our minds to follow him.' Livingstone was interested in their racial origin, and wrote 'Yao' by four and 'unknown' by the Ruttons. He appointed Majwara as his personal servant, and later wrote to Stanley:

Majwara has behaved perfectly—but is slow! slow!! and keeps your fine silver teapot, spoons, and knives as bright as if he were an English butler; gets a cup of coffee at five a.m. or sooner, if I don't advise him to lie down again; walks at the head of the caravan as drummer, this instrument being the African sign of peace as well as of war. He objected at first to the office, because the drum had not been bought by either you or me. Some reasons are profound—this may be one of them.[7]

Each man was given a 50-pound load, with half loads for the Nasik boys. With the supplies brought from the coast, and the goods still at Unyanyembe, a few extra *pagazi* were still required, but were hard to obtain owing to the disturbed state of the country, and some items were left there. Mabruki was also left at Tabora—'has long been sick and is unable to go with us—Very lazy too,' wrote Livingstone.[8] The caravan set off for the south-west on 25 August; soon after, a Ganda boy, Mokassa, joined it.

Livingstone's main aim was to solve the problem of the Lualaba's direction by striking south and carrying out a more thorough explora-tion of lakes Bangweolo and Mweru—and perhaps find his fountains—after which he would turn north to Katanga, back to Ujiji, and thence

90

to the coast, a programme of about twenty months. In spite of the relief brought him by Stanley, his health was failing and only his strong will drove him on against all odds of personal weakness and hard conditions in the endeavour to finish his task. The fact that he was able to journey as far as he did was due in a large measure to the quality of his followers. They were certainly far from faultless, but Livingstone was clearly determined to preserve better discipline than in the past. Two Nasik boys who allowed the cows to stray were given ten cuts by Susi, and men who fired off ammunition needlessly or pilfered stores were punished. Livingstone was particularly angry when some of the men bought children as slaves, and was also severe on thefts from the villages they passed through. On one occasion four men were beaten for this offence and he noted 'Manuasera weakly called out *bassi bassi* enough enough—as if to appear more tender hearted than I.'[9]

On the whole, however, morale and conduct were good despite hard conditions. Travelling in hot dry weather avoided the problems of swampy grounds, but was exhausting—Livingstone felt tired, and a number of his followers were ill. The hot ground caused inflammation of the legs, 'and makes some of my most hardy men useless', but the fit, 'willingly carried the helpless'.[10]

Lake Tanganyika was reached in mid October. Food was a problem and the cows were gradually killed off for food or barter. Farjallah shot a buffalo but most of the men were poor marksmen. In November there was a pause for a few days' rest, when Livingstone issued a bonus of two *dotis* of beads to all save defaulters. One man, sick with dysentery, had to be left behind, but in spite of his problems, Livingstone spared a thought for unfortunates such as the little girl deserted by her mother and found by the roadside, whom he handed over to the care of one of the women of the party.

The rains began in November but Livingstone would not wait until they had ended. Early in December they reached an area devastated by slavers, so that food and guides were increasingly hard to find; Kiteneka, who had been engaged before, in 1867, was a useful exception. They pressed on in spite of sickness. Christmas was celebrated by feasting on a cow, but the weather was deplorable. A few days later Chipangawazi, 'a quiet good man', died. Binti Sumari, wife of Kirango, was ill. Early in January 1873 the last cow died.[11]

Conditions were now appalling, but spirits were kept up—the men 'broke out into a chorus in pitching my tent'. 'Never was in such a spell of cold rainy weather except in going to Loanda in 1853,' wrote Livingstone, but he could still take pleasure in seeing and describing the riot of colour in the flowers. However, owing to a combination of miscalculations, errors in his instruments, and the weather which hampered observation, he had lost his way and was unable to make proper use of the advice of even the reliable local guides. Indeed, from 4 January to 13 February, he had to retrace his steps so often that he travelled less than seventy miles as the crow flies. He had to be carried more and more. One stream was over 300 yards wide:

The first part—the main stream came up to Susis mouth, and wetted my seat and legs—one held up my pistol behind—then one after another took a turn and when he sank into a deep elephants foot print he required two men to lift him so as to gain a footing on the level which was over waist deep. Others went on & bent down the grass to insure some footing on the side of the elephants path. Every ten or twelve paces brought us to a clear stream flowing fast in its own channel while over all a strong current came bodily through all the rushes & aquatic plants. Susi had the first spell, then Farjella—then a tall stout Arab looking man [Mariko]—then Amoda—then Chanda—then Wadi Sale and each time I was lifted off bodily put on another pair of stout willing shoulders and 50 yards put them out of breath—no wonder. It was sore sore on the women folk of our party. It took us a full hour and a half to cross all over and several came over twice to help me & their friends. The water was cold and so was the wind but no leeches plagued us.

Sickness was prevalent, but 'people bear their hunger well collect mushrooms & plants . . .' On 29 January three scouts were sent out and one, Manua Sera, came back having seen Lake Bangweolo to the south, but the expedition did not reach it until 13 February.[12]

Reliable guides were hard to find, but Susi and Chuma succeeded, after several attempts, in reaching the chief Matipa and obtaining canoes to take the expedition in instalments to Nsumbu Island, where a camp was built outside Matipa's town. The donkey came with one batch—he 'had to be tied down as he rolled about on his legs & would have forced his way out'. In the course of this the animal bit the maimed hand of Mabruki Speke, who from Burton's time onwards seems to have been incapable of dealing with animals (see p. 17). 'Susi did well in the circumstances' wrote Livingstone in one of his rare commendations.[13]

Matipa now exasperated Livingstone by his dilatoriness over obtaining further canoes—'Matipa acting the villain & my men afraid of him' he wrote on 18 March. The next day, his sixtieth birthday, he lost patience. He fired a pistol through Matipa's roof and summoned up his men in force: the chief immediately changed his tactics and supplied three canoes in which Susi and Chuma took a party on to Kabinga's. Chuma remained there in charge of the advance party and Susi returned with the canoes; the second batch set off on 25 March. The following day one canoe sank, and 'a slave girl of Amoda' was drowned. The final batch were then sent for. By now they were passing over flooded land south of Lake Bangweolo, well away from the proper route.[14]

The expedition left Kabinga's on 5 April; a small party with the luggage went in canoes, with most of the men going by land, but contact was lost between the two; Livingstone was weak, and 'My men were all done up'. He crossed the Muanakazi on 12 April but, as the Africans told Waller 'said he could not walk. Susi went in front to put up tent and prepare for the Doctor coming. Chuma and men stop behind to carry him. Tried to follow Susi but couldn't walk—complained of throat getting dry. Put Dr on shoulders of Chuma and Chowperi and Chandi carried him thus. Found Susi by Lukulu. Crossed small Lukulu and then big Lukulu. Men had crossed by force and they all met at big Lukulu. The men thought the Doctor had gone by the lake and did not know he was following by land.'[15]

On 20 April, at Muanazawamba's, Livingstone managed to conduct a service, but his strength was failing, and thereafter he could make only a few scrawled entries in the journals he had kept so meticulously. The final stages of his journey were described by Susi and Chuma. The next day, Livingstone 'tried to go on but fell off the donkey. Chuma put down his gun and ran on to stop the men ahead. Susi took off his belt and pistol and carried it. As he lay he said to Chuma "I have lost so much blood my legs have lost all their strength. You must carry me." . . . Took him on shoulders and he held Chuma's head. Susi carried his cap which had fallen . . .' He was taken back to Muanazawamba's, and the chief said 'stay as long as you like—when ready I give guides'. He rested there the remainder of the day. Here he had to abandon his custom of greeting all his men daily—'I cannot say good morning so often'.

The following day his men made a *kitanda*, or litter, with two side pieces 7 feet long, joined by 3-foot cross pieces lashed at intervals, covered with grass and a blanket. This was slung from a carrying-pole, over which was hung a further blanket, as shelter from the sun. For two days the journey continued, and on the 24th a village was reached, and:

Whilst building a hut the Doctor was put in the shade in the Chitanda. Chief hid. All others came near. The Doctor told Chuma to ask about four rivers. 'We don't know. All the men who used to travel are dead. Mlenga's people were the great travellers and whenever an expedition was formed for trading all used to assemble at Mlenga's. The Mazitu now have killed them so that no one can tell you' . . .

93

Doctor told him to bring food and explained he was so sick he could not talk much.

On the 25th only a short journey was possible, but on the 26th they reached Kalunganjovu's, where, apparently planning for future needs, Livingstone 'called Susi and said that as they were short of cloth and beads they had better buy two big tusks to take to Ujiji there to sell them for beads and cloth.'

The following two days he rested; the last entry in his journal was made on the 27th. Chuma and Susi recalled that he told their wives to pound some corn with nuts, but he could not eat it. On the 29th the journey continued to Chitambo's. It was:

> . . . very difficult because the Doctor stopped them continually to put him down but he became drowsy . . . Chuma came on with him and eight men—before he arrived Susi had sent water to him. He called to Chuma . . . Chuma went to him and said 'Sir here I am . . .' The Doctor did not answer. Chuma said 'Here is water Susi has sent.' He said 'Is it cold?' Drank . . . asked to be put down and got out of the Chitanda. Chuma went to lift him but he complained of such pain. He said 'Let me lie flat and put my arms over your neck and then get your arms under me and lift me.'

He crossed in a canoe but could not sit in it and had to be laid down. Chitambo's was reached about 4 p.m.; Susi had gone ahead to prepare a hut and Livingstone was laid in it. He was too ill to see Chitambo when he called next morning; he told Susi he was cold, and a cloth was brought to cover him. He also asked Susi for his watch; he 'laid it on Susi's hand and wound it. Susi noticed his eyes looking no strong . . .' That night Majwara, who slept at the door, called Susi as Livingstone had asked for medicine. They brought the medicine chest, holding the candle close to the labels of the items they took out until Livingstone was satisfied that they had found the right one, calomel. Susi boiled water for him. He asked what a noise was and was told that a buffalo was eating corn in the fields. Susi shut the door and went out. Majwara dozed off and woke about 4 a.m. to find Livingstone in the same attitude, 'kneeling on his bed with his head on the pillow'. He was alarmed, ran for Susi and said 'come and see how the Doctor is sleeping.' Susi, accompanied by Chuma, Manua Sera, Matthew Wellington and Carus Farrar, entered the hut. They 'saw the Doctor fallen forward as if in the act of praying . . . They felt his cheeks and found him dead.' After covering his body with a cloth, they went out and sat by the fire; 'in a short time the cock crew.' It was dawn on 1 May 1873.

94

'The whole camp wept for him,' wrote Carus Farrar,[16] but the immediate problem was how to deal with Chief Chitambo, since he might levy a heavy charge on the leaderless expedition if Livingstone's death was known. Chuma therefore took a gift of cloth and beads to the chief, whom he found in his garden, and according to his own account said 'Our master very sick—he does not like this old smelling town and the rats he wants one built outside.' Chitambo proved amenable and 'sent a man to show them where they might build. It was about 200 yards off where there was a big tree. Built a fence round it. Carried body in Chitanda. Fenced with Msugu.'

Next day one of the party bought supplies in the village and let slip news of the Doctor's death. Chitambo sent for Chuma who again prevaricated, but Chitambo said 'do not be afraid. Before Malenga died we used to go long journeys—we know what it is to travel. We know you don't come to fight.' Susi therefore went to Chitambo with a gift and admitted that Livingstone was dead. The chief replied 'All right—now my people shall mourn.' Drums were beaten for three hours, and the young men fired their guns.

It was resolved to carry the body, with Livingstone's diaries, maps, and scientific instruments, to the coast. Jacob Wainwright drew up a brief inventory. This decision, which led to the most famous and in some ways the most remarkable journey in African exploration, has been much discussed. Matthew Wellington, forty years later, suggested that the Muslim members of the expedition, including the headman (Susi) wished to bury the body but the Nasik boys, who had promised Price 'to bring back the Doctor with us dead or alive' persuaded them to change their minds. There are inaccuracies in his account, and it is hard to credit that the seasoned travellers would have taken much notice of raw recruits. The French traveller Victor Giraud claimed that Chuma and Susi had told him that they had brought the body to avoid punishment and to obtain a reward, but his evidence is not always reliable. As a group of resourceful men, with carbines and supplies, Livingstone's followers could, if they had wished, found employment with Arab caravans in the interior out of reach of the coast and had no need to return to it. The Victorians believed that their reason was to honour their master by taking his body to his own people, and to preserve the records which his more experienced followers had seen him keep so meticulously under conditions of hardship and sickness—and who can say that this was not the truth?[17]

Chuma's and Susi's story is simple. 'Susi said he must not be left so said Muanyaseri'; and Chitambo commented 'if you like to bury him do if not you can carry him away for I believe he is a great man.' The body was placed in a hut, open at the top, about twenty-five yards from the large tree in the enclosure. Here it was prepared by the

95

removal of the heart and internal organs, which were buried some three feet below the floor of the hut. This operation was carried out by Farjallah, who had been Dr Christie's assistant at Zanzibar,[18] with the help of Carus Farrar. Susi, Manua Sera, and Chuma were also present for the burial, and Jacob Wainwright read from the Bible; these six were the only ones in the hut. The body was then covered with salt and left in the sun for two weeks, watched continually by the six men, at night by the glow of candles. Chitambo called daily.

Before they left, Jacob Wainwright carved an inscription, giving the names of the 'heads of departments', on the tree:

DR. LIVINGSTONE
MAY 4, 1873
YAZUZA, MNIASERE
VCHOPERE

Chitambo was given a biscuit tin and newspapers as evidence that Livingstone had been there and was asked 'to keep the grass cut round the tree that the fires should not touch it'. He agreed, but added 'if the English come let them come soon for I fear the Mazitu may come and then if the place is left men may cut down this tree for a canoe.'[19]

On the first day's journey they found it necessary to cover the canvas shrouding the body with tar, and wrapped a length of bark outside it. Two days later they arrived at a town belonging to a kinsman of Chitambo, where they were delayed a month by widespread illness, the symptoms of which were pains in limbs or face. Chuma had a pain in his groin and could not walk; Susi's pain 'changed from one leg to another', and Sangolo was very ill. Two women, Kaniki and Bahati, died; indeed, the sufferings of the women on the journeys before and after Livingstone's death, were severe. 'Chitambo's people said it was a bad country for strangers. Many Arabs had died.' However, the rains ended and there was 'plenty of food, fowl and fish'.

Barely had the march been resumed than Susi became much worse and another twenty days were spent at Muanamazungu's town, still in the Ilala region. The old chief, 'an *excellent* man', called daily and brought food. 'Farijala killed three buffalo there, which pleased the people much.' Another day's journey brought them to Chisalamalama's, where they stayed a day and then were provided with canoes to cross the Luapala. That night:

The donkey was in a shed near the tents of Chuma and Susi. Two lions came; one rushed in and seized the donkey by the mouth. Amoda sang out. They rushed out and found the house down and

96

the donkey gone. Got the men together and lit some grass; when they saw the lion over the body fired a volley and the lion went off wounded. They found the tracks and followed but a native warned them that there were two and that the other might attack them.

A few days' journey on, at Nkoso's, they traded brass and wire for a cow, which they then had to shoot. Wadi Safeni 'catching up his gun from smoking shot a man in the leg.' Compensation was paid, and the man treated by the local method. 'They took earth and made the man sit buried in it up to the chest—put splints on his leg with earth round his leg—lighted fire on his leg on the earth. When it got very hot they took his leg out and squeezed it together, bound it very tight, and put him in a hut. They told Chuma that in this way they could unite any bone—but not the back.'

They passed through the territory of the Wausi, 'who did not like the body to pass', and approached Chawendi's. Two messengers were sent ahead; 'there was a great Pombe drink on. Chief willing they should come—his son, drunk, said no.' They returned to their colleagues and a larger party, Chuma, Amoda, Manua Sera, Safeni and Saburi came to the town and met the chief's son.

He said 'Who told these men to come?' Safeni said 'Don't let these men stop us,' and pushed them away and entered. The son fired an arrow and missed when they attacked. Fought for about two hours. Burnt two villages and drove them away. They got plenty of goats and great threats about tomorrow from the people who fled. Susi who was behind at first heard the guns, and Mabruki Speke was going to shoot a man who caught at his gun but Susi said 'No don't, it may be the guns were fired in rejoicing' . . . The next morning plenty of men came but on getting a charge of small shot they all went saying they didn't want to fight with men who threw things like rain at them.

After seven days' rest at the captured town they moved on. Three days later they rested for two days at Chama's village as Susi's wife was ill, and not long after they had to leave two sick men, Songolo and Damungu, at a village, giving the chief a present of beads.

At a subsequent village, Chiwa's, there was a dispute about their right to carry the English and Arab flags, with Majwara beating his drum, at the head of their column, 'but eventually they passed in peace'. Soon after they struck Livingstone's outward route and began to return in familiar country, though many of the towns and villages were deserted owing to the recent fighting in the area. They eventually came to the town of Kumba Kumba, brother of Tippu Tip, who held

97

sway over a considerable area, and had recently killed the powerful chief Casembe. He warned them against the danger of hyenas stealing the body, so they kept constant watch over it and lit fires. Near here the Nasik boy John Wainwright was lost. Matthew Wellington wrote that he 'died from fever and dysentery' but Chuma and Susi reported that 'he malingered and stayed behind—many paths meet—They burnt grass for him to see smoke and did all they could. They think he ran away.'[20]

A few stages later they came to Chitimbwa's, but the chief said his people were afraid of the body, so they stayed outside the village and remained only one night. From Chitimbwa's they began to descend. 'It was hot and fine now and all the men had picked up well. They looked down on Tanganyika, a beautiful view . . . Came to Kasakalawe's down by Lake, they drank Lake water here.' They decided not to follow Livingstone's difficult route along the edge of the lake but to strike north-east. It was pleasant country—'all flat, and enormous quantities of game in all directions—giraffe and zebra and lions.' There were also buffalo, and the marksmen of the party, notably Asmani, Farjallah and Manua Sera, were able to shoot some, both for their own food and to reward local hospitality. The Fipa people were generally friendly, though at one point they had to pay their first *hongo*—fourteen strings of beads.

On one occasion they saw a large caravan approaching. Susi and a number of men with loaded guns stopped behind with the body, while Chuma and a detachment with the flags went on to meet the caravan which proved to be a friendly Arab trading party, bound for Fipa country. Its leaders had already heard rumours of Livingstone's death, and brought news that there was a new relief expedition, with the Doctor's son, at Unyanyembe. This was confirmed by another caravan a few days later, and at Baula Jacob Wainwright, the most literate of the party, wrote a letter, which was taken on to Unyanyembe by Chuma and three colleagues:

Ukhonongo October 1873

Sir

We have heared in the month of August that you have started from Zanzibar for Unyanyembe, and again and again lately we have heared your arrival. Your father died by disease beyond the country of Bisa, but we have carried the corpse with us. 10 of our soldiers are lost and some have died. Our hunger presses us to ask you some clothes to buy provision for our soldiers and we should have an answer that when we shall enter there shall be firing guns or not, and if you permit us to fire guns, then send

98

some powder. We have wrote these few words in the place of Sultan or king Mbowra.

The writer Jacob Wainwright
Dr Livingstone Exped.[21]

Chuma reached Unyanyembe on 20 October. The man who received the letter, and to whom he told his story, was Lt Verney Lovett Cameron, RN, commanding a new relief expedition. It was not Livingstone's son, but his nephew, Robert Moffat, who had accompanied it, and he had died of fever in May. Cameron and his colleagues, Dr Dillon and Lt Murphy, had been delayed at Unyanyembe since August. Chuma was sent back with supplies, and a few days later Livingstone's followers brought his body into the town. The procession passed through two lines of *askari*, each in red patrol jacket, fez, white shirt and cummerbund; in command, his rank indicated by white NCO's stripes, was Bombay, now Cameron's caravan leader. Two of Speke's followers, Ferrajji and Umbari, carried the colours.[22]

Cameron suggested that Livingstone, like his wife, should be buried in Africa, and warned his followers of hostility in Ugogo; but they stuck to their original decision. It was therefore agreed that Cameron would continue into the interior, but that Murphy, who was unwilling to do so, and Dillon, who was ill, would return to the coast with a few men and with the party carrying the body. They left on 9 November. At the end of the first day they had to halt owing to the illness of Chowpereh's wife, but reached Kasakera a few days later. Here, in view of possible opposition to their progress, they adopted the subterfuge of repacking Livingstone's body to make it appear like an ordinary load. They then made up 'a bundle of grass with cloth, and sent a letter off as if returning the body to Unyanyembe. When they got a certain distance they pulled the bundle to pieces and pitched it far away (the pieces and likewise the cloth and pole) and jumped aside in all directions so as to make it impossible to follow them and returned in the middle of the night into the town.'

By now Dillon's illness had affected his mind, and on 18 November he shot himself. He was buried by Chuma and some of his colleagues, and Livingstone's men resumed their march to the coast. At last, in February, they reached their goal—' "Heria bahari" or welcome sea was the cheering word heard from everybody's lips while approaching Buagamoyo', wrote Farrar.[23] The party of some seventy men and women had travelled 1,400 miles in their nine months' journey; three women had died and at least seven men had been lost on the way, but the body of Livingstone, with his papers and instruments (other than those which had been taken by Cameron) had been brought back to his own people.

Chuma had been sent on ahead, and reached Zanzibar on 3 February with the news that Murphy was nearing Bagamoyo. Kirk was on leave, but the Acting Consul, Captain W. F. Prideaux, sent Chuma back with supplies; he himself crossed to the mainland on the 14th, met the expedition next day, and brought it to Zanzibar on the 16th. Prideaux found Livingstone's followers destitute, and at once paid them the arrears due to them; he also gave Halima a gratuity of 50 dollars; he expected the Royal Geographical Society to meet the cost, but they disclaimed responsibility and the amount was eventually paid by the Government. News of Livingstone's death had been telegraphed to London on 3 January when Mgaia, a messenger sent by Cameron, reached Zanzibar. This was reported at the Royal Geographical Society meeting on 26 January, but the President, Sir Bartle Frere, doubted its accuracy. Fuller details were given in February and on 23 March news was received of the arrival of Chuma at Zanzibar. Some members were still reluctant to credit the fact that Livingstone was dead, and Horace Waller interpreted this as a reflection on the Africans who had brought down the body. 'The task that these men had performed was truly Herculean . . . Chumah and Susi had been with Livingstone for eight or nine years. It was true that they laboured under the great and terrible disadvantage of being black, but still they ought to have accorded to them all the honour which was their due.' The President tried to mollify the indignant Waller '. . . when Livingstone's faithful servants arrived in this country, the Royal Geographical Society would mete out the fair share of praise to every member of the expedition, without distinction of race or colour.'[24]

Shortly after, Waller received a letter from Chuma at Zanzibar, dictated to Captain Brine of HMS *Briton*:

Chuma gives compliments to Mr. Waller. I have been all over with Dr. Livingstone in Africa, and am now in Zanzibar with my wife. I am now by myself. I do not know what work to do. Give my compliments to my sister, who is at the Cape. His name Chasika. I hear it with Dr. Livingstone that letters came to him that Kinsolo, my brother, been shot with a gun. I don't know who shoot him. If please you get answer, send to me at Zanzibar. Susi, Kibanga man, give his compliments to Mr. Waller, and to Dr. Livingstone's son, and now he is in Zanzibar and will wait for a letter. If you have got any business in Africa, let us know. We want to go in Africa again where Dr. Livingstone died. Susi don't know write.

In sending this to *The Times*, Waller commented 'Chuma promised me in a similar epistle that he would stick to the Doctor, come what might.'[25]

1 Bombay. *Photograph by J. A. Grant, Zanzibar, 1860*

2 Speke's 'Faithfuls', Cairo 1863. *Rear:* Ulimengo, Ilmas, Matagiri, Khamsin, Baruti, Mka
Uledi Mapengo, Uledi (Grant's servant); *Centre:* Manua, Sadiki, Umbari, Farhan, Mekt
Front: Mabruki, Mtamani, Bombay, Frij, Sangoro. *From a photograph by Royer*

3 Women of Speke's expedition,
Cairo, 1863. Sikujua, Kahala,
M'Essu, Faida. *From a photograph
by Royer*

4 Livingstone's sketch of Bombay, 1871
(original $3\frac{1}{4}$ in. wide)

5 (*below*) Part of Stanley's list of reinforcements, May 1872, with additions
by Livingstone

6   Jacob Wainwright with Livingstone's coffin and trunk, 1874

7   Model of Livingstone's hut made by Chuma, 1874

8 Jumah   9 Sambo

Both the above were probably sketched on Cameron's expeditions

10 Chowpereh, on Stanley's expe-   11 Wife of Manua Sera
dition, 1874-77

12 Group of Stanley's men, Cape Town, 1877. Manua Sera is the bearded figure; facing him is Robert Feruzi. Majwara sits on the extreme right next to Uledi, in a turban. *Watercolour by Catherine Frere*

13 Susi   14 Chuma

15 Chuma (left), Thomson and Makatubu, 1881

16 (*below left*) Dualla Idris

17 (*below*) Jumbe Kimameta

18   Zanzibari garrison at Vivi, 1880

19   The Rev. W. H. Jones returns to Rabai, 1886

It was, however, Jacob Wainwright who arrived in England with the body of Livingstone, which was under the charge of Arthur Laing, an English merchant from Zanzibar. Jacob's name had been recognised by W. S. Price, the founder of Nasik (see p. 54), then in England, and the Church Missionary Society had telegraphed that he should be sent home with the body. At Livingstone's funeral in Westminster Abbey on 18 April he was a pall-bearer, and travelled in the second coach, which also contained Kalulu. The other pall-bearers were Stanley, Kirk, Waller, E. D. Young, and three friends from earlier days, Sir Thomas Steele, W. Cotton Oswell and W. F. Webb of Newstead Abbey. The inscription on the massive tombstone alluded to the Africans' work in its opening phrase 'Brought by faithful hands over land and sea here rests David Livingstone . . .'[26]

At the Royal Geographical Society meeting on 27 April, Thomas Livingstone, who was then intending to edit his father's journals, was present, with Jacob Wainwright, and in May Wainwright was also present at the Church Missionary Society Anniversary, where his story was told by Price. In a letter to *The Times* Price wrote:

After that sad event, Jacob Wainwright commenced keeping a diary, and continued it for nine weary months, during which they were working their way to the coast, carrying with them the mortal remains of their late master. It is a most interesting record of their journeys, and contains observations of natural features of various countries through which they passed, and some notice of the customs of the different tribes of people with whom they came into contact.

He gave a circumstantial account of this diary, which had been copied in Zanzibar and reproduced in the Indian papers, but had subsequently been sealed up, brought home by Laing, and handed back to Jacob in Price's presence. It would 'shortly be given to the public'. However, it vanished from the record. Horace Waller, the eventual editor of Livingstone's Journals, noted 'it was to the intelligence and superior education of Jacob Wainwright . . . that we were indebted for the earliest account of the eventful eighteen months during which he was attached to the party,' but he never quoted from Jacob's diaries, and drew instead on the reminiscences of Chuma and Susi.[27]

Some gifts of money were sent to Chuma, Susi, Halima and N'taoéka,[28] and the two former were brought to England, after the funeral, at the expense of Livingstone's old friend, James Young of Kelly. Just before Whitsun they visited the Webbs at Newstead Abbey on their way north, and there met Horace Waller. Augusta Webb, later Mrs Fraser, recalled them:

101

Of the two, Susi was much the elder, as well as the taller . . . He looked as if he had gone through a good deal of anxiety in his time, and had a rather lined and careworn face, slightly marked by the smallpox, which, strangely enough, invariably shows its traces more on black than on European complexions. He was also two or three shades darker than Chumah. The latter was of a light chocolate hue, and of a very smooth skin. He was a far more vivacious character, as was easily to be discovered by his bright, dancing, and roving eyes. He appeared to be taking in his novel surroundings with great interest.

One felt instinctively that the two were on the best of terms. Although Susi was evidently the responsible superior, Chumah surpassed him in quickness of perception. Throughout their visit, it was pretty to notice Chumah's deference to his elder. He took care at all times to show he looked on him as his leader.

They were dressed in European attire, in very thick blue serge jackets, with bright round buttons—reefer jackets, I believe they are called—and blue serge trousers. They found even the June weather chilly, but never wore caps or hats even out of doors; and although I have at times seen them with striped red silk kerchiefs knotted round their heads, it was more for the sake of adornment than aught else.

They were immensely proud of their new English clothes, but evidently found them rather irksome; and in spite of their satisfaction in wearing socks and shoes walked as if unaccustomed to their use.

During their stay they were photographed with Tom Livingstone and Horace Waller, and also with some of the relics of Livingstone. Waller had conversations with them every morning, chiefly in English which 'proved so much better than was expected' that he seldom had to resort to his knowledge of African languages. He commented that 'Their knowledge of the countries they travelled in is most remarkable, and from constantly aiding their master by putting questions to the natives respecting the course of rivers, &c., I found them actual geographers of no mean attainments.'

Augusta Fraser recalled that 'On Sunday, as a matter of course, they attended morning and evening service in the Chapel, where their reverent demeanour was remarked by all to be an example to many English churchgoers,' but this is somewhat surprising, since Susi was at this time a Muslim.[29]

On 1 June they were present at the Royal Geographical Society meeting and Frere introduced them cordially, saying that if his audience 'were acquainted with the whole history of these excellent men, they would respect them even more than they did at present, and that they would pay them a tribute such as Englishmen knew how to pay to duties strenuously performed.' They returned for the anniversary meeting on 22 June, at which the President spoke at length of Livingstone, adding:

Thanks to the indomitable energy of this extraordinary man, and thanks, too, to those who, by contact with him, felt their own natures raised to deeds of faithfulness and heroism, David Livingstone's journals were not only kept with scrupulous care to within a few days of his death, but brought hither by his negro followers with a devotion, which, whilst it has excited the admiration of every civilized nation, has perhaps done more than any individual act on record to raise the black races in the estimation of the world. Let us never forget what has been done for geography by the faithful band who restored to us all that it was in their power to bring of our lost friend, and who rescued his priceless writings and maps from destruction.

He also announced:

That the Council had that day unanimously decided that medals should be given to the servants of Dr Livingstone who had come to England, and that a special silver medal should be struck, to be given, as a mark of approbation of their fidelity and courage, to all who accompanied the Doctor in his last great expedition.

Horace Waller then led up Chuma and Susi who received bronze medals.[30]

In July Tom Livingstone finally decided that he could not undertake the editing of his father's journals and the task eventually fell to Horace Waller. He had Chuma and Susi with him for a total of four months. One episode, linking Africa with the drawing-room of Leytonstone Vicarage in a moving way, took place when the Africans had been speaking of slaves who pined away in captivity, 'when Chuma had been telling us about the man dying thinking about his home Alice offered to play for them & played "Home sweet home" and in their astonishment—they had never seen a piano before—they asked if the keys were Ivory! What a flood of thought came up how this Ivory had been subject to the same agony of human heartbreak.' Waller also took them to an agricultural show, and to a workhouse, where they told the children about slavery in Africa.[31]

In September they visited the Livingstones at Hamilton. Anna Mary, the younger daughter, wrote to her friend, the Danish author Hans

Christian Andersen: 'Papa's two coloured servants were here seeing us last week. They were telling us a great many interesting things about Papa, and one of them called Chumah made a little model of the grass hut in which Papa died and showed us the position of Papa's bed in it. It is very interesting to us.' They returned to Africa soon after and reached Zanzibar by 20 October. Jacob Wainwright spent some time in England, and was taken round the country to address meetings under the auspices of the Church Missionary Society. He stayed at Newstead shortly after Chuma and Susi, but his brash manner made a very bad impression.[32]

The selection of a design for the RGS silver medal, and its execution was made the responsibility of J. A. Grant and R. H. Major, the Hon. Secretary of the Society, and the work was entrusted to J. S. & A. S. Wyon, of Regent Street. Round a bust of Livingstone ran the inscription DAVID LIVINGSTONE BORN 1813 DIED, ILALA, 1873. On the reverse was PRESENTED BY THE ROYAL GEO-GRAPHICAL SOCIETY OF LONDON 1874. Round the rim was inscribed FAITHFUL TO THE END and the recipient's name. There was a clip and silver ring, through which ran a cord for suspension round the neck. Sixty medals were struck, and the names, apparently from Prideaux's pay list, added.

Major C. B. Euan Smith, who was acting for Kirk at Zanzibar, received the medals on 29 June, but had some difficulty in collecting medal recipients together, for many had left the island, most of them in Stanley's new expedition. Eventually he presented medals to Chuma, Susi and ten others on the morning of 17 August at the British Consulate in the presence of Bishop Steere and other European residents, and the ceremony was followed by 'a native feast'. W. Salter Price had recently transferred the school for freed slaves from India to Frere Town, near Mombasa, and Euan Smith visited it on 24 September to present medals to the five survivors of the second batch of Nasik boys. One medal was said to be a duplicate, issued owing to a confusion of names. 'I would suggest that the surplus medal occasioned by this fact be given to Halima the female cook who attended Dr Livingstone with such fidelity and for whom I observe no medal has been sent out,' wrote Euan Smith, but it is not known whether this suggestion was accepted.[33]

9

ACROSS AFRICA FROM EAST TO WEST

The expedition which received Livingstone's body at Unyanyembe in October 1873 had been organised by the Royal Geographical Society, using the money remaining from the hastily abandoned Dawson expedition.[1] On arriving at Zanzibar in January its leader, Lt Verney Lovett Cameron, had engaged Bombay for 12 dollars a month 'which at the time we thought of great importance on account of his previous experience'. A Comorian named Issa, formerly an interpreter on HMS *Glasgow*, who had travelled in Manyema and elsewhere, was employed as interpreter and storekeeper. Bombay was instructed to obtain thirty *askari*—soldiers, servants and donkey drivers—but 'a motley crew they proved' having been picked up in the bazaar. These were paid 8½ dollars a month. It was the wrong season for porters, and those engaged, both at Zanzibar and Bagamoyo, were a riff-raff, mostly without experience of travel, who nevertheless charged double rates, 5 dollars a month. Cameron also blamed inflated prices on the fact that he had arrived with Sir Bartle Frere, on an official mission to persuade Seyyid Barghash, Majid's successor, to abolish the slave trade (see p. 133); he was therefore believed to have official status, and hence ample funds.

During February and March Cameron was trying to organise his caravan, both at Zanzibar and on the mainland at Bagamoyo. He had problems with recruiting enough *pagazi*, needed to overhaul his saddles and other equipment, learned the complexities of paying his men in varied types of goods, and endured desertions, pay claims and delays when he tried to set off for the interior. His early impressions of his men were favourable—'our askari seem a very decent set, and most of the pagazi seem cheerful and inclined to work' he wrote on 23 March, but he modified this view when about thirty deserted in March and April. It was the end of May before the varied elements of the expedition were united for the first time, at Rehennko. The total strength was Issa as storekeeper; Bombay and his 34 *askari*; 192 *pagazi*; 6 servants, cooks and gunbearers; 3 boys; a few women, including Bombay's wife; some slaves belonging to the men; 22 donkeys and three dogs. The expedition carried Snider rifles, and during the whole journey the men 'kept their arms under very trying circumstances in a condition that would be a credit to any soldier'.

The journey to Unyanyembe took from 30 May to early August, and Cameron experienced the varied problems of African travel. The Gogo levied their customary *hongo* but when a second payment was demanded in one area he determined to go forward in spite of timidity among his men, and was not hindered. He found that costs in Ugogo had more than trebled since Burton's journey sixteen years earlier.

He also had problems with his men. One party of forty men was sent, under the Speke veteran Umbari, to obtain food at Mbumi, where a villager was accidently killed in a fracas, so that delay, and a payment of compensation, resulted. At another village there was trouble because one of the Nyamwezi *pagazi* had collected ivory on his downward journey but had failed to obtain the promised gunpowder in return for it; Cameron persuaded the creditors to accept payment in cloth. There were some deaths of men and donkeys, and some desertions, a particularly galling one occurring when a gang of Nyamwezi porters, dissatisfied with their pay, enlisted with a caravan that had joined Cameron for protection through Ugogo. Some other losses took place when Cameron forbad the custom of firing guns at the new moon on grounds of waste and danger, with the result that one *askari*, whom he had reprimanded, and some *pagazi* deserted. In July, the *pagazi* refused to pitch tents, though, as Cameron later found, they had been travelling with loads ten pounds lighter than the average. The *askari* undertook the erecting of tents, and servants and gunbearers saw to their contents.

A major cause of indiscipline was that Bombay had 'lost much of the energy he displayed in his journeys with our predecessors in African travel, and was much inclined to trade upon his previous reputation'. He had little authority, preferring to take the line of least resistance, laconically summing up one refusal to work as 'Tell all man, all man say no go'. He drank too much, lacked drive, and got muddled over routes and negotiations about *hongo*. However, interspersed with denunciations on these points, one finds in Cameron's diary that he built 'a very decent hut' and there are other favourable references. Cameron eventually summed him up as 'very well in his peculiar way, but neither the "Angel" of Colonel Grant nor the "Devil" of Mr. Stanley. I generally found after yielding to him that I should have done far better to have adhered to my first intentions.'[2]

As they neared Unyanyembe, morale appeared to improve; on the march 'the kirangosis kept up a sort of recitative, the whole caravan joining in chorus with pleasing effect'. When they reached their destination, Said bin Salim welcomed Cameron and allotted him the house at Kwihara formerly used by Stanley and Livingstone. Staff problems continued and some *pagazi* deserted after pay disputes. Discipline also broke down when some *askari* took the law into their own hands and hanged a *pagazi* upside down as a punishment for theft. Bombay was ordered to put the culprits in chains but reported that the *askari* refused. When Cameron told him to warn those who would not obey that they would be dismissed, he translated this into telling them to go, and they all walked off. Cameron appealed to the Arabs, who seized the troublemakers, and the rest returned to duty.

The expedition was delayed at Unyanyembe by the illnesses suffered by all white men, and desertions and uncertainty among personnel— 130 *pagazi* were engaged but could not be kept together. Cameron considered pushing ahead with a small band of picked followers.

On 20 October Chuma arrived with the news of Livingstone's death. By 9 November Cameron had weighed up the altered circumstances and had decided to go on. Issa had been valuable, keeping reliable accounts and conducting some negotiations, but he wished to return home for family reasons, and he had not got on well with Bombay. Cameron therefore agreed that he should go back with Dillon, Murphy and Livingstone's body. Cameron's leading men were now Bombay, Bilal wadi Asmani, Asmani who had been Stanley's guide and was a useful hunter, with his friend Mabruki, Mohammed Malim, Sambo the Comorian cook who had once served on an English merchant ship, Kombo his mate, and two engaged at Unyanyembe—Hamees a gunbearer, and Jacko a slave boy freed by Said bin Salim. He also had about a hundred *askari* and *pagazi*, 'desertions and engagements causing the total to vary daily', though he had a hard core who had been with him thoughout.

When he left he suffered considerable delays due to desertions, and on more than one occasion he had to use Bombay or Bilal to look after goods left behind or bring up stragglers. 'Bombay has been working splendidly lately, and so has his second, Bilal,' he wrote. It seemed impossible to go by the direct route, so he set off by a more southerly path on 27 November. He began with a hundred men, but in a few days more than fifty had deserted, and to add to his problems the *askari* decided that carrying flags and a drum was work for *pagazi*, not for them. Bombay supported this view, and the eventual solution was to leave the drum behind.

When Cameron learned that Ugara was disturbed he sent Asmani back to Unyanyembe to try to persuade the Arabs to make peace in the areas. While waiting, he spent a miserable Christmas—a dog stole the fish, Sambo upset the soup, and the pudding was not boiled. Asmani eventually brought news that the dispute had been settled, and he had also collected up a few deserters. Soon after setting off on 30 December, Cameron learned that one of his donkeys alleged to have strayed at Unyanyembe had been sold by Umbari and Manua Sera. Umbari had been 'a grumbling, troublesome fellow' and Cameron now turned him out.

The journey continued through January. Bombay lectured the men on keeping a good watch in case of attack by *ruga ruga*, the guerilla bands of the area, and a small Nyamwezi caravan joined them for protection. There was no attack, but the weather provided difficulties with rain and storm. The *pagazi* were resourceful—'I'll back the East African to make a camp against any man'—and when Cameron's tent nearly blew away, some of his followers ran up in time to save it. When the weather improved, Asmani took out a hunting party, and the men, in spite of urgings from Bombay, would not go on until they had a good meal. Cameron had some sympathy with the protesters—'they so seldom get meat to eat'. When the expedition set off again Asmani was unable to find the road, but this was partly due to the depredations of Mirambo; Bombay, who had been in the area before, commented 'all village broke up again'. Food was running short and progress was difficult; Bombay brought up the rear with the slow-moving donkeys.

Early in February the expedition was nearing exhaustion, and though at first annoyed when Bombay suggested delaying an extra day at a place where rations were cheap, Cameron later admitted 'there is a great deal of truth in what he says'. At last, on 21 February, Cameron had his first sight of Lake Tanganyika and arrived at Ujiji; Bombay and the rest joined him next day. Here Cameron took stock; there had been theft as well as half-heartedness in the caravan, and he found only one man had a full load. The equivalent of sixteen loads of beads was missing, but it was difficult to identify the thieves: Bombay had been an ineffective guardian. Where thefts were proved the men were dismissed, and one caught in the act was flogged.

On 13 March Cameron left Bilal in command and began the exploration of the southern end of Lake Tanganyika with Bombay and thirty-seven men in two hired boats which he named *Betsy* and *Pickle*. Two guides were paid $17\frac{1}{2}$ dollars each for the journey whilst the elders who engaged them received 34, and Cameron later gave them extra for their good work.

During the early stages of the journey Cameron was ill. He was looked after by Bombay and Mohammed Malim and soon improved. Most of the crew slept ashore, and had to be roused up on a squally night as 'I had no taste for a cruise on the Lake with no crew but

Bombay and his wife'. Cameron was not very satisfied with his men—
'Bombay certainly seems to feel an interest in the work, but what is
one among so many?' The others were unduly timid, given to theft,
poor oarsmen and 'All humbug and laziness'. One, Mungreza, shot
himself while grasping his loaded gun by the muzzle in order to use
it as a boat-hook; as he was very fat, the bullet caused no serious
damage.

Cameron was a fair-minded man, however, and conceded that 'it is
impossible to be really angry with them, as according to their lights
they do very well. They always look for pitching my tent very quickly;
and at any muddy or bad places . . . I always have a lot of volunteers
to carry me across . . . I like most of them very much, but still do not
put the slightest trust in their pluck . . .' He was, consciously or not,
measuring them against his bluejackets—'Oh! for a whaler and crew
for six weeks!' he wrote, and later 'they went chopping water like
dockyard mateys paid by the hour.' He was perhaps comparing
Bombay with a seasoned petty officer in some of his criticisms; he lectured him 'about the way he gives in to the men, and allows them to
nag at him'. Next day Bombay roused the men without being told,
but he lapsed again, and on one occasion of general dilatoriness
Cameron seized a piece of wood—which he described as more useful
than Bombay—and struck out. The men got to work and 'seem in
a good humour, much more jolly than usual'. He was then 'obliged
to chaff Bombay to get him in a good humour, and he began as usual,
when put out, to forget his English and talk Suaheli.' The south end
was reached on 17 April, the mouth of the Lukuga entered on 4 May—
though it could not be explored owing to vegetation—and Ujiji
reached again on 9 May. Bombay had now been round all the lake
except the north-west end.[3]

Cameron again reviewed the situation; he had only four donkeys
left. He had reduced his numbers to seventy and reorganised the stores
to make fewer loads, though Bombay did some further reorganising
of his own which reversed this procedure. Livingstone had left some
journals at Ujiji, and Cameron sent these to the coast in charge of his
servant Mohammed Malim; he had been a useful man, acting as
tailor and interpreter as well as servant, but he had incurred Bombay's
enmity. He was replaced by Jumah wadi Nasib (or Juma bin Nasibu
as he was more frequently called), and 'most invaluable he proved'.

The usual drinking marked the eve of departure, and Bombay and
his wife were involved in a fight which resulted in spoiling a quantity
of *singo-mazzi* beads, and there was other damage. By 31 May the
expedition was finally assembled on the western shore. They travelled
in company with a trader, Syde Mezrui, and later joined with a larger
caravan for the crossing of the hazardous Manyema area.

Cameron's aim was to reach the supposed Lake Sankorra and thence to go down what he correctly believed to be the Congo to the sea, but he could not get canoes at Nyangwe. Syde Mezrui was adept at begging beads from Bombay and Bilal, but proved to have little influence with the local chiefs; and Bombay's attempts to negotiate were without success. On 19 August Tippu Tip arrived and suggested that Cameron came south with him, so that he could approach Lake Sankorra across the Lomani. They set off on the 26th, Bombay following; when he arrived it was to report the desertion of Asmani, Mabruki and another *pagazi*, with their guns and ammunition.

Tippu Tip's camp was reached on 3 September, where Cameron learned that the direct route to Lake Sankorra was closed; Tippu offered to find guides to take him into Urua, where, it was rumoured, there were Portuguese traders, and whence he could strike up to the lake. The journey was to prove hazardous. The guides, Mona Kasanga and M'Nchkulla, both headmen, and Kongwe, were not very satisfactory and on at least one occasion Cameron insisted on going in what he thought was the right direction; his men were reluctant to follow, and Bombay said they would run away. 'Where will they run, you old fool?' demanded Cameron, and went on.

In a village called Kamwawi he found his pet goat Dinah was missing, and when he made enquiries, arrows were shot at him. Cameron hurriedly assembled his armed followers with their stores and prepared to stand firm. His display of resolution led to negotiations with the village chief; and terms, including blood-brotherhood with Bombay or Bilal, had been agreed when the arrival of reinforcements led to a fresh attack. Cameron threatened to open fire if further hindered, and he was allowed to leave the village, but only in an eastward direction. The next village too proved hostile; Cameron attacked, and though supported only by Jumah, Sambo and a handful of men, drove the villagers back. Bombay and four or five others guarded the stores; the rest fled, but in time rejoined him. Cameron now built a stockade, named Fort Dinah, and held off attacks for two days, though half a dozen of his men were wounded. Eventually peace was made with the chief of the district and it was found that the hostility had been due to a mistaken identification with Portuguese slavers who had recently been active in the area.

The two guides, unsatisfactory in negotiations and anxious only to travel to the places they themselves wished to reach, left the expedition; Kongwe was too much afraid of his more powerful colleagues to help. However, another guide named Ngooni, engaged at Munza in October, led Cameron and his men to the camp of a friendly Arab trader, Juma Merikani, at Kilemba. Here it was agreed that Cameron would travel on with Alvez, an African trader. While waiting to start

Cameron set off on two short trips to visit lakes Mohrya and Kassali, with the aid of Bombay, who proved loyal and helpful.

During this delay he reduced the pay of at least four of his most troublesome men from $8\frac{1}{2}$ dollars to 5 dollars a month. At last, late in February 1875, Alvez left, but after only a short journey halted for nearly four months. Some of Cameron's men deserted, but Juma Merikani would not accept them and sent them back. During this waiting period a fire broke out among the huts. Bombay was busy looking after his own property, but Juma bin Nasibu, leaving his own goods to be burnt, 'followed like a brick' and saved Cameron's journals, books and instruments. Alvez demanded compensation for alleged losses to his own property, but Juma Merikani sent a replacement tent to Cameron, who also obtained grass cloth to replace the clothing the men had lost.[4]

It was 10 June before the march was at last resumed with Alvez. The pace was painfully slow, and Cameron tried to press on with his own men, but only Bombay and a handful followed him and he had to return. Food was very scarce.

An extraordinary episode in September indicated some odd ideas on justice; some of Alvez's men bribed Hamees Ferhan, Cameron's gun-bearer, to steal cloth. When the vigilance of Juma prevented this, they claimed the value of the bribe and of the cloth Hamees failed to steal because he had not kept his bargain—otherwise he would be sold into slavery. As Cameron thought that Hamees, though 'a most shameless thief, was otherwise worth half-a-dozen of the ruck of the caravan', and possessed of 'a wonderful aptitude for making himself understood by all the different peoples we have passed', he paid up, but commented 'to have claims made upon me because a man has failed to rob me quite puts a topper on all my ideas of legal justice'. Cameron also had to pay compensation when an old chief was offended by Sambo's chaffing.[5]

In October they crossed the Kwanza, where some of his men saved two slaves from drowning. Alvez's village was reached that month, and Cameron then purchased cloth to clothe his men, by now virtually without garments other than the Urua grass cloth. On the 10th he set off with Manoel as guide, and some porters of Alvez, Lunda men. The wet and cold took its toll and by mid November illness and fatigue had gripped the expedition. There was one death, and lack of cooperation from the local people.

One hundred and twenty-five miles from the coast the state of the expedition was serious—'a regular broken down lot of pagazi' wrote Cameron.[6] He therefore decided on a forced march with a small party to the coast to obtain assistance. His volunteers were his servant Juma, Sambo the cook, Hamees Ferhan his gun-bearer, Marijani, also known as Antonio, whom he had promoted from *pagazi* to *askari* for his hard work, loyalty and good influence and who could interpret, and Ali ibn Mshangama. With them were Manoel, two of his men, and some Lunda.

They pressed on and after five and a half days, early in November, a welcome glimpse of the sea told Cameron, sick and exhausted, that he had become the first European to cross Africa from east to west. A messenger was sent ahead to Katombela and food was brought out from the town. They then went on, and Cameron soon noted in his diary 'Jumah & Sambo are keeping themselves sober & behaving like men the rest are all drunk.'[7] When the remainder of the men arrived on the 11th they too celebrated the end of the hazardous and exhausting journey by heavy drinking. Cameron had assigned his men the task of making more uniform clothes at Lungi and on 21 November they entered Loanda with colours flying.

Cameron prepared to return to England, accompanied by Jacko as a servant, but for the remainder, he bought a schooner—which he renamed the *Frances Cameron* after his mother—for £1,000 and under Captain Carl Alexanderson they sailed for Zanzibar on 8 February 1876.[8] Like Livingstone, a meticulous recorder of punishment for bad behaviour, he sent the pay list to Zanzibar, where Kirk saw to the remuneration of the men, subject to deductions for advances of goods and for fines for various offences.[9]

Cameron noted of one conversation with Bombay, 'He says Speke's and Stanley's men were better than mine. I hope so for the sake of black humanity,' and he recorded a long tally of faults against most of those who reached the western shores with him, even though they were presumably the best of his followers. Bombay was obviously a disappointment, but Cameron shrewdly compared him to 'the old Scottish servant who, when his master said they must part, replied, "Na, na; I'm no gangin'. If ye dinna ken whan ye've a gude servant, I ken whan I've a gude place." ' He had the virtue of enduring, and this encouraged others to do so. Of the fifty-four men (and perhaps some women also) who reached the west coast, forty-nine (including twenty-three of the thirty-five *askari*) had come all the way; the many desertions were therefore primarily of those engaged en route, and Bombay's hard core, however he recruited them, stuck it out.[10]

Of the other men, Sambo Musa the cook had defects and merits. His skill was limited; he wasted honey, let meat go bad, mixed dough with castor oil, failed to render elephant palatable and made coffee too strong, but he was brave and loyal. Juma bin Nasibu, too, was courageous and as a capable massager ('shampooer') was able to ease Cameron's aching limbs as the journey neared its end. Ferrajji, Speke's 'faithful', acquired a nickname, Mhogo Chungo (two Swahili words meaning green-stemmed, or bitter, Cassava) by which he was afterwards known. Cameron recorded nothing of his activities, but he was one of the few whose pay records bear no deduction; he reached the west coast, returned to Zanzibar, and had many years of travel yet to come.

10

THE JOURNEY OF LAKES AND RIVERS

After the burial of Livingstone, Stanley's thoughts turned to the unsolved problems left by his death, particularly the detailed configuration of Lake Victoria, the outlet of Lake Tanganyika, and the nature of the river system of the western portion of central Africa, which might or might not be established by Cameron's expedition still in the heart of the continent. He persuaded the *Daily Telegraph* and the *New York Herald* to join in financing an expedition under his leadership, and left England on 15 August 1874. His equipment included a Yarmouth yawl called the *Wave*, a gig, and a forty-foot cedarwood barge, intended for exploring the great lakes, which had been made by James Messenger of Teddington in five sections for transport overland. This was named the *Lady Alice* after Miss Alice Pike of New York, whom Stanley hoped to marry. As boatmen he took two brothers, Frank and Edward Pocock from Lower Upnor, Kent; a third young Englishman who accompanied him was Frederick Barker, a clerk.[1]

Stanley arrived at Zanzibar on 21 September 1874 in circumstances vastly different from those of his first visit. Not only was he a traveller of assured reputation, but he had a pool of African labour on which he could draw. He stayed with Augustus Sparhawk, the US Consul, and the morning after his arrival veterans of his own and Livingstone's expeditions visited him there. The first meeting was taken up with the distribution of gifts, but later there was a *shauri* or conference with the leading Wanguana at which Stanley explained his ideas and reassured those who were apprehensive of the extent of the proposed journey. Even allowing for a degree of journalistic exaggeration in his account, it is clear that Stanley enjoyed these discussions. With Europeans he was often conscious of his own humble origin and could be aggressively self-assertive; among Africans, though at times a tough, even harsh, leader, he was more relaxed. On this occasion the Wanguana had confidence in him from their previous experience, and agreed to re-

114

enlist. He asked them to find another '300 good men like yourselves'.

Recruiting was interrupted by Stanley's expedition to explore the Rufiji River, in the *Wave*, between 30 September and 15 October. On his return he was visited on 20 October by Chuma and Susi, just home from England. Whether there was any question of his employing them is not known, but it is possible that they had already agreed to enter the service of the Universities Mission.[2]

The post of Chief Captain was assigned to the experienced Manua Sera. 'The courtly, valiant, faithful Chowpereh—the man of manifold virtues, the indomitable and sturdy Chowpereh', whose wife had been redeemed from slavery by Stanley, and whose two-year-old son he now vaccinated, was enrolled. Other chiefs were Hassan Wadi Safeni, Mabruki Speke, Farjallah Christie, Amoda, who had accompanied the Rufiji journey, Gardner, Ulimengo and Sarmean, now better known by his nickname of Kacheche or 'The Weasel'. In all he had twenty-one, drawn from those who had served with him before.

He found that rates had gone up—instead of $2\frac{1}{2}$ dollars a month he had to pay 5, or in some cases 7 or 8. He blamed this inflation on Cameron's over-generous pay. When engaging his men he undertook to care for them in sickness and in health, and to administer justice with impartiality and patience. By now he had acquired enough practical experience to plan a careful distribution of loads. The heaviest, 60 pounds of cloth, were allotted to the most muscular men; the shorter carriers were assigned 50-pound sacks of beads; the youths the 40-pound boxes of stores, ammunition and sundries. Older men were chosen for the instruments, books and photographic equipment, and the chronometers were the special responsibility of one selected for his steadiness and cautious tread. The boat sections were found to be far too heavy, but a young shipwright at Zanzibar, Bob Ferris, cut down the length and divided each section into two. The boat-bearers were men picked for their strength and reliability, two pairs to each section so that they could take turns. They were paid more than any of the chiefs except Manua Sera, had double rations, and shared with the chiefs the privilege of bringing their wives.

Stanley crossed to Bagamoyo on 12 November. Here problems began, when the 'boisterous intemperate fools' of the expedition, influenced by drink and drugs, ran riot in the town on a pre-expedition spree. Stanley arrested some of the offenders, others were punished by the Governor, and the expedition left on the 17th. Even so, the Governor had to send a body of Baluchi soldiers to demand the return of fifteen local women who had attached themselves to the expedition.

The party that left Bagamoyo was over 350 strong, Wanguana, Nyamwezi, and coast men recruited in Zanzibar and augmented on the mainland. First came 4 chiefs, then 12 guides, dressed in red, led by Hamadi their chief, holding his ivory horn, used to warn of danger or the approach to a camp site, and preceded by a drummer boy. The main body of 270 porters followed, among them 3 pupils of the UMCA—Robert Feruzi who had accompanied one of Cameron's companions to Unyanyembe as a servant, Dallington Maftaa and Andrew. Here too were the boats, an inflatable pontoon (which was never used) and the *Lady Alice* with its stalwart bearers. Thirty-six women and 10 children followed, and the rear was brought up by Stanley and his 3 English colleagues with their gun-bearers, Mabruki, Majwara, Billali and Kalulu, and 16 more chiefs. The company, straggling out over nearly half a mile, included many who had previously been with Stanley, 34 of them also with Livingstone.

The early stages which Stanley took at an easy pace brought out the good and bad qualities of the caravans—illness due to lack of condition, or the effects of *bhang* smoking (notably among the men from Zanzibar) began to take effect. Stanley vaccinated all who had not had smallpox. Sick men were discharged and some replacements recruited as the journey to the interior continued. In spite of the zeal of Kacheche, the 'chief detective', some fifty men succeeded in deserting during the twenty-five days' journey to Mpwapwa. By Christmas the heavy rain, and shortage of food, had adversely affected morale; an attempted mass desertion of fifty men was discovered and the leaders were chained and flogged.

In January 1876, inadequately directed by unreliable guides, the expedition entered the dense bush of Uveriveri. Simba, in spite of 'having a reputation among his fellows for fidelity, courage, and knowledge of travel' was lost with four comrades; and six others died in camp at Suna. The Rimi people were incensed by the theft of food by some of the Wanguana: though Stanley had the chief offender flogged, the hostility was such that he pressed on, with the worst cases of sickness carried in hammocks, among them Edward Pocock, who died of typhus on 17 January. He had been the bugler, rousing the expedition each morning, and a popular man among the Africans—who called him 'Bana Mabruki'.

On the evening of 21 January the expedition camped at Vinyata. Here they waited a day while Manua Sera, Kacheche and three others were sent back to search for Kaif Halleck, Livingstone's letter-carrier who, handicapped by asthma, had been lagging behind. They returned the next evening to report that his body, with over thirty wounds in it, had been found on the edge of a wood between Izanjeh and Vinyata. However, the local 'magic doctor' had paid an apparently friendly visit and Stanley, bearing Livingstone's example in mind, hoped for peace. The following day, a dispute arising from the theft of some milk by one of the Wanguana was settled by a gift of cloth, but soon after

Soudi, a Zanzibari youth, ran into camp with several wounds and reported that his brother Suliman had been killed. After this sporadic hostility had developed into a direct attack, which was repulsed, the expedition built a stockade and cleared the adjoining ground. The situation was serious. Since leaving the coast twenty men had died and eighty-nine deserted, and sickness had left its mark. Stanley could reckon on only seventy effective fighting men, the rest being 'invalids, frightened porters, women, donkey boys and children'.

The possibility of being starved out, however, made him resolve on positive action, so he divided his force into seven detachments of ten, each led by a chief with a messenger for contact; four were to attack, two were reserves, and the seventh was to guard the camp. On the morning of the 24th the camp was again assaulted, but this time he sent out his four attacking parties east and north. Farjallah Christie, leading the first detachment, blundered into swampy country too far left and the whole party was killed save for the messenger. The second group under Ferahan was attacked by the victors of this encounter, but put up a stout resistance and, though Ferahan was wounded by a spear, he and his comrades joined a young boatman, Murabo, who was gallantly defending a small *boma*. A reserve party under Manua Sera came to the rescue of this section.

The third detachment under Chakanja went in the wrong direction and lost six men: the survivors joined with the fourth, which drove the enemy out of their main village and fired it. Their leader, Safeni 'whose services were most efficient and signal' behaved 'prudently and well'. This was the first occasion on which Stanley noted the qualities of this man who was to become one of the most valuable members of the expedition. Hassan wadi Safeni, who had travelled in Manyema with the Arab Muhammad Bogharib (see p. 90), had been engaged by Livingstone at Unyanyembe and was one of those who had carried him in the last miles of his journey.

At the end of the day the casualty list was twenty-one soldiers and one messenger killed and three wounded. Farjallah Christie, Chakanja and Ulimengo—'the incorrigible joker and hunter in chief of the Search and Livingstone's expeditions' and indeed a veteran of Speke and Grant's journey—were among those killed.

The following day Manua Sera led a party of forty to burn the surrounding villages and seize food. In the following weeks several batches of porters were recruited, but desertions were still a problem, and after three had been recaptured, one, who had taken a box of ammunition, was punished by vote of the expedition, a majority of eighty to fifty-one favouring chaining and flogging to execution. Though food supplies improved, deaths from disease continued, and two days' journey beyond Mombiti, Gardner Livingstone, as he was now called, died of

E

typhoid after eleven days' illness. He gave his estate of 370 dollars to be divided, half to Chuma and half to his fellow Wanguana for a mourning feast. He was buried under a cairn of stones and the camp named after him.

The next stage was through pleasant country and on 27 February Frank Pocock sighted Lake Victoria. Singing an extemporised song, the expedition descended to the lakeside town of Kageyi, where they were welcomed by Kaduma, the local ruler, and Sungoro Tarib, an Arab resident. Here they took stock; they had travelled 720 miles and now numbered 166 having lost 181 members since leaving the coast, and the Sukuma auxiliaries were paid off.

They had now reached the first objective of the expedition and early in March the Lady Alice was floating on the Speke Gulf. A call for volunteers to man her was fruitless. Wadi Safeni picked some men but they were inexperienced, so Stanley himself, with the aid of Kacheche, who sought out those with some knowledge of boating, selected a crew of ten men and a steersman. It included a combination of seasoned travellers—Zaidi Mganda, Wadi Safeni (who acted successively as steersmen), Kirango and Amoda, who had been in Livingstone's crew in the Lady Nyassa (but who did not apparently distinguish himself in the Lady Alice), and younger men from Bagamoyo—Wadi Baraka, Murabo and Marzouk among them. Robert Feruzi, who as a mission pupil had some linguistic ability, was also taken. A fisherman named Saramba, 'with a head of hair resembling a thick mop', who had acted as a boatman for Sungoro on some of his trading expeditions, was taken as guide.

The Lady Alice sailed up the east coast of Lake Victoria and at the end of March reached the outlet of the Nile at the Ripon Falls, and thus established the validity of Speke's claim that this was the same lake.

Stanley had sent a message of goodwill to Mutesa, who still ruled Buganda, and on 2 April his envoy, Magassa, brought a welcoming reply. They were able to talk in Swahili, and Stanley and his party travelled to Usavara where Mutesa was awaiting them. Stanley was escorted by his boatmen, armed with Sniders. Prepared by Speke's account for a blood-thirsty savage, he was greatly impressed by Mutesa's appearance and manner, and the general atmosphere of culture in his court. Mutesa had become a Muslim, but Stanley envisaged the influence such a man could exert and endeavoured to preach the Christian Gospel to him. Robert Feruzi spoke the words of the ten commandments in Swahili to Idi, the Kabaka's writer, who wrote them down in Ganda.

Stanley left Buganda on 17 April; Mutesa promised him thirty canoes for the main expedition to join them, but these were not forthcoming, and as he was growing anxious about the fate of those left behind, he began the return journey in the *Lady Alice* down the west coast of the lake. On 28 April, when in need of food, they approached Bumbireh Island where Wadi Safeni and Wadi Baraka endeavoured by words and gestures to indicate that they were friends and hungry. As they drew into the shore, however, a shouting mob of villagers seized the boat, dragged it about twenty yards on shore and surrounded it. The crew kept calm, which 'acted as a sedative on the turbulence and ranting violence of the savages', and after a while a message from the ruler arrived demanding payment before the boat could leave. Wadi Safeni, 'a born diplomatist', acted as Stanley's spokesman. 'His hands moved up and down, outward and inward; a cordial frankness sat naturally on his face; his gestures were graceful; the man was an orator, pleading for mercy and justice.' Wadi Baraka also exhibited courage and composure. Hopes of a peaceful solution dwindled when the oars were seized and the local warriors threatened attack. Wadi Safeni was again employed to play for time while Stanley organised the rest of the crew to push the boat back to the lake. As it began to move, Wadi Safeni was called and raced after it to the water's edge, while Stanley covered the embarkation with his gun. Both scrambled into the *Lady Alice* and, using the bottom boards as paddles, the crew drew away from the shore while Stanley dispersed the pursuers with his elephant rifle. 'The crew was composed of picked men, and in this dire emergency they did ample justice to my choice,' he wrote. They were later able to land on an uninhabited island where they found fruit and berries and Stanley shot a brace of duck: farther down the lake, Saramba was able to obtain food for the party, but the crew of the *Lady Alice* were in an exhausted and emaciated state when they reached Kageyi again on 6 May.

To them the main expedition looked in robust health, but the previous two months had not passed without loss. Frank Pocock and Frederick Barker had been left in command of 166 men. Manua Sera, who had carried out several responsible tasks in the earlier stages, was in effective command—Pocock called him 'such a nice man; he is like a father', able to speak all the 'lingos' encountered. When Manua Sera discovered that three local chiefs were planning an attack on the camp arms were distributed, spies sent out, and the danger passed. Pocock had suffered from fever in April but had recovered, and towards the end of the month Frederick Barker had an attack of fever and died suddenly. Six members of the expedition had died of dysentery—among them Mabruki Speke—'one of the most trusted men of my present following'. 'Could an epitaph be written over his grave: Here lies the most faithful and true servant,' wrote Stanley in his diary.[3]

Rumours that disaster had overtaken Stanley had led to an incipient mutiny under a noted troublemaker, Msenna, but Stanley's return stabilised the situation. As the promised canoes from Buganda did not arrive, Stanley negotiated with Lukongeh, King of Ukerewe, for the loan of twenty-seven canoes to take his expedition to Buganda. Lukanjah and Mikondo, kinsmen of Lukongeh, would at the same time undertake an embassy to Mutesa. The Kerewe canoe men, however refused to go and when the first part of the expedition, some 150 men, women and children, with the main supplies, left Kageyi on 19 June, the crews were Stanley's porters, most of whom were inexperienced. On the evening of the 21st the flotilla was making for Komeh Island after dark when one of the canoes sank, followed by four others, with some supplies and rifles, but no loss of life. This was due in no small measure to the energetic and skilful efforts of two coxswains of canoes who were working with crews whose capabilities they knew. These were Uledi, a man of about twenty-five, and his younger brother Shumari, who in spite of the wild confusion caused by the capsized canoes, manoeuvred their way successfully in the dark and picked up many of those clinging to upturned boats.

Stanley eventually established a base in what he termed Refuge Island where he left Pocock, Manua Sera, Lukanjah and Mikondo with forty-four men in a stockaded camp while he returned to Kageyi with the rest of his men in seventeen canoes to collect the remainder of the expedition. The crew of one canoe deserted and went to Unyanyembe but all the rest eventually arrived safely. On 6 July they left Kageyi and returned to Refuge Island where Lukanjah, Mikondo and Manua Sera had preserved good relations with the neighbouring mainland chiefs.

After a farewell feast on Refuge Island, the advance party moved on to Mahyiga Island where Stanley remained with a garrison of forty-five men under Wadi Safeni and four local guides, while Manua Sera took back sixteen canoes to fetch the remainder. At last an escort of Ganda arrived but since they too had been attacked at Bumbireh Island, Stanley organised a joint punitive expedition against it. His force comprised 250 Ganda spearmen and 50 of his own men with guns, and the island was raked with fire from the canoes.

On 5 August the *Lady Alice* and a flotilla of thirty-seven canoes sailed from Mahyiga Island with 685 on board, and in due course reached Dumo, Buganda, where a camp was established and placed under Pocock and Manua Sera. On 15 August Stanley visited Mutesa in the hope of obtaining guides to Lake Albert. Majwara, now Pocock's servant, went with Stanley, and while in Buganda he was given a wife, Tuma-leo, by Mutesa.[4]

Stanley was cordially received and promised an escort to the lake;

in return he resumed his efforts to convert Mutesa. Accompanying him was a pupil of the UMCA, Dallington Scopion Maftaa, 'probably only fifteen, with a face strongly pitted with traces of a violent attack of small-pox'. He was one of fourteen youths released from slavery by HMS *Daphne* and handed over to the UMCA in November 1868, and his name may be a corruption of that of the missionary, the Rev. C. Alington. Bishop Steere recalled him as 'an old scholar of ours whom we never thought likely to do us much honour', but Stanley considered him 'as bright and intelligent as any boy of his age, white or black'. He translated extracts from Pocock's Bible into Swahili, and Mutesa's writer Idi made a fair copy on paper provided by Stanley. 'When completed, Mtesa possessed an abridged Protestant Bible in Kiswahili, embracing all the principal events from the Creation to the Crucifixion of Christ. St. Luke's Gospel was translated entire, as giving a more complete history of the Saviour's life.' On 12 October the Kabaka declared that he renounced Islam in favour of Christianity. Stanley agreed to allow Dallington to enter Mutesa's service to act as a Scripture Reader pending the arrival of missionaries. Meanwhile he sent for Fred Barker's prayer book, and as he left for Dumo on 13 November he had the satisfaction of seeing a church being built.[5]

Pocock had endured a difficult three months at Dumo. A young boatman without experience of travel, he had been placed in command of a substantial body of men in the middle of Africa with no guidance save very occasional letters from Stanley and the aid of the resourceful but unscrupulous Manua Sera, whose undoubted loyalty to the expedition did not prevent his pursuing his own interests. 'There is not one man in the caravan but will do anything for me . . . If a man steals I punish him accordingly,' wrote Pocock to his family, but the reality was not quite so simple. Occasional indiscipline was checked—he knocked down a man who struck him and Manua Sera beat the culprit; Msenna, a notorious bully and troublemaker, was disarmed by Manua Sera and theft was punished. Less easily controlled were some of the women. Muscati, wife of Wadi Safeni, not only refused to make flour, but set her hut alight by making a fire in it, and a few days later repeated the offence—'I put water on it, but she made fun of me' commented the perplexed Pocock. Bwana Muri had trouble with his wife, and eventually offered her for sale. On the other hand 'Joe Perry' (i.e. Chowpereh), who had returned from Buganda, was married on 12 November. Manua Sera was dilatory in preparing carrying poles for the boat and Pocock wrote, 'Today I shall stop telling and lay the blame on him if they are not cut when Master comes back.'[6]

The usual sickness and death plagued the camp but the most serious problem was that of food. Stanley had arranged with the

Ganda for a regular supply to be given free but in practice this was not always forthcoming or was charged at an exorbitant rate. Pocock also discovered that the representative who had been left to supply food had been taking a rake off and that Manua Sera had been aware of this but had kept quiet in return for receiving special items himself. When supplies were inadequate, the Wanguana went out foraging and asked Pocock for guns. He had, on Stanley's instructions, taken in the twenty-four muskets and fifteen Sniders and had issued firearms only to Manua Sera, Zaidi, Mabruki Manyapara, Mabruki Unyanyembe, Bwana Muri and Wadi Rehani. He refused guns to the others and was disconcerted to hear that Wadi Rehani and Manua Sera had lent their guns to Zaidi (the boatman) and Jumah Kirangozi respectively. Pocock could 'speak a little of the lingo' but when he tried to establish the truth of the matter 'Amice Amfalla told one tale, Manwa Sera another, I don't know who to believe'. Amice Amfalla and another man guilty of threatening the local inhabitants were later put in chains.

When Stanley returned he spent a few days reorganising the camp, and set off with the expedition on 27 November, hoping to meet Mutesa's promised escort under Sambuzi to take them to the Luta Ngigé which Stanley believed to be Lake Albert. By 16 December the promised escort had still not arrived and Manua Sera was sent in charge of a party to Mutesa to obtain news. He came back on the 18th to report that the escort was not yet ready, but Mutesa had assured him 'that he wanted a road to Albert Nyanza more than the white man because the white man only wanted to pass once but he wanted the road to make trade'. Stanley and Sambuzi met at last on the 23rd though it was a few more days before the escort numbers were complete.

Two days later Stanley sent Dallington to Mutesa. He had originally promised to send him back from the Albert Nyanza but, Pocock wrote, 'the Sultan was so impatient to hear the Christian religion that Mr. H. M. Stanley sent him from here, not only for the Sultan but for the good of the expedition.' 'I regret much indeed to part with the boy,' wrote Stanley, 'for he was a faithful, good and honest lad, a credit to the labours of the English Mission at Zanzibar.'

Dallington remained with Mutesa for more than five years. Though, particularly at first, he appears to have taken his missionary role seriously, writing to Bishop Steere in April 1876 for teaching materials, he became increasingly involved in Mutesa's diplomatic manoeuvres and acted as his English secretary (see p. 139). Some two dozen letters, written in his individual brand of English, have been identified—among them messages to Queen Victoria, General Gordon and Emin Pasha.[7]

Stanley had 180 men in the body of about 2,800, including women and children, that entered Unyoro in January 1876. On 11 January a lake was sighted; Stanley believed it to be the Albert Nyanza and he named the spot Beatrice Gulf, but it was, in fact, Lake George. The precipitous edges made it difficult to take the boats down; Manua Sera was despatched with the Ganda Lukoma to reconnoitre. The party 'went to the margin & drank the water' but Stanley himself did not reach the shore. His hopes of further exploration were foiled when Sambuzi, fearing conflict with the Nyoro, resolved to take the escorting party back to Buganda. Stanley held a *shauri* with his leaders and Kacheche, as their spokesman, said that the faithful ones would go on with him, but they doubted its practicability and more than half the expedition would go back with Sambuzi. Stanley accepted the inevitable, and returned with the escort—a hard march, which entailed one skirmish with the Nyoro. When they parted from Sambuzi, Stanley halted for three days' rest, sending Kacheche and two others to Mutesa to report the unsatisfactory conclusion of the expedition. He also sent Mutesa a Bible. Pocock wrote 'I consented to send mine with a wish that it would be the means of bringing him to the Christian faith & at the same time please him & do us good in the end. I hope it will bring him to the light of the world . . . The Bible was given to my brother on his leaving our native village by a friend of his.' Mutesa, indignant at Sambuzi's action, sent a letter written by Dallington offering fresh help, but Stanley did not risk further disappointments.

At 6 p.m. on 29 January Amoda, Livingstone's follower for many years, died. Pocock attributed his illness to grief at the loss of his slave Majariwa, who was drowned at Dumo on the same day as Amoda had gone with Stanley to Buganda. 'When his master received the news he took ill and never recovered.' The next day 'we carried his body about 5 miles in the wilderness & buried it'.

The expedition resumed its march and on 24 February reached the Arab trading centre of Kafurro where Stanley was welcomed by the Arabs and introduced to the benevolent Rumanika, King of Karagwe (see p. 31). Pocock put the boat together on Lake Ruanyara (Speke's Lake Windermere) 'the first white man ever afloat on this Nyanza'. A race between Stanley's crews and Rumanika's canoeists was held before he successfully circumnavigated the lake (8–12 March). When he left on 25 March Rumanika supplied three guides to Uhimba. The journey continued without undue incident save for another provocation from Msenna who tried to incite desertions. The count was now 175 men.

At Serombo, in mid April, news was received of the approach of Mirambo, now a very much more powerful leader than in 1871. Stanley arranged to meet him and was impressed by his quiet authority. Manua Sera presided over the ceremony of blood brotherhood between the two. Early in May Stanley learned that the Swiss trader Broyon was at Urambo and sent Robert with two others as a messenger. A day or two later Stanley met Maganga 'the dilatory Chief of one of my caravans during the first Expedition' (see p. 76) who helped ensure him a welcome from the local chief. Travelling conditions in April and May were difficult: wading through mud and water lowered morale and caused sickness, and there were several desertions—one chief, Zaidi Mganda, was ready to desert so he was degraded and his command given to Chowpereh.

At noon on 27 May the expedition reached Ujiji. Stanley circumnavigated Lake Tanganyika from 11 June to 31 July 1876 in the *Lady Alice* and a canoe, *Meofu*, lent him by Muini Kheri, governor of Ujiji, in replacement of one stolen. His picked crew was composed of Uledi the coxswain, with his brother Shumari and cousin Saywa; Murabo, Mpwapwa, Marzouk, Akida, Mambu, Wadi Baraka, Zaidi Rufiji and Matiko. Billali and Mabruki came as gun-bearers, and for guides he had Parla who had accompanied Cameron in 1874 and Ruango who had been with Stanley and Livingstone in 1871. Wadi Safeni, who had travelled in the area, was coxswain of the canoe, and pointed out parts of the route Livingstone had followed from the south end of the lake towards Lake Bangweolo in the last months of his life.

For the third time Pocock had to take command of the majority of the expedition and did well under difficult conditions. His chief assistants were Manua Sera and Kacheche. At times Pocock enjoyed watching the bustle of the market from the expedition *tembe* near the lakeside, but he, like Manua Sera, suffered from fever. The misery of the slaves appalled him—'the cruelty with which they are treated is enough to make one's flesh crawl in his bones to see & hear it . . . All the land is foul with monstrous wrong and desolation of the sons of Hell.' Smallpox swept through the camp and seven of the expedition as well as many Arabs died. In addition five men sent to Unyanyembe for letters did not return.

Stanley was anxious to move off after his journey round the lake but an attack of fever prevented him from going until 25 August. He then found that proximity to an Arab settlement, with its opportunities of alternative employment and its softer conditions, had had its customary effect in encouraging desertions; fear of the unknown country ahead and the ravages of smallpox had also contributed to lowering morale. Pocock, with Kacheche, Manua Sera, and Wadi Rehani recaptured some deserters, but the total strength was now only about one hundred and thirty, of whom barely forty were reliable.

In October Stanley reached the Lualaba which Livingstone had believed to be the Nile, and shortly after leaving it he encountered Tippu Tip, who had already met Livingstone and Cameron. Believing that a stronger force was necessary, Stanley, after hard bargaining, persuaded Tippu Tip to travel with him for the next three months. Giving up the idea of reaching Lake Albert, he decided to follow the Lualaba.

Tippu Tip was accompanied by about a dozen Arabs and four hundred men, women and children. The slow pace irritated Stanley and conditions of travel through damp jungle were appalling, especially for the boat-carriers with their heavy loads. On 19 November they again reached the Lualaba, but when Stanley decided to travel down it and asked the expedition to agree, thirty-eight, led by Uledi and Kacheche agreed and ninety-five did not. When Stanley tried to bargain for canoes with the local villagers his party was attacked, possibly because of the depredations of slave-raiders in the area. Attempts to obtain food locally met with fear at best and hostility at worst, and smallpox raged in the expedition.

On 4 December, at Ikondu, Stanley found a large abandoned canoe which Uledi and a few colleagues repaired sufficiently for it to be used as a floating hospital. At Vinya Njara a desperate fight took place but after Stanley had been joined by Tippu Tip, the local Chief sought peace and made blood brotherhood with Wadi Safeni.

At this stage Stanley ended his agreement with Tippu Tip and appealed to his own men to go on; Manua Sera and Uledi declared their loyalty. The end of the association with Tippu Tip was marked by a feast, at which sports were held, including a women's race in which Muscati, the wife of Wadi Safeni, gave an ungainly display and Khamisi won. At the end of December Stanley's flotilla, one hundred and forty-nine men, women and children in the *Lady Alice* and twenty-three canoes set off.

The first seven months of 1877 were occupied in travelling down the Congo—arduous, difficult and dangerous. The constant falls made it necessary to carry the boats overland or to shoot the rapids where possible, and the flotilla was gradually reduced by the loss of canoes. The varied tribes on the river banks were sometimes friendly but more often hostile. Communication with them was made difficult by the lack of interpreters: Katembo, one of the two cannibals engaged as guides through Tippu Tip, did useful work but could not always make himself understood. Sign language was sometimes effective. Stanley gathered what vocabulary he could and tried mixtures of languages at times. Occasionally local guides were employed, but they were seldom satisfactory. Thirty-four men died by drowning or were killed in some of the thirty-two fights which took place.

This period placed a great strain on the leaders of the Wanguana who had now been away from home over two years. In a depressed mood, Stanley wrote in December that he had thirty-two effective

125

men—one hundred and nine were 'mere dummies', and he noted examples of foolish behaviour. Pocock, however, wrote in May of 'stout hearted Wanguana, although some were cowards, but the greater part brave. When we have been surrounded by fifty or sixty canoes the[y] have acted with the coolness of old veterans.'

Stanley himself described as 'first class men' Manua Sera, Wadi Safeni, Wadi Rehani, Kacheche and Uledi. Manua Sera had commanded canoes, including at least two river battles, and had led flanking parties in land operations. While Stanley was constructing a new canoe at Nzabi in May, Manua Sera brought the rest of the canoes overland. Nevertheless, he had a surprisingly reckless streak in his canny nature. In November he rashly shot rapids, and not only was the canoe overturned, with the loss of four Sniders, but the survivors were attacked and saved only by the arrival of Uledi and his colleagues. Manua Sera resented Stanley's reprimand and threatened to join Tippu Tip, but did not do so; the following February he lost another Snider through carelessness.

Wadi Safeni was one of the steadiest and most reliable men, often helping in negotiations, and on more than one occasion he made blood brotherhood with a local chief. He was kind-hearted and his talents included some medical knowledge. Wadi Rehani, the storekeeper, had been a staunch leader in the fighting at Vinya Njara in December 1876 and was given independent command on occasion. Kacheche, the detective, was used for pursuing deserters and inflicting punishment. He was in charge of sentries when there was conflict with the Bakumu, and was sometimes sent with exploring parties or separated portions of the expedition. His resourceful persistence discovered a blacksmith and material suitable for caulking boats.

The truly heroic figure is Uledi, the coxswain, 'short, and of compact frame . . . his face was marred with traces of smallpox.' He showed courage in adversity, resourcefulness in descending the rapids, and skill, with his close colleagues and relations Shumari and Saywa, in building a canoe. On several occasions his perseverance and courage helped to avert loss of life on the Congo. The most spectacular was in January 1877 when the canoes were taken down a stretch of rapids near Ntunduru Island. One, with three men on board, was upset: two of the crew were rescued by Manua Sera and Uledi but the third, the chief Zaidi, was swept on and saved only because the fragments of the canoe were caught on a rock on the very edge of a sheer drop. Efforts to float out a canoe on a rattan cable or throw over poles tied on creepers were frustrated by the turbulent water and eventually Stanley prepared a canoe, linked to the shore by cables of rattans and tent ropes fore and aft. Uledi and Marzouk volunteered to attempt the rescue but again and again the current drove them aside. At last

Zaidi managed to hold a rope thrown from the canoe, but was at once swept over the falls and the strain broke the cables. His rescuers managed to bring the canoe to a rocky islet fifty yards from shore and haul Zaidi up. The situation was still desperate and, after establishing a precarious link by throwing a length of cord weighted by a stone, and making some vain attempts to utilise creepers, Stanley had to leave the three for the night as darkness fell. The next morning more rattans were gathered and with the cables made from them, all three men were hauled back to safety, through the turbulent water. Uledi was also active in other emergencies, and saved in all thirteen lives.

On 28 March the expedition was descending falls which were navigable only by canoes hugging the right shore: several had arrived safely when one with six men on board was seen shooting down in midstream at top speed to be overturned and lost in the falls. A second, containing two men, followed but they managed to steer for the left shore which they reached comparatively safely. Soudi, the survivor of wounds in January 1875, was in a third canoe which was let go by the carelessness of the rest of the crew and was also swept out of sight over the falls. Among the valued men lost in the first canoe was Kalulu. He does not appear to have played a significant part in the expedition, and indeed deserted at one stage, but Stanley continued to take an interest in him and only a few weeks before the fatal accident wrote to Alice Pike, 'You would wonder to see how tall he is grown, he has shot up like a palm tree.' He gave the name Kalulu Falls to the scene of his death. Pocock too was affected and wrote on 1 April, 'Last night I dreamed I saw Kululu in camp.'[8]

A few days after the disaster the two men from the second canoe appeared, together with Soudi, who had not merely saved his canoe but had survived a brief captivity by villagers. In spite of this good news, the morale of the expedition was deteriorating under the strain of the arduous journey and of widespread illness. Stealing from the local population damaged the already precarious good relations and Pocock recorded thefts from the stores of the expedition by some apparently reliable members—'In my opinion they are hand in hand with the whole of the chiefs.' A climax came on 27 May when Uledi the coxswain was found to have stolen beads. Stanley wrote an elaborate account of his discussion with the chiefs regarding Uledi's punishment, and their eloquent pleas as to his devoted service, which resulted in his pardon and continued valuable membership of the expedition.

Even Uledi's skill and courage, however, could not avert the tragedy of 3 June. Frank Pocock had been suffering from ulcerated feet and was unable to walk. Stanley, after an unsuccessful attempt to take the *Lady Alice* down the Massassa Falls, went overland, leaving instructions with Uledi to attempt the river route in a canoe. The latter took the

Jason, one of those built at Nzabi, and just before starting, Pocock asked to be taken in it. Manua Sera, in command of the canoes, and Uledi tried to discourage him but he insisted and, when the crew hesitated to attempt the falls, goaded them into risking the descent. The canoe was sucked out of control into a whirlpool and overturned. Frank Pocock came up unconscious, and Uledi's desperate attempts to rescue him were in vain. Two more of the crew of ten were also drowned. Frank Pocock, saddled with responsibilities and problems far beyond anything he could have contemplated, had matured into a resourceful and trustworthy man, popular with the Africans and relied on by Stanley, more perhaps than he had realised. The needless loss distressed him deeply, and he could hardly keep his hand steady, or write coherently, when he recorded the events in his diary. The dispiriting effect on the Wanguana was soon apparent. The expedition was split in three, with dangerous falls to navigate, and Stanley, at Zinga with a handful of men, was informed by Manua Sera that the rest at Mowa had mutinied. He was on the verge of another attack of fever and wrote in despair, 'They are faithless, lying, thievish, indolent knaves'. However, Manua Sera, the chiefs and boatmen were loyal, and the former brought up the rearguard; a day or two later Stanley wrote, 'my people anger me, oh so much, and yet I pity and love them.' On 20 June the crisis was reached when Stanley gave his men the choice between going on with him and leaving—thirty-one under Wadi Safeni decided to leave, but Manua Sera and Kacheche stood by Stanley and helped to persuade the thirty-one to change their minds —Wadi Safeni took the lead in doing so.

On the last stage down the river thefts by members of the expedition from local villagers grew so serious that Stanley eventually abandoned five men who had been seized by them for stealing, though all of these later escaped. A more serious loss occurred on 25 July when Wadi Safeni, perhaps the steadiest of Stanley's leaders, 'one of my favourites for his cleverness and cheerfulness', who had recently shown signs of mental disturbance and had been confined, broke loose, and, declaring that he was going to find the sea, dashed off into the jungle. Men were sent after him, but 'the sage Safeni' was lost.

On 31 July Stanley abandoned the *Lady Alice* above the Isangila cataract where she was eventually broken up for the sake of her copper nails. The next day he led his expedition—one hundred and fifteen men, women and children, forty of them ill—away from the river. On 4 August he sent four volunteers—Kacheche, Uledi, Muini Pembe and Robert Feruzi—accompanied by two guides, ahead to Boma with a letter asking for help. The guides absconded, but the four men pressed on and found their way to the town, whence the first two returned with a party bringing food supplied by two merchants. Refreshed and encouraged, the expedition resumed its journey, and Murabo the boat-boy extemporised a song retailing the exploits of the past 1,000 days, with its chorus:

> Then sing, O friends, sing; the journey is ended;
> Sing aloud, O friends, sing to this great sea.

Boma was reached on 9 August and after two days the expedition crossed the mouth of the Congo, thence to Loanda. Here Stanley declined the opportunity of going straight back to England, for some of his followers had died even after reaching the coast, and he decided to accompany the survivors to the Cape in HMS *Industry* in which they had been offered a passage.

The expedition was heartily welcomed at Cape Town and its members had their first experience of a steam-train and a theatre. Sir Bartle Frere, the Governor, was absent, but Lady Frere arranged functions for the Africans, and her daughters Lily and Catherine painted water-colours of some of them. Stanley decided to take his men all the way to Zanzibar, and they arrived there on 26 November. The last casualty, Wadi Safeni's widow Muscati, died just after landing, but the remainder—eighty-eight men, fourteen women, three children and three infants born on the journey, returned safely. Robert Feruzi had married in the interior; his wife, Hasina, gave birth to a daughter who was named Alice after the expedition's boat, but the infant died. Hasina, 'a pretty little gentle creature, with a skin just like brown satin', survived, and was later baptised in Zanzibar as Caroline, after her godmother, the missionary Miss Thackeray.[9]

Two days after arriving at Zanzibar Stanley received a letter from Kirk. On his return from finding Livingstone Stanley had made many outspoken criticisms of Kirk, but the Consul-General wrote in cordial terms, 'I feel assured that in asking you to give the medals personally into the hands of such of Dr. Livingstone's followers as remain among your men I am inviting you to do an act agreeable to yourself nor could they be committed into other hands or be distributed at a more appropriate time than this.' Stanley replied that this would give him pleasure, 'but I assure you that it would be a still greater pleasure to be a mere witness while you personally distributed them.' Stanley went on to urge the claims of the men concerned to extra pay on the basis that Livingstone had promised them a higher rate than they eventually received—'I should be pleased to receive a word from you in relation to these poor yet worthy men's claims' he concluded. Kirk was unable to give an immediate decision, as Prideaux's pay lists had been sent to London, but he invited Stanley to provide further details and also took a statement from Manua Sera on behalf of the claimants.[10]

At 9 a.m. on 3 December Stanley presented the medals to the fourteen survivors from the thirty-four entitled to them who had set off with him three years before. The settlement of pay took five days—not only was there the distribution of wages, but the money due to those who had died was handed to their widows or family, if adequately identified. Stanley noted with pleasure how his followers had recovered their health after the privations of the journey. 'They had never boasted that they were heroes, but they exhibited truly heroic stuff while coping with the varied terrors of the hitherto untrodden and apparently endless wilds of broad Africa,' he wrote. When he left on 13 December a deputation—Uledi, Kacheche, Robert, Zaidi and Wadi Rehani—called to assure him they would wait at Zanzibar until they knew that he was safely home. The last words of his story of the expedition, *Through the Dark Continent*, were of its success, 'aided by their willing hands and by their loyal hearts'.

Kirk was left to clear up the claims to extra pay for the Livingstone veterans. Its basis, as put forward by Manua Sera, was that he and his colleagues had represented to Livingstone that $2\frac{1}{2}$ dollars a month was the rate for going to Unyanyembe, 'a place on the known trade road', but that they should have an increase to 5 dollars—the amount that those already with Livingstone were receiving—for venturing beyond it. He had not at first agreed, but at Zombe, in Fipa, had done so. However, Prideaux had paid them only at the $2\frac{1}{2}$-dollar rate, save for Majwara who, on account of a memorandum left by Livingstone, had been given back pay at the rate of 5 dollars.

Kirk wrote home asking for guidance: on the prompting of the Foreign Office the Treasury agreed to meet the claim if Kirk was satisfied, and Prideaux's pay-list was sent out on February 1878. When Kirk looked into the details it emerged that Majwara had been given only the standard $2\frac{1}{2}$ dollars, but Manua Sera and Chowpereh, the 'heads of departments', had received 5 dollars plus an extra 20 dollars per annum as authorised by Livingstone, 'all which facts he carefully withheld from Mr. Stanley and myself'. 'Yet,' added Kirk, 'as I think the bargain was an unfair one from the beginning and the men did their work beyond all that the contract implied and in doing so saved much anxiety on account of the fate of Dr. Livingstone whose death might otherwise not have been satisfactorily ascertained & secured the great traveller's journals which are of much value, I think Your Lordship will consider that I am truly carrying out your orders in paying these men a small gratuity . . .' He therefore paid all those on the $2\frac{1}{2}$-dollar rate a gratuity of 25 dollars each 'for which they have shown themselves most thankful'. This was given to eleven who had been with Stanley and seven who had remained at Zanzibar.

In addition to attempting to obtain more pay for some of his followers, Stanley showed his gratitude to all who survived by sending seventy-eight rings, to be distributed by August Sparhawk, the American Consul in Zanzibar, who had been very helpful to Stanley and had engaged Majwara, Billali and Mabruki as servants. Some, intended for the leading men, were larger than the rest, and Sparhawk, who received the consignment on 30 May 1878, invited Manua Sera, Kacheche and Uledi to be umpires and advise on their allocation. A number of veterans gathered in Sparhawk's office. Sparhawk wrote to Stanley:

I then passed round one ring of each, and as I saw most everyone hefting the rings, I gave them a lecture, telling them that it was not the intrinsic value of the rings in Rupees and Pice that they must think of but that they were 'Alama za Bwana' [Tokens of the Master]. That there were expeditions now constantly being made up at the french house and at the Agents of the Missionary societies and that any one calling himself one of Bwana Stanley's men, on showing one of these would be engaged immediately, and on probably better wages than others were receiving. Then commenced the distribution. The Umpires giving me the name of each and their work on the road, and whether to give a 1st or 2nd ring, and I distributed 44 rings that day, and up to date have given out 67 rings, leaving me now on hand 11 Large. When I got to Choperry I did not hesitate, but immediately passed him a large ring, you can't fail to remember bluff old Choperry. When he got his he put it on one of his large brawny fingers down as far as the second joint, and then stood looking at it, till I had written down his name, when he said 'Bwana, what shall I do with this'. I explained to him again what it was for, and how it might help him if he wanted to go to 'Bara' [the mainland] again. He said 'Yes, truly, but I don't want to go to Bara again, and if I do, and no one will take me, I will stay at home. With the money I got from Bwana, I bought a house, and a little land, on which I grow mahago etc. and when I am not at work on that I work and dig for others for pessers [money] and what sort of a thing is that for me to wear in such kind of work? I shall rather have the money for it.' Well, I said you can keep it in your house. He answered 'A no, that wouldn't do, my wife or I might lose it, and it's got a big name on it, No, I would rather sell it, and if you won't give me something for it, I will sell it to someone else.' So after more talk I bought it of him giving him two Rupees for it. It weighed $1\frac{1}{4}$ Rupee. Then I told them all that if there were any others who wished to sell their rings at any time to bring them to me for it would be very bad for them to sell your rings in Town. Since then I have had three small rings brought to me which I have purchased and I know that several europeans have purchased one also.

Some men, however, kept their rings. H. H. Johnston's headman Ali Kiongwe had one in 1884.[11]

Sparhawk also wrote to Stanley about Kirk's activities. J. P. Farler of the UMCA had criticised Stanley's conduct on the basis of Robert Feruzi's account of the trans-African journey, and the Secretary of State, Lord Derby, instructed Kirk to investigate. Sparhawk learned that various Stanley veterans were being interrogated, and asked the men concerned for details. In his view, the version of events these men gave was the same as Stanley had told him, but he was uneasy about Manua Sera—'I can't help thinking that the latter is a big rascal and too fond of money' and noticed that after their conversation, Manua Sera had continued to call on Kirk, though by the back streets, and had afterwards been evasive about having done so. When Kirk made the final distribution of pay to Livingstone's followers, he gave none to Manua Sera or Chowpereh, and the former, omitting to mention that they had received their share years before, explained to Sparhawk that this was because he and Chowpereh wouldn't tell lies about Stanley 'to please Kirk'. Kirk in fact drew up a strong indictment of Stanley's conduct on the basis of the accounts he was given.[12]

In November 1879 four men reached Zanzibar from the interior. They were Khamseen and three others, the survivors of the five sent to Unyanyembe from Ujiji in June 1876 who, delayed by fighting and other causes, had failed to overtake Stanley's expedition. It is not known whether their claim to be paid for the whole of this period was ever met, but Khamseen received his Livingstone Medal from Kirk on 4 November, probably the last man to do so.[13]

11

VETERANS OF EXPLORATION IN MISSION SERVICE

The 1870s saw not only several notable journeys of exploration, but also a great development of Christian missions, whose members travelled widely in the course of their work. Experienced Africans were much sought after, and a number of veterans rendered good service. The records of such activities are the main sources of the rather scanty information on their lives when not on major journeys.

In 1870 Johann Rebmann still maintained the Church Missionary Society station at Kisulidini, faithfully assisted by Abbe Gunja (see p. 7), who lived until 1881. The Roman Catholic Holy Ghost Fathers had established themselves in Bagamoyo, and the UMCA had developed their base at Zanzibar. On St Bartholomew's Day, 25 September 1864, they received their first charges, five slave children released to them by the Sultan, one of whom, Robert Feruzi, became a noted caravan leader both for explorers and for the Mission itself. Other boys were trained at the school at Kiungani and the Mission's work and responsibilities grew.[1]

A fourth Mission, that of the United Methodist Free Church, had been set up under the guidance of J. L. Krapf, though ill-health had limited his stay to a few months in 1862; since then, two dedicated men, the Rev. Thomas Wakefield and, from 1863, the Rev. Charles New, had worked at Ribe, fifteen miles from Mombasa, and had also travelled in the Galla country.[2]

Two events gave a new impetus to missionary endeavour. Early in 1873 a mission led by Sir Bartle Frere arrived in Zanzibar to persuade Sultan Barghash, who had succeeded his brother Majid in 1870, to impose further restrictions on the slave trade (see p. 105). Eventually he signed a treaty which closed the Zanzibar slave market and prohibited the export of slaves from the mainland. Almost at the same

133

time, Livingstone died in the heart of Africa, and when the news of his death reached England early in 1874, a new enthusiasm for evangelising the continent stimulated a series of missions.

Bishop Tozer resigned from the leadership of the UMCA owing to ill-health in 1872; after some hesitation Edward Steere, who had always been the strong man of the Mission, accepted the post and returned to Zanzibar in March 1875 after his consecration as Bishop. At the Mission festival on 24 August Chuma and Susi were guests of honour. After the festival the Bishop, with three colleagues, crossed to Lindi, to start an expedition to assess missionary possibilities in the Nyasa country. With them went Chuma, Susi and twenty Zanzibari porters, but owing to illness and other causes only the Bishop, Chuma and their carriers set off on 1 November. 'I had about forty men as porters, under the command of James Chuma as captain of the expedition, and two coast men, said to have great experience, as guides', wrote the Bishop. 'These last turned out to be merely expensive ornaments, but Chuma was throughout the soul of the expedition and success without him would have been all but impossible.' The route lay through the Mwera forest, across the Rovuma, which was forded, and through country which was in a disturbed state as a result of intertribal conflicts. Chuma made a 'lie down' (u-lalo) or primitive bridge across the flooded Lukwisi River by cutting down a tree which fell across the river and held in place by the branches gripping the bottom. At the ford of the Luatize, which Chuma remembered crossing with Livingstone in 1866, they met a slave caravan.

Mataka's was reached early in December. The chief 'understood my Swahili, but would not talk it, preferring to use Chuma, himself a Yao, as an interpreter'. After their first meeting, Mataka sent him a present of food and pombe, the native beer. 'I like it in moderation, and Chuma made me with it and some flour I had brought capital little loaves which were very acceptable as a relief from the endless rice and fowls, which are the staple food, and the weariness, of every European in tropical Africa.' Mataka was willing to allow a mission to settle in his country; the Bishop left after two weeks' stay and reached Lindi on 21 January. They had covered about 350 miles.[3]

Chuma accompanied another party in June 1876 to Magila, a mission station in Usambara. There were sixteen porters. 'We always said evening prayers—the Bishop, I, Chumah, and two of our Kiungani boys whom we have brought up here—and the hymn we sang was commented on by the villagers afterwards, who compared our singing with that of the Arabs, giving ours the preference,' wrote Chauncy Maples, one of the missionaries. They remained there about a fortnight.[4]

The following October Steere attempted to take up the work in the

Nyasa area. He left Zanzibar on the 16th with the Rev. W. P. Johnson, James Beardall, four Kiungani scholars, fifty-five freed slaves whom he hoped to settle on the mainland, and seventy porters under Chuma. He also took draught oxen and a donkey and cart, which had to be abandoned owing to the impediments of the wooded country. Johnson was to spend more than half a century in Africa, but on his first experience he commented of the Zanzibar carriers, 'they did not seem at all like the band one would have imagined helping missionaries, for though Chuma was a well-known man, his followers were hardy ruffians', and at one stage he experienced an hallucination that Chuma was plotting against the missionaries. Extra carriers offered themselves in good numbers, and after a week a caravan of about 200 moved south. Chuma managed his 'ruffians' well, foraging for food when supplies ran low. When they reached the mountainous district of Masasi the freed slaves, who had come from this region, asked the Bishop to settle there; in view of accounts of famine farther south, he agreed. One man who came to welcome him, saying that he had been set free by the British, proved to be one of those liberated with Chuma. The Bishop spent a month establishing the station at Masasi before returning to Zanzibar with Chuma who was sent back twice with various commissions. In July, a new party went to Masasi—Chauncy Maples, J. A. Williams, nine freed slaves, six boys, the men from Mataka's, and fifty porters under Chuma. On the journey Maples had 'an interesting talk with Chumah about his former life with Dr. Livingstone, and at the school at Bombay, where he was baptised. I I think he feels that he is engaged in mission work, as indeed he is, while helping us to get up the country in this way.' On his return to Zanzibar in December Chuma was able to give Kirk valuable information about conditions in the interior, and the names of some of those near the coast who were still engaged in the slave trade.[5]

Chuma continued to be a regular source of communication between Zanzibar and Masasi, and when Johnson was taken ill at the close of 1877 he 'and some of his most trusted men took me down to the coast without my having to walk at all, carrying me on a native bedstead'. In July 1878 he took the Rev. H. W. Woodward to Magila.[6]

The perils which could attend mission service were illustrated at this time. Tom Snowball or Sudi, a Yao sent to Livingstone by Stanley, remained with him to the end and received his medal in August 1875. He travelled with Bishop Steere to Mataka's as a porter in 1875-6, and later helped with bullock transport for the UMCA in Zanzibar and acquired skill as a brick-layer; he was described as 'a merry fellow'. When baptised by Bishop Steere on 30 June 1878 he rejected his old name and took that of Peter. He married Mary Hatosha, a girl from Mbweni, the UMCA school in Zanzibar.

135

On 15 August 1881 Peter Sudi and his wife sailed in a dhow with goods for W. P. Johnson who had been sent to Mataka's the previous year; Mary suffered from seasickness, and the master of the dhow offered to show them an overland route. He landed them at Ras Ndege and sailed off having sold them into slavery to a local Arab. They were then parted; Peter succeeded in running away but was again seized as a slave, taken to Pangani, and shipped to Pemba. Here he managed to get a message to the British Vice-Consul, Frederic Holmwood, who arranged his release and sent him back to the mission on 14 December. On 14 March following two men were imprisoned by Barghash for selling him.

There was no trace of Mary, however, and on 22 February 1882 Peter again sailed in a dhow for Lindi and travelled to Masasi. Here he was one of the five men who went with the Rev. Chauncy Maples in his vain attempt to avert the Magwangara attack on the mission, and presumably came down in the party which arrived at Zanzibar on 20 November. Soon after his return news was received that his wife had escaped, and reached the coast at Mboamaji, whence Peter fetched her back to Zanzibar.[7]

Another of Livingstone's followers, Wekotani, came into contact with a mission founded in his memory, the Livingstonia Mission on Lake Nyasa. James Stewart was a prime mover in this, but the first leader, chosen for his practical skills, was E. D. Young, who was released by the Navy from coast guard duties from 1875 to 1877. Following the successful example of the *Search*, a metal boat that could be taken up in sections was made; she was the *Ilala*, and was driven by steam. Among the crew was Lorenzo Johnson, the cook from Mackenzie's expedition (see pp. 45–47).

Young followed the same route as in 1867. He found that Moloka had been murdered, but under the leadership of Ramakukan the Makololo gave every assistance. They helped enlist porters, of whom some 800 were used to take the *Ilala* and one wooden boat up the Murchison cataracts. The price for a 50-pound load was six yards of calico, worth about sixpence a yard, and later twenty porters were taken on permanently at one yard a day. Young had a steelyard for ensuring accuracy in weighing loads and thus preventing disputes. Not one item was lost. He established the settlement by the lake, and in October 1876 arranged for 1,000 porters to transport two boats and other material brought by the first party of reinforcements. On 2 November he handed over to James Stewart, and returned home.

He had met Wekotani at Mponda's in October 1875 and found him a most useful helper, both as an interpreter and for information on the country. He was on the *Ilala* for her first voyage on the lake and helped to obtain food at Mponda's when that chief proved uncooperative. He brought the Mission useful local information in March 1876 and in August accompanied Young down to the Shire to meet the Mission reinforcements. In September, when they were occupying adjoining huts, Young heard Wekotani singing a hymn which he had remembered from his days with Bishop Mackenzie's mission, and he also repeated the evening prayer taught him by David Livingstone.[8]

The Church Missionary Society also undertook new initiatives and sent W. Salter Price to establish a settlement for freed slaves in the Mombasa area. He took Jacob Wainwright with him and arrived at Mombasa, where he was greeted by some of the former Nasik boys who had settled there, on 15 November 1874. The next day he crossed to Zanzibar where he met Chuma and Susi, who were awaiting the return of Bishop Steere. On the mainland Rebmann, prematurely aged and blind, retired (he died in Germany in October 1876) but the small community at Kisulidini continued under the leadership of George David, a former Nasik boy who had been his assistant. Jacob Wainwright was assigned to teaching there; 'Poor fellow!' wrote Price, 'he has had hard times of it since coming to Mombasa: a great change from the life he had in England; a greater perhaps even than ours, but he has borne it admirably.' Carus Farrar had had a brief career as an engineer on a ship, and had spent a few months in India, but by early 1875 he was back in Africa, and in March was confirmed at Zanzibar. He became Price's servant at Mombasa; when the missionary fell ill, his wife heard Carus 'earnestly pleading with God in my behalf'. Among other duties he was used to carry mail to and from Zanzibar. Another Livingstone veteran Richard Rutton, who was house servant to J. T. Last, was married on 30 March to Janet, Last's cook.

More batches of men arrived from Nasik, the last forty strong, in January 1876. Its leader was one of the outstanding former pupils of the school, William Henry Jones (see p. 54). He was rescued from a slave ship in 1854 and landed in Bombay. When Isenberg took the first Africans to Nasik, he began training as a blacksmith; from this he acquired his nickname of 'Fundi' (Craftsman) Jones. In 1864 he was sent to help Rebmann; from December 1867 to January 1869 he and his wife Jemima were in Zanzibar assisting in the UMCA schools, but then returned to the CMS. He was sent back to India to bring over the Africans from Nasik. This influx, however, with the locally freed slaves who were also sent to the mission, caused accommodation problems. In May 1875 Price was able to acquire land about a mile north of Mombasa for a freed slaves' settlement, which was named Frere Town in honour of the man who had advocated such an idea. Here, on 24 September 1875, Euan Smith presented the five Nasik 'boys' with their Livingstone medals (see p. 104). A school was set up under J. W. Handford, and when Jacob Wainwright, who had been

137

'patiently plodding on' with a handful of pupils at Kisulidini, was transferred there Handford found him 'a great help'. In September 1876 he was still at Frere Town where Matthew Wellington and Carus Farrar had set up a general shop. Carus later moved to Kisulidini and became one of the four elders responsible for supervising it under the general guidance of Isaac Nyondo, Abbe Gunja's son (see p. 133).[9] Majwara became a cook at the CMS station at Mpwapwa in 1878-79.[10]

Meanwhile, Stanley's message urging the evangelisation of Uganda had reached England, and in November 1875 the CMS decided to respond to it. Six months later a party, under Lt Shergold Smith, left England. After the CMS had rejected Cameron's suggestion that a 'respectable Arab' should be engaged as headman, it was suggested to Price, who had been asked to make preparations, that Bombay or Jacob Wainwright might be recruited. Jacob was unwilling to go; the Secretary of the CMS wrote to Kirk, 'I heard with much regret that Jacob had been huffed about something . . . I fancy that the new young schoolmaster whom we sent out has driven him with a rather heavy hand and scared the lad.' Price accordingly crossed to Zanzibar and on 5 May 1876 he saw Bombay 'and engaged him to lead our expedition to Uganda. At first he said his heart was set upon going to England, to see Captn Grant and Speke's grave &c, but finally he agreed to go with us first to Uganda.' The next day a curious situation arose. The Rev. Roger Price arrived to organise an expedition for the London Missionary Society. He sought out Bombay and offered him a post. Bombay was 'bewildered at having to do with two persons of the same name but settled it in his own mind that it was only one concern' and signed. When the confusion was explained, Roger Price released him, and an agreement was signed at the Consulate with the CMS.[11]

Shergold Smith was somewhat disconcerted to find that this had already been done, since Cameron had warned the CMS that Bombay was 'a drunken jealous old fellow'. Opportunities occurred of assessing Bombay's abilities during preliminary journeys in the steam launch Daisy to test the navigability of the Wami and Kingani rivers in June and July. Bombay was in command of the crews, and was used as a negotiator, though A. M. Mackay, one of the missionaries, noted his 'very imperfect knowledge of English'. Towards the end of the journey, in Mackay's words 'My men stormed more than wind and rain and sea together at their disappointment at not getting to Bagamoyo that day, but having quieted the roughest—including Bombay—by fining them part of their pay, I lay to till daybreak.' The problem of how to deal with Bombay might have become difficult had it not been resolved by the Royal Geographical Society conferring a life pension of fifteen pounds a year on him. 'Bombay has been paid off', wrote Shergold Smith on 22 August. 'He is getting old and having received a pension from the Geogr. Socy. for life is not unwilling to enjoy his *otium cum dignitate*. We must all wish him that for his faithful services in the past.'[12]

About this time Bombay wrote to Grant, 'Bana Grant, I, Bombay, send for my old master plenty salaam. I have been many years with white men, Cameron, Speke, Stanley &c, but have not yet seen England their home, and as I am getting old, I should like to see the land of my old master before I die.' Regrettably he was not able to do so, but settled down to enjoy his pension in Zanzibar.[13]

The Mission party was duly recruited, and included twenty freed slaves and some of Cameron's veterans. However, a decision to avoid Unyanyembe created problems, for Nyamwezi porters would not enlist for the new route, and the Sukuma porters who were engaged demanded extra favourable terms for a limited amount of work. Cameron had advised against Zanzibar porters, but some of these had to be engaged. The equipment to be taken included a large printing press requiring twenty porters, but there were not enough to carry it.[14]

Illness, inexperience, trouble with *hongo* and porters delayed the mission on its upward journey, but Kageyi was eventually reached. Mackay, the engineer, had to turn back through illness, and Shergold Smith launched the *Daisy* as a sailing boat as no one else could instal the machinery. Smith and C. T. Wilson crossed to Buganda in her in June 1877, having received three welcoming letters written by Dallington Maftaa, two on behalf of Mutesa and one from himself: 'To my dear Sir, I have heard that you are in Ukerewe, and this king is very fond on you. He wants Englishmen more than all. This is from your servant, Dallington Scopion.' At Mutesa's court, Dallington translated the letters of greeting from Barghash and from the CMS. The mission encountered many problems and setbacks, including the murder of Shergold Smith and O'Neill in Ukerewe in December 1877.[15]

Mackay, on recovering his health, had spent some time in the coastal area, arranging transport of goods to the mainland, and later, from April to August 1877, organising a gang of forty men to build a 250-mile road inland through Mpwapwa. Susi aided him in these activities, but in October fell into disgrace by helping himself to a case of cognac from Mackay's supplies.[16]

Kirk used the presence of the CMS in Buganda to develop diplomatic contacts. Archibald Smith, of the trading firm of Smith Mackenzie, was the CMS agent for sending up supplies, and he engaged Kacheche on this work at 7 dollars a month. Kirk sent a letter of greeting to Mutesa on 2 September 1878 and on 3 March 1879 Mutesa wrote a cordial reply which was brought down by Kacheche, accompanied by twenty Ganda representatives. They reached Zanzibar in October, and left under Kacheche's leadership on the return journey the following month, with gifts and further letters from Kirk. Some of the property was lost in a fire on the journey, and they returned to Zanzibar in February 1880 to obtain fresh copies of the letters.[17]

Dallington Maftaa suffered from temporary blindness in December 1878 and was successfully treated by Mackay who had just arrived at Rubaga. He was away from the capital for a while in the early part of 1879 but for most of the time he continued as an interpreter and was helpful to the CMS missionaries in this capacity—one remarked that he spoke English 'much better than I expected'. Mutesa was capricious in his attitude to the missionaries; they were temporarily banned from the court in December 1879, and Dallington 'who has from the first been so useful as an interpreter, and who openly identified himself with the Mission on the day of the crisis, also found the palace closed against him'. This crisis passed, but there was another difficult period just over a year later. The missionary Charles Pearson wrote on 5 January 1881, 'Mtesa said (to Mufta), "You don't like me now." Mufta said, "Yes I do; but the English are my friends." The Katikiro said, "Are you not our slave?" Mufta rejoined, "No, I am a free man; I am nobody's slave," and when we came out of court he went to the Katikiro and said he no longer wanted the piece of ground which he had from him.'[18]

In March 1881 a caravan brought from the coast by the Rev. P. O'Flaherty and Charles Stokes, a lay missionary who later became a noted caravan leader, was accompanied by Jacob Wainwright. Jacob had lost his earlier mission post some time before on account of his becoming 'impudent and forward' and early in 1879 he was acting as a door porter to one of the Zanzibar traders. In August 1880, however, he had been engaged by O'Flaherty, and he now acted as interpreter; in May 1881 O'Flaherty wrote, 'Jacob Wainwright, who is a great comfort to me, and who goes with me to the palace as my Kiswahili interpreter, teaches a class in my house.' In November, Dallington, perhaps feeling that his post at the capital was somewhat precarious, accepted the offer of the *kitongole* chieftainship of Mutezi. Mackay was disappointed: 'Of course his liberty is gone for ever, as he is now virtually a slave of Mtesa's, and dare never more leave the country. I only hope he will not return to complete heathenism. I have entreated that lad, spoken with him earnestly, and sometimes even scolded him for his godless life, after all the teaching he got at the Mission in Zanzibar, but all seemingly in vain. May the Good Shepherd bring back this stray sheep.' In December Jacob Wainwright succeeded Dallington as scribe to Mutesa. 'He was bribed to leave me I learn now by the Arabs', wrote O'Flaherty. 'Let us hope this salt may not lose its savour.'[19]

Uganda was also one of the goals of the expanding Roman Catholic missionary activity in east Africa. The White Fathers sent their pioneer party to Zanzibar in 1878. In June, their caravan, 450 strong, left Bagamoyo. It was led by a *kirangozi* carrying a banner made by Carmelite sisters near Algiers, representing the Sacred Heart.

The journey to Unyanyembe was marred by sickness among the missionaries and disputes between the porters and it was decided that in future expeditions the Fathers would be accompanied by Papal Zouaves, who could provide a practical lay element.

At Tura there was a mass desertion, and three priests had to go on to Unyanyembe to obtain porters to enable the remainder to complete their journey to set up two separate missions, one to Lake Tanganyika, one to Lake Victoria. The mission in Buganda came into conflict with the CMS representatives but despite doctrinal differences the Tanganyika party was warmly welcomed by Edward Coode Hore, a lay missionary of the London Missionary Society.[20]

The LMS enterprise had begun with the arrival in April 1876 of the Rev. Roger Price. He had spent seventeen years in South Africa, and believed that ox-waggons might solve the problems of transport. Chuma and Susi gave him some help in recruiting and he led a trial expedition from Saadani to Mpwapwa and back, and decided that its success justified using ox-waggons for the major LMS expedition to Ujiji. The following year he brought thirteen Africans and some trained oxen, from south Africa to Zanzibar, and early in June they crossed to the mainland. He engaged Juma bin Nasibu (see p. 112) in July. At first they had a fierce dispute as to whether Juma's duties included looking after the oxen, but once this was settled, they worked fruitfully together. 'Captain Juma, my factotum, is doing well', wrote Price in August. 'He is an immense service to me in directing my vehicles. He has a capital idea of a waggon road; he has been sole director of the van to-day, as I had to look after the rear.' Nevertheless, the experiment was a complete failure, owing to sickness among oxen and drivers; by the end of the year, Price had returned to England, but before doing so he transferred Juma's services to his colleague J. B. Thomson.[21]

The remaining missionaries set off on Christmas Day with a caravan of the customary type—150 men, eventually led by Juma bin Nasibu; on the last stage to the lake he was the leader of 240 men, and had four 'petty officers' in the words of Edward Hore, a former merchant seaman. Juma was sent off to fetch men and stores, arrange *hongo*, and was generally reliable. Another man who was to give good service to the Mission was Ulaya, at first as cook, and later in more responsible posts. Indeed, Hore spoke highly of the Zanzibaris—'who, by their tact, devotion, and endurance, have often been the chief aid to success on our journeys and voyages, and in a number of critical positions'. Some of them remained with the mission and were used for boat crews by Hore, who found that, even if lacking some of the skill of the local men, they were more dependable. Juma continued with the mission and by 1881 he was regarded as so reliable that he was sent up to the lake with a caravan to take charge of the station in the absence of Europeans, so many having been removed by illness or death. When Hore returned to Ujiji from leave in February 1883 he found 'the Mission property intact . . . the result of the faithful care of Juma.'[22]

In 1884 Hore brought his wife and infant son from the coast to Ujiji, in a 'bath chair'. He re-engaged Juma, even though he was in disgrace for dabbling in the slave trade. In Mrs Hore's words, 'We argued, however, that while he was in our service he was well employed, and if we should reject every man of doubtful character we should scarce have a caravan at all.' Juma recruited some of the men, and led the advance party of 200. He was valuable in the crisis when heavy rain flooded the camp, and in other ways. Ulaya led the rear party of 200 and was left in command when Hore went off on the lake in April. In February 1886 he was sent 'as the very best escort we could offer' to the coast to meet a newly arrived missionary.[23]

The mission also recruited others who had been in missionary service, notably some of Livingstone's followers—Shabani, who took charge of the boat but died of smallpox in 1883; Majwara, who was drowned with six colleagues when a canoe capsized on the lake in October 1886; and Jacob Wainwright. It is not known when Jacob left Mutesa's service, but during the 1880s he joined the LMS at Urambo. Though slow, he was able to help the mission by translating hymns and passages of scripture. At the beginning of April 1892 he died from the effects of burns and scalds caused by falling on a fire and overturning a pot of water. His had been a tragic life. His educational abilities were obviously limited, but by reason of the attention paid to him in England after Livingstone's death, he received an exaggerated idea of his future prospects. The contrast when he returned to Africa seems to have unsettled him, and so began the drifting career that ended in tragedy at Urambo.[24]

Jacob was buried by his hut, his grave marked at first only by a borassus palm. In 1923 Dr A. J. Keevill came to Urambo as a member of the Moravian Mission which had taken over the station from the LMS in 1898. Learning the position of the grave from a patient, Kilwile, who had helped to bury Jacob, he wrote an article on the subject which led the congregation of the Moravian Church at Winston-Salem, North Carolina, USA, to present a metal tablet which in 1931 was set in concrete over the grave. In 1938 the area was evacuated owing to the prevalence of sleeping sickness, and the solitary memorial now stands remote among the elephant grass.[25]

12

'CHUMA'S WHITE MAN'

While this missionary expansion was taking place, other events were foreshadowing the 'Scramble for Africa' of the 1880s. King Leopold of the Belgians arranged an International Geographical Congress in Brussels in 1876 and this set up the International African Association which, working through national committees, was intended to promote the exploration of that continent by opening lines of communication and establishing 'scientific and hospitable stations', at suitable points. Five Belgian expeditions were eventually sent to east Africa.

The British delegation, which included Grant and Cameron, was at first enthusiastic, but in the new year of 1877 doubts arose and the Council of the Royal Geographical Society, which had been entrusted with forming the British Committee, decided instead to establish an independent African Exploration Fund.[1] The Society appointed Keith Johnston, thirty-four years old, an experienced geographer and cartographer, efficient but somewhat withdrawn, to command a new expedition, and he arrived at Zanzibar on 5 January 1879. His assistant was Joseph Thomson, a Scottish geologist, still a few weeks short of his twenty-first birthday, naive and puppyish, friendly, eager and alert for new experiences. Their aim was to explore the country between Dar-es-Salaam and Lake Nyasa to assess the possibilities of a regular route, and if possible to continue to Lake Tanganyika.[2]

As a first stage they looked for a caravan leader. Susi, Chuma and Jacob Wainwright were names familiar from Livingstone's journeys, and Chuma was selected. Thomson wrote:

Among the guild of Zanzibar porters there is certainly none to equal Chuma as a caravan leader, especially for white men. His long experience under Livingstone as an interpreter of the geographical questions so necessary to be asked, gave him a very fair notion regarding these things, so that he is able at once to pick up a European's meaning when an ordinary native would only look at him in blank perplexity. He is well acquainted with English, and about a dozen native dialects.

143

Chuma was, moreover, a natural orator, and could exercise this ability on the men of the caravan or in negotiations with African rulers.

Full of anecdote, and fun, and jollity, he was an immense favourite with the men, and yet he preserved such an authority over them that no one presumed to disobey his orders. If any one was rash enough to do so, woe betide the offender! Chuma went straight at him; and though not tall or muscular himself, he speedily humbled the strongest.

Chuma had his faults—he was not always truthful:

His off-hand statements required to be accepted with judicious reserve. Lies came natural to him, not indeed from any premeditated purpose, or from desire of gaining profit or pleasure to himself, but simply because they seemed to be always nearer his tongue than the truth. Yet it was almost impossible to catch him tripping— a fact which often made matters extremely exasperating, when we knew that, however plausible his story, it was untrue. Chuma was also extremely fond of acting the big man, and right well he could do it. To keep up his dignity he deemed it necessary to be somewhat lavish in his expenditure, so that we required to be continually on the look-out, and to keep a firm hand upon him to check his extravagance.

Susi's state was less happy; he had 'fallen into very bad drinking habits, and was in a state of destitution through his debaucheries.' He was anxious to join the expedition but, though Thomson thought him potentially even more able than Chuma, the fact that he would have to serve under someone who had been junior to him in the past made it prudent to reject his offer; Jacob Wainwright was also thought unsuitable.

The preparation of the caravan was undertaken with great care. At that time Barghash was conscripting 'idlers' into his army, and 'all the nondescript villains and scamps of the town were eager to get engaged as porters, to escape such a fate'. Potential recruits, however, had to be recommended by a man of known reliability and this was noted on the list which Johnston drew up. Of the 128 men eventually chosen, a quarter were vouched for by Chuma; many by Cameron's servant Juma bin Nasibu, and others by the leading men of the expedition. Some had been with traders such as Broyon and Morton (a former UMCA lay missionary), or missionaries like Mackay and Last. Mabruki Nasolo and Ramathani, as well as Chuma, had travelled with Livingstone, and Songoro Nasaro with Cameron. Litala Sudi was a UMCA pupil and there was also Andrew, the erstwhile UMCA boy who had been with Stanley and later with Wakefield and the CMS (see p. 116).[3]

Thirty-eight of the men were Yao, nineteen from Nyasa, seventeen from Zanzibar. There were eight Nyamwezi and, from farther afield, seven Konde and four Ganda. The remainder were from varied areas. One or two of the original 138 were unable to go because they were slaves, but other slaves were engaged on the same basis as free men after having made suitable arrangements with their masters. The rate of pay was 10 dollars a month for Chuma, 6 dollars for five headmen, 5 dollars for the rest, all with rations supplied, and four months' pay was given in advance. The list was drawn up on 17 April, and was ratified by the porters in the presence of Kirk, who took a great interest in the preparations. The five headmen were led by Makatubu. He was keeper of the stores and measured out goods for barter. 'A capital fellow was Makatubu, full of life and energy, and seemingly ever on springs, never grumbling at hard work.' His defect was lack of authority with the men. Nasibu, 'tall and Arab-like', was strong and could give sound advice, but was devoted to sleeping and drinking. Asikari, a former slave at the Zanzibar court, was a picturesque dandy, but the remaining two—Stamboul, 'formerly slave-driver, now adjutant and drill-sergeant' and the giant Bedue, a practical hunter and a good needleman, were 'working officers'.

Uledi, 'my good servant', stuck to Thomson throughout; mission-trained Litala, the cook, was bad-tempered and impudent, but looked after Thomson's little luxuries. Another noteworthy man was Brahim or Ngombe, one of the ten *kirangozis*, 'butcher and bully'.

The trade goods purchased at a cost of nearly £500 were systemati-cally organised, though even so changing fashions had their effect—beads bought on Chuma's advice for barter at Lake Tanganyika proved to have gone out of favour. Each bale of mixed cloth was wrapped in *merikani*, then sewn in matting. Thomson painted a number on, and Johnston kept the tally. The average load was 60 pounds, making with personal gear a total weight of about 80 pounds per porter. The expedition had thirty Sniders supplied by the Govern-ment, twenty old Enfields bought in Zanzibar and twenty-two ancient flintlocks and other primitive weapons. About half the men had handled guns before. In Kirk's view, 'no better organized caravan ever left the coast for the interior'.

On 14 May the expedition embarked; Thomson noted that some of the wives broke down on parting—'After the terrible loss of life in connexion with Stanley's expedition and others, it seemed to be some-thing of a forlorn hope to join a European caravan.' At Dar-es-Salaam numbers were made up to 150.

145

In some ways the pattern of travel was changing: coins were coming into use instead of barter along the coast and many more expeditions were being organised. Thomson met no less than seventeen Europeans—missionaries of various denominations and employees of the International African Association—in the interior. But porters were still needed, and the problems of organising a caravan were unaltered. There was the usual squabble about distributing loads, but,

> . . . here Chuma was in his element. He danced about with indignation, seizing this man by the ear and that by the throat, and dragging him to his appointed load, while he volleyed out his threats, or lashed them with his satire. He was ably seconded by the headmen, who, thoroughly enjoying the pleasures of command, seemed to glory in laying hands upon mutinous porters. In an hour, however, the noise and confusion died away. Each man knew his load, and had apparently become reconciled to it.

On 19 May all was ready, and the caravan wound out of Dar-es-Salaam. It was led by the vanguard with miscellaneous goods, including a patent collapsible boat—later named *Agnes* in honour of Thomson's mother—carried by two men. The main body was headed by a drummer followed by the *kirangozis* with feathered headdresses and crimson robes, one carrying the union jack, and the main body of porters. The rear was brought up by five donkeys, Johnston and the headmen. Thomson thought donkeys were more trouble than their carrying capacity justified, and that they encouraged laziness.

In due course camp was pitched, and at sunset the caravan band, consisting of a native drum, a *zomiri* (resembling a clarinet) and a *barghumi* or antelope's horn, struck up, and the flag was lowered. The men were resourceful campers, operating in *khambis* or messes, whose members shared the preparing of food or shelter. A favourite recreation was dancing in which,

> . . . every muscle is brought into play. The feet stamp into the ground, like the hoofs of circus-horses, and arms and legs are thrown about in that alarming manner only to be seen in Parisian dancing-gardens. The ground becomes literally ploughed up, while shouts and recitatives are kept lustily going, and time is beat by clapping hands. The exertions of an ordinary working week seem to be comprised in three hours of such breakdowns.

Other evenings were quieter:

The ruddy camp-fires light up the hollow with weird effect among the skeleton-like bamboos . . . Animated groups of laughing story-tellers crouch round the fires, awaiting the cooking of their supper. Some are moving about like ghosts in their white shirts; while others twang away for hours on rude stringed instruments, accompanying somewhat monotonous, though not unpleasing, songs . . .

At times Thomson seemed to be living a boy's adventure story, but he had to grapple with stern realities. Both he and Johnston suffered from illness, aggravated by being taken on the wrong road by an incompetent guide. For three days they had to stay in camp, while Chuma kept a firm grip on the situation. Johnston was anxious to resume the journey, and the village of Behobeho, pleasantly set in a forest clearing, was reached on 20 June, but he was now seriously ill, and eight days later he died.

Joseph Thomson, twenty-one years old, now had to decide whether to go on. He had two assets, his own courageous and eager temperament, and the experience of Chuma, who, as Keith Johnston wrote in his last letter, was 'working splendidly'.[4] He therefore decided to go ahead, though by the circuitous route through Kuti where food was more plentiful and conditions safer. However, soon after the journey was resumed, there was an alarm that the Henge were hostile. Thomson asked Chuma to explain to his comrades the importance of maintaining unity at this juncture; drums were beaten, and in the firelight he climbed on some bales and harangued the men. His oratory swayed them and after Makatubu and one of the *kirangozis* followed with similar courageous speeches, Thomson felt renewed confidence in his followers. When the journey was resumed there was a false alarm of an attack and considerable panic, but Chuma and a few of the men helped to quell this. In an effort to improve matters, Thomson took Chuma and another man as interpreter, and persuaded the Henge of his pacific intentions. Good relations were sealed by Chuma making blood brotherhood with the chief's son.

On 18 July the route lay along the Msendasi Valley, a thickly wooded area in which a party of pioneers, with axes, bill-hooks and knives, was organised to clear the way, though the remaining sharp ends were painful to bodies and destructive to clothes. The *Agnes* was used for the first time in crossing the Ruaha, and after initial inexperience in handling her had been overcome, proved very useful, though taking the last surviving donkey across gave problems. Thomson obviously enjoyed the 'jollity and excitement' of the horseplay and jokes that accompanied the crossing. Unlike Cameron, with his naval background, he had no preconceived ideas or standards and took his men as he found them, an attitude which stood him in good stead in his relations with them. There were some setbacks, however; not long

147

after, the men refused to go on without a day's rest, as some had been ill, and Thomson reluctantly agreed. To his chagrin, the same evening, a lively and noisy dance was held in which the sick men proved as vigorous as any.

A few days later volleys of gunfire signalled their entry into the main town of the Henge, Mkomokero. Here Thomson met the chief Komokero; Chuma translated Thomson's words into Swahili, another interpreter repeated them in the local tongue to the chief's son, who passed the message to his father, and so in reverse. This cumbersome practice was followed in other areas also. The chief asked him to stay for a while, and it was four days before he went on with local guides who were not satisfactory and soon had to be replaced. On the way, a porter who stole was flogged, but when Thomson made enquiries as to how another porter had obtained some beads, there was an indignant outcry about his allegedly false accusation, and Thomson disarmed criticism by declaring that he was a mere boy, needing guidance and not hostility.

The edge of the plateau was reached in August. After 350 miles Thomson could claim with justifiable pride that not a man had died or deserted—one who was thought to have done so near the coast returned after having visited his sick wife—no cloth had been stolen, and there had been no conflict with the peoples encountered. The ascent was hard going, but the beating of the drums, the chants of the *kirangozis*, and the jokes and chaffing of Chuma kept morale high. On the higher gound, conditions were miserable, with cold and wet weather, an incorrect route, and shortage of food—one goat had to be divided among 150—but 'the Zanzibar porters, who have so frequently been vilified till they have appeared the very incarnation of all that is bad in man, acted like heroes'. Though they seemed to expect three large meals a day when doing nothing, they endured limited rations uncomplainingly on the march.

On 17 August 'our brave little band' reached the plateau, disappointingly bleak. A problem now arose within the caravan. Misdemeanours had hitherto been punished by flogging, administered by Chuma; Thomson noted that those who suffered did not seem to bear any grudge, but he disliked the amusement of the sufferer's colleagues, and looked for a more civilised means of maintaining discipline. On 28 August he ordered the men on after a halt; they had reached the end of their tether and refused. He therefore decided to fine them. Virtually the whole caravan went on strike; they laid down their weapons and loads and made off in the direction of Unyanyembe, leaving Thomson with his six headmen, cooks, two boys and one porter who had his wife with him. The only course was to submit; he sent Chuma after the strikers and followed himself. On the understanding that future punishment would be physical, not financial, they all returned.

The expedition halted at Uhenge, where it had to wait for the arrival of Mamle, the chief. Thomson sent three men to the coast with letters and instructions to return to Ujiji. The village chief was friendly and enjoyed looking at Thomson's photograph album, particularly the young ladies whom Chuma described as Thomson's wives. Entertainment was also provided by Sirkali, a former slave in Barghash's palace, who drilled the men in comic imitation of the Sultan's troops. When at last Mamle came, blood brotherhood was made between Chuma and the headman of Uhenge.

The journey was resumed and on 20 September they caught a first glimpse of Lake Nyasa, an occasion celebrated by a drinking session on local *pombe*. Thomson arrived at the northern extremity of the lake, the first European to do so, on the 22nd.

He decided to continue to Lake Tanganyika, but during the journey fell ill and thought in his delirium that his men were deserting. This was an illusion, but in fact he did become short-tempered as a result of his illness and at one stage quarrelled with Chuma; as Chuma could make conditions very awkward for him, Thomson was glad to smooth things over. The close association between them, the most fruitful in African exploration since Speke and Bombay, was not broken again. Thomson had his own ways of maintaining control—malingering porters were given castor oil, and he stuck to the old method of buying food in bulk and issuing rations instead of handing out cloth with which the men could buy their own—a growing custom which was pushing up the cost of travel.

On the morning of 3 November the caravan, with its band playing its loudest and guns firing, made its way through the forest to Lake Tanganyika. The men danced energetically in celebration; Thomson called the roll, made a speech, and shook hands with every man 'which made me feel that, whatever might be the colour of our skin, there existed no barrier between us, nor any difference but that of degree between our respective feelings and sentiments.' A general distribution of cloth followed. Pambete, the same spot at which Livingstone and Chuma had reached the lake in April 1867 (see p. 66), had deteriorated since that time. While there, Thomson was saved from a crocodile by the prompt aid of his men. On 10 November he went north. Some of the porters were tiring, but rallied for a ceremonial entry into Liendwe, a flourishing trade centre. Here Thomson, ever anxious to cover new ground, decided to explore the Lukuga with a smaller party carrying light loads and to leave the rest, with the main stores, under the command of Chuma.

There was a good response of volunteers and thirty-seven, under

F

149

Makatubu, were chosen. The band played them off on 16 November. They carried the *Agnes* which proved very useful, though on the higher ground eight men were needed to carry her instead of the usual two. Though Thomson set off with confidence in himself and in his men, it was hard going, and he usually had at least five men sick. His guide had a more satisfactory journey; scattered about the country he had numerous wives whom he collected as he proceeded. Despite some false alarms all went peacefully. However, on 6 December a porter, died of a haemorrhage—the only fatality on the expedition.

By 23 December the men were fatigued and reluctant to go on and only did so when Thomson showed he was willing to continue alone. On Christmas Day, after 'a feast as good as circumstances would allow', they reached the Lukuga and made useful observations on its flow. Thomson then went on to Mtowa, by the lake, where he met two agents of the London Missionary Society. On New Year's Day 1880 his letters were brought across the lake by the men he had sent to the coast in September and who had arrived at Ujiji on Christmas Day. He later learnt that, despite their good conduct while they were with him, one of them had killed a Msagala in order to abduct his wife in Ugogo. Leaving the rest under Makatubu, Thomson crossed to Ujiji with his servant Uledi in a boat crammed with slaves. A storm arose, and Juma bin Nasibu, who was on board, helped to safeguard Thomson's box of diaries and, on landing, hurried on to tell the LMS missionaries of his arrival. They made him very welcome, and he returned to Mtowa on 17 January.

He now decided to make a detour, returning to Liendwe via the Lukuga, Lualaba and Lake Mweru. His men, including Makatubu, were most reluctant to go. 'In this nasty situation I began to appreciate Chuma's value more justly; for now, when the entire work fell on me of forcing the men to do this or that, I felt half the pleasure of travelling gone.' They eventually refused to go to Manyema and were extremely reluctant to venture south into Urua.

It was a disastrous enterprise, and Thomson had to turn back on 20 February, ten miles short of the Lualaba, because of the disturbed state of the country. Guides were unreliable, ammunition was almost exhausted, and both outward and return journeys were plagued by exactions and thefts. In one village there was an outcry against Brahim, a *kirangozi*, by a jealous husband whom Thomson had to pay heavily to placate. Later, the expedition escaped from hostile villagers in the *Agnes*, under the protection afforded by the guns of some of his men. Thomson, pressing on ahead with Uledi, re-entered Mtowa two months after leaving, not like a lion, but 'like a sheep from the shearers'.

The opportunity of going back to Liendwe in the canoe of the LMS missionary Edward Hore (see p. 141) made him decide to dispense with most of his men, and he sent all but ten off to the coast via Ujiji, with cloth and a discharge paper; looking at the Urua episode in retrospect, he described them as 'good fellows who had stuck to me so well through thick and thin'. He then took passage in Hore's decked canoe, the *New Calabash*, to Karema, and noted that Hore, a former merchant navy officer, expected his crew to respond like trained sailors.

The International African Association's station at Karema had been founded in August 1878 by Capt. Ernest Cambier, the only member of the first IAA expedition to penetrate far inland. His original caravan of 90 Zanzibaris and 350 Nyamwezi had been reduced by desertions, but he had retained some Zanzibaris to garrison the new post.[5]

Most members of the first expedition suffered in health and three died; another unfortunate traveller in the area at that period was an eccentric Frenchman, the Abbé Debaize, who left Zanzibar in August 1878 with a 'well-equipped and numerous party', but suffered from the desertion of at least one hundred and fifty of his men, and died at the London Missionary Society station at Ujiji on 12 December 1879.[6]

The second IAA expedition, which reached Zanzibar during the first half of 1879, was the most interesting, since it involved an attempt to solve transport problems by the introduction of trained elephants. Keith Johnston had considered this idea, and thought there were points in its favour—if an elephant carried the equivalent of fifteen loads, the saving in porters' wages in one year would be greater than the cost of buying the animal, but he did not pursue the matter, and it was left to the IAA to make the practical experiment.[7]

Two male elephants, Mahonghi and Naderbux, and two females, Sosankalli and Pulmalla, with thirteen mahouts, were brought from India under the command of Captain F. F. Carter. On 1 June they were deposited from the ship's derricks in shallow water in Msasani Bay, four miles north of Dar-es-Salaam. The expedition, comprising 700 porters, set off inland. The journey was not easy, with the elephants sinking into soft ground; Mahonghi died of heat apoplexy at Mpwapwa, and Naderbux farther inland on 23 September. The two females made an impressive entry into Unyanyembe and were then taken towards Karema. Sosankalli died on the way in December, but Pulmalla, the oldest, reached Karema on 29 February 1880, a few weeks before Thomson's arrival.

Thomson continued his journey in the *New Calabash* and reached Liendwe early in April, to be greeted with cheers and welcoming shots by the men. All was well—no desertions, no casualties, and a neat, well-laid out circle of houses, with one prepared for him. Chuma—'a treasure that cannot be valued too highly', had

. . . acted with much care and moderation, in spite of his somewhat extravagant character. The only fault I had to find was that he had carefully selected all the bales with fine cloths in them, and being of a very gallant nature, with a soft side towards the female sex, he had been somewhat lavish in his gifts to such Liendwe damsels as had the good fortune to attract his attention. I found that he had earned great popularity among the natives; and immensely to my amusement, I heard myself described as 'Chuma's white man . . .'

An all-night dance celebrated the return.[8]

Thomson could not, as he intended, return direct to Kilwa owing to conflict in the intervening country but had to go north-east to the old arab caravan route via Unyanyembe. He went with a guide to Lake Rukwa, and was the first European to visit it. Shortly after he met Tom Cadenhead, a young Scot who was on his way to join the elephant expedition. Unsuccessful from the beginning, it came to a tragic end. A contingent sent to bring up more elephants became embroiled in a conflict with some of Mirambo's forces and Carter, Cadenhead and several porters were killed after desperate fighting. The last elephant, Pulmalla, was safe at Karema, but shortly after this she too died.[9]

Thomson resumed his march to Unyanyembe on 29 April. He had badly blistered feet, and his men were suffering from various diseases, including cracking of the heels, though they kept up a good pace, the fit helping the sick. Illness did not prevent the porters provoking some annoyance by their free ways with local women.

Thomson had issued cloth to repair losses of clothing, and ever a believer in making a brave show, he entered Unyanyembe in style on 26 May; Brahim, carrying spear and shield, led the way, clad in scarlet *joho* (a long cloak), leopard-skin and feather headdress. The caravan band, in black *johos* and leopard-skins followed; then the flag, with armed escort, gaily dressed *kirangozis*, porters in their new clothes, and finally Thomson in his tweeds, surrounded by white-robed headmen. Thomson was allotted the *tembe* at Kwihara used by so many explorers; three days later he paid a ceremonial visit to the Governor, Abdullah bin Nasib, with an escort of thirty men, who received lavish hospitality as they were taken round Tabora.

On 7 June he set off again, the caravan augmented by some of the men he had sent to the coast from Lake Tanganyika and whom he had found still at Unyanyembe. After a stop at the mission station at Mpwapwa they were heartened by the fertility of the mountain area of Usambara compared with the desert plateau of Ugogo. Thomson was pleased to find that in the last stages he could out-walk his followers. At Bagamoyo he called the roll for the last time; all but one of the 150 had survived the journey. They crossed to Zanzibar in three dhows, arriving on 16 July, and after seeing to the pay of his porters, Thomson left for home.

In its conduct and humanity, if not in its significance, this was one of the most successful of all African explorations. Thomson gave unstinted praise to his men:

Chuma and my second headman Makatubu have worked like heroes, and I should indeed be but a poor mortal if I did not acknowledge the fact that the success of the Expedition has been to a large extent due to them,

he wrote. Chuma

. . . was ever at my elbow, with his ready tact and vast stores of information—ever ready to guide and direct me.

He also praised the rank and file:

I cannot express, in too appreciative terms the honesty and faithfulness which characterized my men, and the really genuine character which lies at the bottom of their semi-savage nature . . . the Zanzibar porter is infinitely better than he has been usually represented . . . We hear frequently about their troublesome conduct, desertions, obstinacy, &c. But we are never told how much they have to bear from their masters . . .'[10]

In the Royal Geographical Society, tribute was paid to Chuma by Waller, Farler and Maples, and Waller also wrote to the Society, 'Too often these poor fellows are allowed to sink out of sight simply because they have no one to speak for them . . .' The decision was taken to award Chuma a sword and silver medal; Makatubu a 'second-class sword' and a silver medal; the remainder bronze medals and certificates.[11]

During his journey, Chuma had sent money back to his wife in Zanzibar but when he returned he found that she had died. In July he declined an invitation to accompany a Church of Scotland mission of enquiry to Blantyre, as interpreter, but the following month Chuma, Makatubu, and sixty of their followers joined an expedition under Captain Temple Phipson-Wybrants, to explore the Sabi River in Mozambique, but it was a total disaster; Phipson-Wybrants died on 29 November, two other Europeans also died, and the personnel had to be picked up from Chiluan.[12]

They had not long been back in Zanzibar when, in June 1881, Thomson returned there on a two-year contract from the Sultan to

153

examine the mineral resources of the mainland, beginning with alleged coal deposits on the Rovuma River. He was pleased to be able to distribute the medals and swords, and to be photographed with Chuma and Makatubu. He engaged them, and fifty-four of their comrades, for the expedition, and another twenty men were added. He had to enlist the aid of the Sultan's troops to rout them out of the drinking shops of Zanzibar so that they could sail for Mikindani, which they reached on 13 July.

The town had grown since Livingstone's days, but Thomson spent little time in it. Burrowing its way through dense undergrowth, the expedition struck up to the confluence of the Rovuma and Lujende rivers, reached on 3 August. The coal deposits proved illusory, but they followed the Lujende up, cut across to the Rovuma, back to the confluence, and to the coast by a more southerly route, which involved some hazards from lack of water. Tungi Bay was reached on 10 September, after an eight-week expedition in which 700 miles had been covered. His tried followers had been excellent, and the whole enterprise was efficient, but it did not produce the hoped-for coal; the Sultan therefore dispensed with Thomson's services and he returned to Scotland at the end of the year.[13]

13

SUSI'S JOURNEYS

In the early months of 1879 Susi, five years after being acclaimed for his devotion to Livingstone and his leading part in bringing back the body, appeared to be in a hopeless position; he had left missionary service in disgrace and was rejected by Johnston and Thomson. On 30 March, however, Henry Stanley landed in Zanzibar with the intention of enlisting 'as many of my old comrades as might be willing to try their luck on the great river again'. He had returned to Europe in January 1878 full of enthusiasm for the possibilities of developing the Congo and, finding little response in Britain, had welcomed the interest shown by King Leopold, and had entered the service of the Comité d'Etudes du Haut-Congo which the King had set up to investigate the commercial possibilities of the area.[1] He now sought experienced Africans to pioneer the establishment of settlements and communications there, but maintained an air of secrecy about his aim which was reminiscent of his first arrival eight years earlier.[2]

He had problems in selecting his leading men. Manua Sera, even if in Zanzibar at the time, had ruled himself out, having, as Stanley knew from Sparhawk, given Kirk information detrimental to Stanley's reputation: the same applied to Kacheche who in any case had gone to Buganda (see pp. 139–40). Uledi was on the mainland, and Johnston had recruited many other experienced men. Stanley had never employed Susi, but he knew his strengths and weaknesses from Livingstone's day, and in spite of his fallen condition, appointed him 'head chief of the foreign native employés'. Among veterans of the Congo journey he engaged were Wadi Rehani as 'quarter-master and commissary-general'; Robert Feruzi; the gun-bearer Mabruki; Soudi; and Kadu, once a page to Mutesa who had become the expedition's drummer and an entertaining narrator of his country's legends. Another to re-enlist was Hamadi, one of those left in 1877 after being seized by the natives for theft; he and his companions eventually escaped, and he had just returned to Zanzibar. Stanley also engaged a seventeen-year-old Somali,

Dualla Idris, son of the police chief of Somaliland, who had already travelled to America.[3]

Early in May Uledi, the coxswain of the Congo journey, arrived at Zanzibar and was promptly thrown into prison and 'ignominiously chained' on the orders of Henri Greffulhe, a French merchant.

In his misery he sends me word of his condition but fails to convey to me the cause of this treatment,

wrote Stanley to Greffulhe.

I should esteem it a great favour if you would kindly explain to me why he has been arrested and chained, and his neck fastened between the prongs of a 'heavy tree'. If it is for robbery, and you will mention the sum, I promise to make up the sum he stole. If it is not for robbery will you kindly tell me in what way I can assist this unfortunate man.

Stanley left on the *Albion* shortly after with sixty men, having contracted with Frank Mahoney, an American, to bring eight more, including Uledi, who sailed on the *Asiatic* at the beginning of June. There was apparently some unresolved problem, for Hathorne, the American consul, wrote, 'Greffulhe had his spies here on the beach, but I gave the principal one the choice of going on his own accord or being kicked away.' Of Stanley's sixty-eight men, three-quarters were veterans of his last expedition, the rest were their friends.[4]

Travelling by the Red Sea, the Mediterranean and west Africa, he arrived at Banana Point on 14 August with all his men in good health. His task was a complex one. With a number of Europeans of various nationalities, his Zanzibaris, and such local labour as he could engage, he had to make treaties with local chiefs, establish stations, and build up communications by river and land. He began his journey upstream on 21 August and reached Vivi on 26 September. Here he negotiated treaties and established his first station. When he left in February 1880 he handed the command over to Sparhawk, who had come from Zanzibar. The Zanzibaris had already shown their value, by local knowledge derived from their earlier experiences, working with local labour on roads and as police. They had quarters at one end of the platform on which the headquarters was constructed. More had arrived; the roll in February was twelve Europeans, eighty-one Zanzibaris, one hundred and sixteen men from the coast and six from the interior.

From Vivi Stanley began the construction of a road to Isangila where he established a second station. Leaving a small force at Vivi, he took one hundred and six men to begin with and augmented them with local labour. His 'disciplined and trained Zanzibari chiefs' such as Wadi Rehani, proved valuable in supervising transport and labour.

In February 1881 he set off towards Manyanga with one hundred and eighteen men, about half Zanzibaris, the remainder local recruits. On the journey he lost an old comrade when Soudi, who had been wounded in Ituru in 1875 and nearly drowned in 1877, was killed by a wounded buffalo. Stanley sought news of Wadi Safeni, but could learn nothing of his fate. Manyanga station was established on 1 May: Robert Feruzi was appointed headman and attended the Bible class established by the nearby Baptist Mission.[5] Soon after Stanley had a severe attack of fever, in which he was looked after by Mabruki and Dualla.

After his recovery he welcomed the arrival of Otto Lindner, a German official of the CEHC, who had enlisted seventy-two Zanzibaris in February on a three-year contract at 5 dollars a month, and travelled via Capetown. Leaving the majority at Vivi, he brought twenty-four with him, 'some of whom were ancient comrades of mine'. By July Stanley had one hundred and thirty-eight imported Africans beyond Vivi. He had found the men from the west coast undisciplined and the Zanzibaris provided his main source of strength, though their numbers were too limited.[6]

In July 1881 he reached Stanley Pool and made the acquaintance of Sergeant Malamine Kamara, a Senegalese placed in command of the station at Ncouma by Savorgnan de Brazza, who had secured it by a treaty with the chief Makoko the previous October. Malamine displayed qualities of resource and initiative comparable with those of the leading Zanzibaris.[7]

In August Stanley was furious to learn that a young Belgian Lieutenant had let discipline slide at Manyanga, so that after a drunken debauch fire broke out in which the sixteen Zanzibari guards lost their houses and possessions and one, Khamis, was burnt to death. 'I feel outraged that my fine people who have laboured now over 2 years should be allowed to die thus from the sheer idleness and inefficiency of the chief in whose charge they were left,' he wrote.

Meanwhile, anxious to establish a station at the Pool, he entered into negotiations with the chief Ngalyema of Ntamo. In these he employed both the veteran Susi and the promising youth Dualla. They proved perceptive observers and in October Susi brought the disquieting news that Ngalyema, after initial friendliness, was turning hostile. Eventually he came to Stanley's camp with a number of armed men, but the latter dispersed most of his men in huts, save for a handful in the open, under Susi 'who was so very clever, and could well enter into the elaborate joke I was perpetrating'. When Ngalyema and his men arrived truculently, Stanley awaited a suitable moment, then his men burst from cover, yelling and waving weapons, until called to order by 'Susi and

157

his brother captains'. Though Stanley did not mind making a demonstration of strength of this sort, he much preferred to maintain peaceable relations with those he encountered.

Haggling with Ngalyema, in which Dualla played a useful part, continued on and off for some time; meanwhile Stanley was able to engage some useful local men. On 9 November he sent Susi, Wadi Rehani, and eight other men to reconnoitre the country round Kintamo to find a suitable spot for another station. They returned with information of a broad plain-like ridge, about a mile from Kintamo and overlooking Stanley Pool. Stanley established his fourth station on this site on 1 December; the following April he named it Leopoldville (now Kinshasha). Susi and Wadi Rehani had supervised much of the labour in constructing it, and in April blood brotherhood was made with Ngalyema, Susi improving the occasion by soliciting divine 'unheard-of atrocious vengeances on Ngalyema if he dared make the slightest breach in the sacred brotherhood'.

In more routine ways, too, the Zanzibaris had been a major element in establishing the structure of the state. They were the backbone of the transport system, manning the whale-boat and other craft, taking supply caravans, frequently without European supervision, between stations, and building grass-hutted camps along the route. W. Holman Bentley, the Baptist missionary, saw much of them—'Some of the Zanzibaris were fine fellows', he wrote; and he heard stories of Livingstone from Susi, and of Stanley from Uledi and Robert Feruzi. Stanley, he noted, spoke Swahili fluently, 'was accessible to them, and was very much liked by his men'. He continued the practice which had begun on his 1874–77 expedition of sitting with his men round the camp fire as they exchanged stories and legends. Though engaged in one or two skirmishes, the Zanzibaris were normally peaceable 'and seemed to have made many friends; they were patient with the extortionate people, surprising us with their forbearance. They were often hungry, but they would quietly put their beads away and walk on, when the natives would not take eightpence for the penny loaf.' They played a significant part in making each station conform to Stanley's aim of being 'a well-governed community of soldier-labourers'.[8]

Meanwhile, Stanley was becoming increasingly concerned about the repatriation of his original Zanzibaris. As far back as June 1881 he had warned Colonel Strauch, Secretary of the Association International du Congo, the new body concerned with its administration, that their term of service expired on 16 May 1882; they expected to be sent home then. He was anxious for proper arrangements to be made; their departure would leave a serious gap, and he thought plans for their replacement were inadequate. When Lindner suggested offering extra pay for an extension of their services, he wrote:

158

I beg of you never to hint to any Zanzibari going home such a thing, because it is impossible that he should listen to it *respectfully*, as that you yourself would after a three years' absence from your family. When their time is up, they must be allowed to depart with all kindness and courtesy. Whatever is good for their comfort must be done, but no attempt civilly or otherwise must be made to impede their departure.

At most, he thought a delay of 'a month or so' might be accepted if a definite date was given.

He was not blind to his men's shortcomings and in a letter to one officer warned him of certain 'famous malingerers'. He did, however, regard them as potentially more useful than the callow and inflexible young officers he sometimes had as his subordinates. Indeed, he also compared the latter with local labourers—'What a moral lesson for vapid-minded white men might be drawn from these efforts of untutored blacks to get through their tasks!'[9]

In January 1882 news had come of the arrival of 100 new recruits, engaged at Zanzibar in August 1881, but they were a long time in coming up-river, and in March Stanley sent 'a detachment of first-class men' to hurry them up. He found the numbers had dwindled for various reasons, and he would receive only part of the batch. Among those whom Lindner had kept back were some he urgently required, and he wrote for them—Chowpereh, Nubi and Kombo in particular: 'Nubi and Chowpereh are sailors; I want sailors. Chowpereh has been with me since December 1870. Going on 12 years.'[10]

In April, having stationed a garrison of reliable Zanzibaris at Leopoldville, in quarters at the foot of the hill, he went on up the river and established Mawata on 1 May; on the 26th he discovered and named Lake Leopold. Here Dualla and Uledi saved a fisherman from drowning. Soon after, Stanley was taken ill, and was conveyed downstream by his time-expired Zanzibaris, whom he had been assembling.[11]

At Vivi, early in July, he was relieved to learn of the arrival of Lt Valcke with 225 Zanzibaris he had recruited in May. He arranged that the original recruits should return to Zanzibar under the command of Albert Christopherson, a young Danish sailor who had proved a loyal and resourceful colleague, and had won the confidence of Africans. He himself then sailed for Europe. He summed up:

Through the fidelity of sixty-eight Zanzibaris, and the faithfull co-operation of a few Europeans, five stations had been constructed, a steamer and sailing-boat launched on the Upper Congo, while another small steamer and lighter maintained communications between the second and third station. A waggon-road had also been made at great expense and time between Vivi and Isangila, and Manyanga and Stanley Pool.

Stanley returned to the Congo in December 1882 with Dualla still acting as a valuable aide, and before leaving for Europe in June 1884 founded new stations and concluded a number of treaties. In the ensuing years further groups of Zanzibaris—a term used to include a variety of Africans enlisted on that increasingly cosmopolitan island, as well as those normally living there—were recruited for the Congo, and for several years they were an important element in the Force Publique established in 1886. Tributes were paid to their resourcefulness and ability by many European administrators and travellers.[12]

The pioneer contingent of Zanzibaris had returned to their home in the middle of 1882, and Susi found his old comrade Chuma dying of tuberculosis. He was tended in the UMCA hospital by a missionary nurse, Ellen Sherratt, who later married the missionary and trader Charles Stokes. Chuma's will, in the handwriting of Archdeacon Jones Bateman, was preserved in the Consular records:

This is the last Will and testament of me James Chuma of Zanzibar I give devise and bequeath all and every my house at Mwembemali and all the things that are in it to my wife Salima binti Sitakishauri without reservation. The above mentioned house and all that is in it I wish my ndugu Baraka and Abdallah Susa to sell and take the whole proceeds before the English Consul, that he may send the said proceeds to my wife above mentioned. My silver sword which I have left in Baraka's house, I wish sold similarly and the proceeds transferred to my wife after the manner abovementioned. I wish however from the money to be transferred to my wife there be first subtracted ten dollars and given to my freed slave Zafarani, and twenty dollars similarly subtracted and given to Kate wife of Francis Mabruki of Mbweni. And also half of the remaining sum to be set aside for my ndugu Baraka and Susa and be given to them.

In token whereof I James Chuma hereto set my hand, the twenty fifth day of September in the year of Our Lord Eighteen hundred and eighty two. We the undersigned witnessed altogether and at one time on the above mentioned day to the fact that James Chuma signed this will and declared it valid. In token whereof we hereto set our hands.

This was signed by Chuma in very shaky writing at the beginning of the second paragraph and witnessed by Archdeacon Jones Bateman and another witness signing in Arabic. The value of the estate, the modest amount of 309 rupees, was received from Bombay, presumably acting as the doyen of the community, in December, and distributed early in 1883.

Chuma, in spite of his remarkable career, cannot have been much more than thirty at the time of his death. The fate of his sword is unknown, but one would like to think that it is valued for more than its weight in silver.[13]

This reference to Bombay is the last we hear of that stalwart, save for his death on 12 October 1885. Stanley wrote of him:

He had his failings but he had also virtues. He was brave & manly. He was faithful, and was incorruptible in a sense . . . He was a fine old gossip, delighted to talk of past days & old times. Seen at such a time Bombay was a dear even lovable man, and as I recall them romance lends a charm to them & softens many asperities of my journey . . . peace be to his old head. May his failings be forgotten and only his virtues remembered.[14]

Soon after Chuma's death, Susi became an active helper to the UMCA, and with Robert Feruzi, 'both as satisfactory and good servants as we could wish for', was a leader of monthly caravans from Zanzibar taking goods, and occasionally workers, to the up-country stations. On 8 November 1883 he went with the Rev. H. Clarke to the Newala Mission, to which the Masasi station had been moved. He was admitted as a catechumen on 3 January 1884, in Zanzibar. 'As a free-born man of great influence and standing in his own quarter of the town, he will have no small share of persecution to undergo . . .'[15]

Bishop Steere had died in office not long before Chuma. On 25 February 1884 Charles Alan Smythies, his successor as Bishop of Zanzibar, arrived on the island. Susi was to become 'the invaluable servant of the Mission' and 'our faithful attendant' and to render to him the quality of service that Chuma had done to his predecessor. Their first expedition together seems to have been in July 1884 when the Bishop, concerned at the consequences of a dispute over the succession to the Kilindi chieftainship, visited Kimweri, grandson of Krapf's acquaintance of the same name (see p. 6), and one of the protagonists, and secured his agreement to refrain from attacking the peaceable Bondei people near the mission. Susi continued his travels on behalf of the Mission during the following year.

The year 1885 was important for the Mission, for its members reached Lake Nyasa with the mission steamer *Charles Janson*. Susi left Zanzibar for Quilimane with A. Read, the engineer, on 25 February. Bishop Smythies sailed in June and travelled up the Zambezi and Shire by a series of slow and unsatisfactory boats. Early in July Susi went on ahead with the Rev. G. H. Swinny, one of the missionaries, and they visited

Bishop Mackenzie's grave. The Bishop was close behind, and landing from the steam launch *Lady Nyassa*—not Livingstone's vessel, but one belonging to the African Lakes Company—he too climbed the steep bank and walked through the tall reeds to the cross which had been set upon the lonely grave. More than twenty-three years had passed since the death of the first Bishop; now the fourth Bishop had reached the scene of the pioneer efforts, and Susi too had come back to the land where, at the same period, he had entered Livingstone's service.

On 10 September the Bishop, with Susi and twenty-five men left the mission's base at Matope, on the upper Shire, to walk back—a journey of forty-five days. Early in this journey Susi was used as an envoy to the allegedly hostile Kalinga. Later the party travelled through areas devastated by the Magwangwara (Ngoni), some of which Susi recalled from Livingstone's time as being well populated. They visited Masasi and Newala, went down to the coast, and returned to Zanzibar on 18 December. 'Susi was with me all the time, and I found him invaluable,' wrote the Bishop.

In May the following year the Bishop set off on a second visit to Nyasa with seven other missionaries and thirty porters under Susi. The Bishop undertook an extensive tour, but Susi returned to Zanzibar in charge of a party of porters, and on 23 August, the eve of the Mission's Festival, he was baptised there by the Rev. H. C. Goodyear who wrote, 'Susi received the name of David, in memory of that great hero who first taught him about Jesus Christ, and into whose labours it was therefore my privilege to enter. It was indeed a glorious service. He was so intent . . .'

Nothing is recorded of Susi in the next two years, but in 1888, following the establishment of German rule on the mainland, there was an uprising under Bushiri. Bishop Smythies decided to bring the women missionaries down from Magila. On 11 November he crossed to Pangani on the Sultan's steamer, accompanied by Nasr bin Suliman, father of the *Liwali*. 'It was thought better that no white men should go with me,' he wrote, so he took Susi and Petro Limo, nephew of the Bondei chief and later a Canon of Zanzibar. They anchored off shore, and Susi was sent ahead to prepare the way. Several days of negotiations followed their landing, on the 15th a mob assembled round their house and the Bishop was told by Susi 'that they were trying to force their way in to kill me'. This threat was averted by the personal intervention of Bushiri, and the next day the Bishop was able to go up country and bring down the ladies; he himself remained on the mainland.

Susi died on 5 May 1891 after a long illness and increasing paralysis. He was nursed by Miss Campbell, received his last communion from the Rev. Spencer Weigall, and was buried at Ziwani by the Bishop. 'The Consul came and we had both Kiungani and Mkunazini choirs, and

162

walked in procession from the church round by Mnazi Moja, the people very well behaved and respectful.' He left a small son 'to whom we hope to act as guardian when he gets a little older; he will be well off to start with as things go here.' The Bishop concluded, 'Susi had been a good friend to me from the first, and I shall miss him more than any of our people.'

14

THE NORTHERN ROUTE

Though Rebmann first saw Mount Kilimanjaro in 1848, and Krapf caught a glimpse of the distant peak of Mount Kenya the following year, only spasmodic attempts were made to explore the northern area in the ensuing thirty years.

The first venture was made by Baron von der Decken, whom Speke and Grant met at Zanzibar in 1860. Initially he set off for Lake Nyasa to seek the scene of Roscher's murder (see p. 24). As an escort he took some of the Baluchis who had accompanied Burton and Speke, though he could not agree terms with Jemadar Mallok to lead them (see p. 20). However they proved mutinous, and the porters stole his goods and deserted, so he soon had to turn back. He therefore decided to explore a different area and, with Richard Thornton, who had arrived in Zanzibar from the Zambezi (see pp. 40, 44), set off in June 1861 for Mount Kilimanjaro. Their party was fifty-five strong—a headman, two assistant headmen, five servants and forty-seven porters, some of whom were slaves engaged from their masters. Thornton armed and paid for seven of the men—three Africans, three Comorians (one as interpreter) and Segwati, his Zambezian servant. They ascended Kilimanjaro to more than 5,000 feet and confirmed that it was snow-capped.[1]

Thornton returned to the Zambezi but von der Decken waited until he was joined, the following August, by two colleagues and again set off. In charge of his caravan was Sadi ben Ahedi, an experienced trader in the area. In a fresh attempt to climb Kilimanjaro the party reached 14,000 feet. Von der Decken's intention to continue to Mount Kenya was, however, frustrated by rumours of the hostility of the Masai who lived in the intervening territory, and he returned to Zanzibar.

In April 1863 he met the Rev. Charles New (see pp. 86, 133), who arrived on the island on his way to join the Methodist mission at Ribe, and aroused his interest by describing Kilimanjaro. Von der Decken then undertook the Somali expedition on which he was murdered. New awaited the opportunity to make his own attempt on the mountain, and

164

in 1871 he was able to realise his ambition. He set out in July. He, too, engaged Sadi whom he described as 'about forty-five years of age, tall and well-timbered; features, half African, half Arabian; complexion, black as a coal; beard, short and thick.' The value of his experience was, in New's opinion, outweighed by his cowardice and scheming nature. New placed greater reliance on his own followers. The chief of these was his cook, Tofiki, a Muslim Mgindo who had been in the service of the mission since 1863, 'shrewd, thoroughly honest, courageous, and as true as steel'. Aba Shora, a Galla, had fled to the mission with his wife and child when his life was in danger, and had become devoted to those who had protected him. In addition there were thirteen men of varied abilities and qualities, most of them from the Ribe area.[2]

New made two attempts to climb the mountain; on the second, on 20 August, he set off accompanied by Sadi, Tofiki and two guides provided by Mandara, or Mangi Rindi, the chief of Moshi, and seven Chaga carriers. By the morning of the 28th not only the dilatory Sadi but even the hardy Chaga men refused to continue. New and Tofiki struggled on to the snow line and the latter triumphantly carried lumps of the white 'rock' back in his blanket as proof of their success.

After his abortive involvement in the Livingstone Relief Expedition of 1872, New went on leave. On his return to Zanzibar in 1874 he organised an expedition to investigate missionary prospects in Usambara; in forty-five days he travelled via Pangani and Vuga, ending at Mombasa. His party included Mabruki Speke, Farjallah as cook, and other Livingstone veterans. As conditions there were disturbed, his thoughts turned to the Chaga country, which he considered would be a healthy spot for a new settlement, and he left Mombasa on 3 December 1874. Unfortunately Stanley had engaged the experienced men whom New had hoped to take, and his thirty-three followers proved unsatisfactory. There were some desertions, and the exactions and hostility of Mandara, when New reached Kilimanjaro, still further undermined their loyalty; two of his leading men intrigued with Mandara against him, and there were more desertions, so that he could count on only three men, among them Uledi 'the faithfullest of my faithfuls', and three Christian lads. He left at the end of January, seriously ill and was devotedly tended by Uledi, and his comrades. One of the Christians, William Chai, was sent to Wakefield for help, but New died on 14 February 1875, before reaching Rabai.[3]

Over the years an exaggerated idea of the ferocity of the Masai developed, probably fostered by traders such as Sadi who wished to keep possible rivals out of their own areas of profitable activity, but in the 1880s a number of caravans, with varied purposes, made their way to Kilimanjaro and beyond, and several headmen acquired a specialised knowledge which led to their engagement on more than one journey.

165

In June 1882 the Royal Geographical Society appointed Joseph Thomson to lead a new expedition to Lake Victoria through the Masai country and to Mount Kenya, as yet unvisited by a European. When accepting, he asked the Society to write to Zanzibar to request that Chuma and Makatubu should be paid a retaining fee, but on his arrival there in January 1883 he was faced with the news that Chuma, his trusted and experienced colleague, was dead.[4]

To replace him was difficult—Makatubu was hard-working, intelligent and loyal, but lacking powers of leadership, so he was appointed second-in-command, in charge of the goods. However, Manua Sera, 'short, and well up in years' was available, and was appointed leader. The result was something of a parallel to the relations between Cameron and Bombay—'He turned out as lazy and unprofitable a personage as could be well conceived, though, to give him his due, he was honest and intelligent . . .' He was content 'to be looked upon as purely ornamental, and was treated accordingly'.

With him came Kacheche, also somewhat of a disappointment, 'rather below the average in size, characterized by a sly expression'—he had strange ways but was put in charge of the commissariat and intelligence department, and was good at obtaining and distributing food. Brahim (Ali Ngombe), the tough, rollicking 'bully of the caravan and the idol of the men', a trouble-maker on Thomson's first expedition (see pp. 145, 150), was boldly promoted 'my aide-de-camp, my personal road assistant, and hunting companion. A more generally useful man I have never had, and I would not have exchanged him for any ten men in my caravan.' Mzee Uledi, a man with Arab blood, was a steady worker who, being handy with cloth, was made Makatubu's assistant, and completed 'as thoroughly good a set as I could have hit upon'. Thomson had one European colleague, the Maltese James Martin, an illiterate but resourceful ex-sailor whose acquaintance with several languages, local knowledge and general handiness, made him an invaluable subordinate.

The need for guards in the Masai country, and the possibility of having to check desertion under such circumstances, made it necessary to have a body of *askari*. Ten were appointed, 'all faithful men and true', who were placed under the giant Bedue, bold, but lazy. He and Brahim were courageous companions of Thomson on his many hunting excursions to feed the caravan. A Nasik boy, Mark Wellington, honest, but slow and stupid, as cook, and Songoro 'simply perfection as an up-country servant' completed the ranks of the main body of specialists.

Far less satisfactory were the *pagazi*, of whom there were one hundred and thirteen, plus a gun-bearer, two boys and a donkey boy. Thomson thought that coast men might be better in some ways than Zanzibaris, but that the latter would be more accustomed to Europeans. He himself

166

understood their ways, but the men he obtained were vastly different from the picked body of four years earlier. Other expeditions had recruited the good men and, in spite of offering an extra dollar a month, he could only obtain 'the very refuse of Zanzibar rascaldom . . .' On Barghash's orders they were taken to the palace to be registered; the Sultan imprisoned some as they had not received their masters' permission, and though they were released at the request of Colonel S. B. Miles, acting in Kirk's absence, several deserted.[5] As guide Thomson obtained, through Wakefield, an ivory trader named Muhinna with a valuable first-hand knowledge of Masai routes and language, but 'a cunning, unprepossessing expression'.

Apart from the problems of personnel, Thomson had cause for concern in the news he received at Zanzibar that the German explorer Gustav Fischer had already started for the Masai country. Fischer had initial problems in recruiting and retaining men at Pangani, but eventually assembled a caravan of 230 men by advancing them materials for barter in return for a share of their trading profits.[6] Thomson's caravan left Mombasa on 15 March, accompanied by thirty Taita to carry food as far as Ndara. The early stages of the journey emphasised Thomson's doubts about the quality of his men. Kacheche endeavoured to keep them together by telling them of the need for unity in the face of dangers ahead, but two deserted. It was an exhausting journey, water was scarce and the headmen had to help carry goods.

At Ndara Thomson, with Brahim and two Taita, climbed the Mrumunyi and then visited the CMS station. Here the Taita porters were paid off, but their discontent with the type of cloth supplied would have led to fighting with the Zanzibaris if Thomson had not intervened. The journey was resumed and on 31 March Taveta, with its pleasant woodland setting, was reached. Before leaving it, Thomson had to prepare his goods for what he learned were Masai requirements—the cloth sewn into garments called *naiberes*, and beads strung in uniform lengths. These tasks were allotted among the men, but soon beads began to vanish at an alarming rate, and Thomson ordered the sturdy Brahim to thrash two men from each mess, stopped rations and collected all guns to discourage desertion. The next day matters had improved.

Learning that the Masai were great talkers, Thomson engaged a second guide, the experienced Sadi ben Ahedi, once von der Decken's companion, hoping that his abilities—he was thought worth 15 dollars a month—would outweigh his dubious reputation. Accompanied by Muhinna and Brahim, he next visited Mandara and camped nearby. The journey had its share of frustrations. He attempted to climb Kilimanjaro, but did not reach the summit. Mandara, despite the efforts of Muhinna and Makatubu, skilfully contrived to extract valuable 'gifts' from his dwindling stores and Thomson was thankful to leave him

167

eventually. At Kibongoto he learned that the German explorer Gustav Fischer had been involved in a fight with the Masai in the area ahead. Initial contacts with the Masai, with Sadi and Muhinna as interpreters, seemed friendly; then, however, came news that they were up in arms seeking vengeance for the Fischer affray. Thomson suspected Sadi and Muhinna of stirring up trouble for their own ends, but could see no alternative to retreating, and the caravan was back at Taveta on 12 May.

Three days later Thomson set off to the coast to get reinforcements, leaving Martin in charge. He took Muhinna, Makatubu, Brahim, Bedue, Songoro, two *askari* and four porters. It was a rapid, gruelling journey; Thomson, with the faithful Songoro in attendance, set the pace, and in one march of twenty-two hours estimated that they covered seventy miles. In six days he arrived at Mombasa, a distance of about two hundred miles. He was unable to obtain a replacement for Muhinna and, after considerable trouble, could engage only sixty new men, of doubtful quality, chiefly from Mombasa and the missions at Rabai and Frere Town. He left on 19 June and was soon faced with a demand from the Rabai men for more pay or lighter loads, but he refused to entertain this request. When he reached Taveta, he found that Martin had kept all in good order, in spite of illness and shortage of food. Mandara had proved unexpectedly helpful over food supplies, and Kacheche had also been useful.

Thomson still distrusted Muhinna and Sadi and was relieved to meet a Swahili trader, Jumbe Kimameta, who was about to lead a caravan into Masai country round the north of Kilimanjaro. He was a little, pock-marked man, blind in one eye, but intelligent and apparently reliable, and Thomson was glad to give up his customary independent travel and join him for protection as far as Lake Naivasha. Before leaving on 17 July he weeded out the worst men and others deserted. He was left with 140 out of nearly 200 he had had in all.

The journey was resumed on 11 August. The early stages were marked by the usual disputes and threats. There was a fortnight's rest at Ngong, and when setting off again in late September, Thomson noted the improved capabilities and morale of his men. The route lay through Kikuyu country to Lake Naivasha. One night the Kikuyu raided the camp—Thomson, with 'my brave fellows' Brahim and Makatubu, rallied his men, but two of his porters were killed or captured. Not long after this lions attacked the caravan.

In the next couple of months Thomson let the trading caravan under Jumbe Kimameta pursue its slow course, while he made several forays of exploration, often with only a handful of followers. With Brahim, Songoro and two other picked men he climbed Mount Longonot. Later he ascended Eburru with eight of his men and a Masai guide, and attempted Mount Kenya. However, the exhaustion of supplies and the hostility of the Masai forced Thomson to abandon his intention of climbing it and he rejoined his main party under Martin near Lake Baringo.

Lake Victoria was now within reach, but the peoples of Kavirondo were said to be hostile and Muhinna would not go on. Thomson therefore weeded out 'the weak and sickly' and, leaving them under one of Stanley's men, set off on 16 November and reached Kwa Sundu, better known as Mumia's, on 3 December. Two days later he reduced his following again, to fifty, and left the rest in the charge of Makatubu. He went on to Lake Victoria but in the lakeside village of Massala had to resort to threats to recover stolen goods, and left without regret on 13 December. After collecting his men from Kwa Sundu, he made a detour to Mount Elgon. Near it, on 31 December, he was injured by a buffalo while hunting and had to be carried; he noted the willingness of his men to do this as an indication of improved morale.

On rejoining the men left at Lake Baringo he found that one had died, but the remainder were well. However, food was short and Makatubu was unable to gather sufficient supplies. The journey to the coast was overshadowed by much illness, two further deaths, and a serious attack of dysentery which compelled Thomson to stay at Mianzini where he was looked after by Martin and Songoro for six weeks. For a short time he again travelled in company with Jumbe Kimameta.

It was the last stage, and Thomson wrote of his porters that they 'worked like heroes', 'laughed at hardships' and 'were regenerated morally and physically'. Makatubu, in spite of his fiery temper, had worked well, and had saved one man from a buffalo's attack. The only loss on the final stage was the two last donkeys, apparently poisoned. Though there had been death and desertion, there had been no serious conflict and no bloodshed, and when Thomson reached the coast at the beginning of June he could look back on another successful achievement.

As Thomson came down to the coast, another caravan was going up-country; it was an expedition sponsored by the British Association and led by a young man named Harry Johnston who was to investigate the natural history of the Kilimanjaro area.[7] He had some thirty men from Zanzibar and others from Rabai. The latter proved to be lazy and incapable on the journey to Kilimanjaro and some deserted. The Zanzibar men indulged in 'noisy behaviour and continual squabbles' at Mombasa but otherwise gained Johnston's warm approval. On the Congo two years earlier he had been favourably impressed with the Zanzibaris and this expedition confirmed his view. 'As a rule the Zanzibar porters are faithful, trustworthy men—I have always found them so, and have even discovered very fine qualities in their nature too. At any rate, if they fall out with a white man it is generally his

169

fault; a very little discipline, together with a kind and quiet manner, will always keep them in order.' They lived on modest rations, were handy at hut-making and could 'plant gardens, make roads, trap animals, cure skins, construct bird-cages, wash clothes, mend them, make them, cook a dinner, and arrange a nosegay with equal facility.'

When they reached Moshi the coast men were intimidated by threats of the redoubtable Mandara, and Johnston was glad to pay them off; the Zanzibar men stood by him. He spent the next four months—June to September 1884—at Kitimbiriu, some two miles from Moshi, where Mandara allowed him to form a settlement.

He now had thirty-two men, including several Zanzibaris who had served with Stanley, and had engaged a headman named Ali Kiongwe, 'whose name means in Swahili a "headstrong jackass", and who was therefore politely called by his inferiors "Shaongwe".' He was about thirty, wore a ring indicating that he had been on Stanley's first Congo journey, and had latterly been in the service of the UMCA and CMS.[8] Johnston found him good-tempered and respectful, and 'if lenient to his own occasional dishonesty he watched well that no one else robbed me'. He proved a useful intermediary with Mandara and others. Second in command was Abdallah, who had also been on the Congo, a man of some learning and fastidious in his habits. Though 'rather a rogue', he 'was on the whole a very good fellow' and generally supervised the work of the Kitimbiriu settlement. He also undertook negotiations in Kiongwe's absence. Mabruki and his slave Athmani were engaged as natural history collectors, the former at a high wage since they had done this work for Fischer. Johnston found them idle, however, and they eventually left him to join Mandara whom they attempted to turn against their former employer. On the return journey Johnston met them taking slaves to the coast and since it had become illegal for a subject of Zanzibar to trade in slaves, was able to release their captives.

The cook, Ferrajji, was the veteran of the expeditions of Speke, Stanley and Cameron. He was 'a busy old man', the strongest in the caravan, satisfactory save for his housekeeping extravagances; his assistant Cephas was a Nasik boy, clever and adaptable. Johnston had a useful personal servant, David Virapan, a Roman Catholic Tamil, whom he had engaged at Aden. He was well-educated, spoke good English and other languages, and acquired some proficiency in natural history work.[9] Other reliable men were Ibrahim, 'the best man in the caravan', short, fat and good-tempered, in charge of constructing Johnston's house, and Kadu Stanley, the 'bright, willing' Ganda youth who had served with Stanley twice (see p. 155) and who was placed in charge of the garden.

While the settlement was being established, Johnston sent twenty men under Kiongwe to fetch the loads left behind by deserting porters;

on his return they ran into a party of local warriors in arms against Mandara but Kiongwe kept his head and, after sending two men on to warn Johnston, managed to avoid the enemy and arrived safely. He later successfully brought reinforcements from the coast and with their aid Johnston was able to leave Mandara's district at the end of September.

Johnston had been unable to reach the summit of Kilimanjaro from Mandara's territory. Now, leaving a small party at Taveta under Abdallah, who looked after the settlement well, and the rest of his party at Maranu, he attempted to climb Kilimanjaro with four local guides and three of his own men, but they were afraid to go on and, though he reached the ridge, he could not manage the summit. He continued his natural history work for a while, but conditions in high altitudes were bad for his men, and at the end of October he left and returned to Taveta by a different route.

Johnston paid off the majority of his men at Pangani, hoping to renew 'our journeyings and companionship', but because of illness and lack of funds he had to return to England. He had left four men at Taveta and they were paid off by Bishop Hannington of Eastern Equatorial Africa. James Hannington had been in Africa before; in 1882–83 he spent nearly a year as a member of the CMS Uganda mission but was invalided before reaching Buganda. He landed at Mombasa as Bishop on 24 January 1885 and visited Taveta in the course of his first journeys, on which his followers included some of Thomson's and Johnston's men.[10]

On 23 July he left Rabai for Buganda, and thought the Masai route preferable to the unhealthy southern area he had passed through in 1882. At one time he had contemplated travelling with Jumbe Kimameta, but decided that the latter's exploitation of superstition to give him a greater hold over his followers made him an unsuitable companion. The Bishop therefore took an independent caravan. His assistant was 'Fundi' Jones (see p. 137) who had returned to India for three years but had been back in Africa since 1881, and whom the Bishop had made deacon on 31 May. There were one hundred and six Muslims from Zanzibar and Mombasa, sixty-six men from Rabai and fifty-four from Kisauni. His six headmen included as principal Brahim (who had probably been with him in 1882) and Bedue, and there were six under-headmen.[11]

The journey was hampered by lack of food; the Kikuyu at first kept away out of fright, and when confidence was established with them, Hannington was hard put to it to keep the peace in the face of their persistent theft; Brahim opened fire on one occasion and was severely reprimanded. On 8 September there was an attack on his stragglers, but it was beaten off without loss. The Masai however were not hostile, though their lively curiosity proved something of a trial.

171

Hannington, a warm-hearted but impulsive man, somewhat given to over-emphasis, wrote in his diary of 'my wretched crew of head men' when they failed to prevent one porter decamping with the medicine chest. After losing his temper he found an improvement, but on the whole morale was bad, and he specifically referred to the 'shiftlessness of nearly all the Rabai and Frere Town men'. Brahim was rash and not always honest, but he showed courage in rescuing a gun from a hut fire and was a trusty hunting companion.

Kwa Sundu (Mumia's) was reached on 8 October 1885, and Hannington decided to go on to Lake Victoria with a reduced following. He left on 12 October with fifty men—twenty-six from Zanzibar, twelve from Frere Town, eleven from Rabai, and one lad from Kavirondo. Jones was left with a hundred and fifty-two men, including Bedue as leading headman.

On the 21st the Bishop reached Luba's, a village subject to the authority of Mwanga who had succeeded Mutesa as Kabaka of Buganda in 1884. His initial reception was unfriendly, and during the day, when walking with Brahim and some of his men in an attempt to catch a glimpse of the distant Nile, he was enticed apart from them, seized and bound. He was imprisoned, with his Goan cook Pinto, for a week in conditions of increasing wretchedness, then on the 29th, on orders received from Mwanga, was taken out of the village and, with Pinto, speared to death. The majority of his followers were then massacred, but three escaped and brought the news to Jones, waiting at Kwa Sundu. One further survivor arrived, but after waiting another month, Jones led the remainder back to the coast.

On 4 February the despondent caravan wound into the straggling settlement at Rabai, led by a *kirangozi* whose blue pennon (the colour of mourning) bore the word Ichabod in white letters. The porters were 'lean and weary, and travel-stained, clad for the most part in hides, for their clothes were worn out, and limping along by the sides of their kind friends who had relieved them of their loads'. 'Fundi' Jones, wearing a battered white helmet, brought up the rear and was greeted by the Rev. W. E. Taylor near the unfinished church. The Rev. J. Handford at Frere Town wrote, 'The manner in which Jones overcame all obstacles and dangers, and brought the caravan safely back is deserving of the highest praise.'[12]

In spite of the Bishop's murder the slaughter was not so great as was at first feared; a few men were not taken out with the rest, and at least ten younger ones were reprieved. Almass, the Bishop's boy, and Kikutu, his chairbearer, reached freedom together. Brahim, spared for his supposed skill in making guns, also escaped. Others settled in the village and were still there years later.[13]

A year after the death of Bishop Hannington, Count Samuel Teleki von Szek, a wealthy Hungarian nobleman, and Lt Ludwig von Hohnel, undertook a lavishly financed journey of sport and exploration. With nearly 500 loads to carry—including a steel boat in six sections requiring eighteen men, and a canvas boat—and some 300 firearms, a substantial caravan was required, and recruitment was speeded up when it became known that Stanley would soon be seeking men for an expedition to relieve Emin Pasha.[14]

Jumbe Kimameta had come to Zanzibar to clear up his debts, and was glad to accompany Teleki and Hohnel for 2,000 dollars. He arranged for the purchase of suitable goods for barter, and helped recruit porters, but had no direct responsibility for the caravan and was allowed to take some of his own followers to engage in trade. Hohnel found him 'a thoroughly good fellow'. Teleki enlisted eight Somalis on his outward journey, following Burton's advice to have a small personal escort from a race other than the rest of the caravan. The chief was Dualla Idris, now 24, elegantly dressed, intelligent, courageous and influential with the men. He had spent two more years, 1882–84, on the Congo where he had witnessed a number of the treaties Stanley made there in March and April 1884. More recently he had shown his organising ability and judgment in charge of the armed guard and camel transport of an expedition into the interior of Somaliland led by F. L. James.[15] 'He had a clear dark skin, almost black in parts; his eyes were jet black, and though their usual expression was earnest and penetrating, they often sparkled with merriment,' wrote Hohnel. He, like Jumbe Kimameta, proved a valuable negotiator during the journey. The other Somalis acted as personal servants or undertook general supervisory duties, particularly in maintaining discipline, and by the end of the journey 'became the most important portion of our followers'.

Hohnel had hoped to engage James Martin, but when he visited him at the country house provided for him by General Lloyd Mathews, the Commander of the Zanzibar Forces, under whom he had formerly served, found that he was already committed. However, he had with him some African veterans from whom Hohnel, if a little disillusioned by their unromantic appearance, engaged Manua Sera and Bedue. Manua Sera was the eldest of nine guides; he was paid 13 dollars a month and promptly demanded 19, but he overrated his indispensability and, when told he could go if dissatisfied, accepted the lower sum. Makatubu, paid at the same rate, occasionally displayed his fierce temper, but in Teleki's hunting expeditions which were a major feature of the expedition, he proved by his physique, resourcefulness and energy 'one of the most valuable men'. Bedue, too, despite occasional laziness, was a 'lynx-eyed' and courageous hunter, and his knowledge of the country from his service with Thomson was valuable. Other guides were Ali Schaongwe (presumably Johnston's Kiongwe) and Tom Charles

173

who, though very strong and scarred from brawling, proved too tender-hearted to inflict corporal punishment. He and Manua Sera had recently returned from a hunting trip up the Wami River with the sportsman Frederick Jackson.[16]

The cook was the apparently indispensable veteran, Mhogo Chungo, or Ferrajji. He was 'not what you would call a first-rate caterer for the table, but from long experience he was quite unrivalled in knowing how to manage in the wilds; he always carried his own cooking-apparatus, one of the heaviest of all the loads.'

Nine askari at from 6 to 9 dollars a month and two hundred Zanzibari porters at 5 dollars were also employed, and more recruits obtained on the mainland, to a total of about three hundred, including seven donkey men with twenty-five animals. Among those engaged were Almass Bischibu, whose name commemorated his former employment by Bishop Hannington, and some who had travelled with Fischer.

The first part of the journey from early February 1887 to February 1888 was over ground mostly covered by Fischer, Thomson and others. The pace was leisurely, partly to allow time for Teleki's hunting, and partly because of man-power problems. At Kwa Mgumi there was as unfortunate episode when a 'black Helen' was carried off from the village to the camp by old Manua Sera 'who acted the part of Paris and Achilles alike in the imbroglio', rousing the men of the expedition to resist the resentful villagers. Firing began, and there were fatal casualties on both sides before Teleki could intervene and end hostilities, but Manua Sera, though in the thick of the fight, was unhurt.

The expedition stopped at Taveta from the end of April to mid July, in a semi-permanent camp site, with huts and boundary hedge, laid out by Manua Sera and Makatubu. Here they met three English hunters, whose followers included James Martin, and Kacheche as headman of the Africans. Sir John Willoughby, leader of the party, thought the latter 'a wily old nigger with a foxy expression', was dishonest and stirred up discontent among the men.[17]

Various parties were sent out from Taveta—Makatubu and Ali Schaongwe took men to recover goods left at the coast; and Teleki and Hohnel, leaving Dualla in command, travelled to Mount Meru. On the homeward journey the donkeys and cattle were reluctant to cross the many streams. 'Our old guide, Manwa Sera, had behaved with such pluck and dexterity in the emergency that he had wiped out a long score we had against him.' An attempt to ascend Kilimanjaro, with four guides who had accompanied Johnston, was unsuccessful. At Taveta there was a quarrel between Dualla and Makatubu after which the latter and Manua Sera refused to participate in anything until an unsympathetic answer to a letter of complaint they had sent to the Sultan of Zanzibar was received, and they returned to duty.

174

The journey was resumed with local guides in July, and in Kikuyu country there were several skirmishes before blood brotherhood was made with a Kikuyu leader. Further expeditions, to Mount Kenya and the Guasu Nyoro River were undertaken before the whole caravan was reunited near Lake Baringo on 7 December. For three months they were based there, and Teleki went on many hunting excursions. During this time a long journey came to an end; early in 1888 Manua Sera, who in twenty-eight eventful years had accompanied Speke, Stanley, Livingstone, Thomson and others, died of tuberculosis, after some months of failing health. Ali Schaongwe was appointed senior guide in his place.

Others were also ill, there was extensive famine, and attempts by Makatubu and Dualla to obtain food were only partially successful, but Teleki and Hohnel were anxious to continue into unexplored territory to the north. Leaving some sick men, with animals and goods, under a reliable *askari*, they resumed the march on 9 February with 230 men, including local guides.

During the seven months before its return to Lake Baringo on 30 July, the expedition underwent great hardships, chiefly from shortage of water, and there were numerous deaths—at least thirteen in March alone. On 5 March, with the aid of a guide, Lembasso, they reached a large lake which Teleki named Lake Rudolf, after the crown prince of Austria–Hungary, but it was brackish and provided no answer to the problem of thirst. One waterhole was found by the head of the straggling caravan. 'As ever at critical times, Maktubu proved himself equal to the emergency', and 'as if hunger, thirst and fatigue were quite unknown to him', went back three or four times during the night to fetch men from the dried-up watercourse where three-quarters of the caravan were lingering in demoralised apathy. Once they had refreshed themselves, he sent them back for their loads until nearly all were assembled at one place.

Lembasso took them on to a second lake, which Teleki named Stefanie; here they turned back, and after experiencing local hostility, floods, desertions and smallpox they reached Lake Rudolf again. Lembasso was paid off, taking with him the most attractive of three Samburu women who had attached themselves to the caravan. After an excursion into Turkana country they reached Lake Baringo, and returned via Taveta to Rabai, where they arrived in October 1888.

Among the survivors was the Speke veteran Mhogo Chungo, though on one occasion his skill at fire-lighting failed, and 'patent lighting apparatus charged with petroleum' was used. In 1890 he was engaged at 11 dollars a month by Captain Frederick Lugard, to accompany him to Buganda for the Imperial British East Africa Company. Lugard wrote disgustedly that 'Mahogo' was 'a fraud and cannot cook a bit, and is lazy besides and consumes twice as much stuff as he should.' However he was 'a droll character . . . and it is very difficult to be angry with him.' In January 1891 he returned to the coast, and perhaps took a well-earned retirement. He had been accompanying caravans for more than thirty years.[18]

On their homeward journey Teleki and Hohnel called at Aden and met Dr Carl Peters, who was in the course of organising the second expedition for the relief of Emin Pasha. The first, and major, expedition was led by Stanley.

15

THE EMIN PASHA
RELIEF EXPEDITIONS

Stanley's Emin Pasha Relief Expedition marks the end of an era; it was not an exploration, but it was the last journey of a famous explorer; and it exemplified the changing pattern of European involvement in Africa. Emin Pasha, a German originally named Edward Schnitzer, had been Governor of Equatoria, a province of the Sudan under Egyptian rule, which included parts of what is now Uganda. Cut off by the Mahdi's forces after General Gordon's death in 1885, he had preserved a precarious independence, and as news of his survival became known, a combination of humanitarian, political and commercial motives resulted in the organisation of a relief expedition. Joseph Thomson offered to lead one by the Masai route, but the command was given to Stanley. He was still in the employ of King Leopold, who insisted that he should approach the beleaguered Emin via the Congo—where, it was pointed out, he had the advantage of river transport for much of the way. Stanley appointed a number of soldiers and civilians as his staff—at one time he had twelve—and left England in January 1887.[1]

As an escort, and to give credence to his claim to represent the Khedive, Stanley had sixty-one Sudanese soldiers, or Nubians as they were sometimes called, from Wadi Halfa. Thirteen Somalis were collected by Major Barttelot, the second-in-command, and joined at Aden on 12 February; and there were two Syrian interpreters. The main force of Zanzibaris was recruited by Edmund Mackenzie, of the firm of Smith, Mackenzie & Co., who was asked to obtain six hundred men and 'twenty young lads as officers' servants at lower rate than men'. Stanley arrived at Zanzibar on 22 February and left three days later. Frederic Holmwood, British Acting Consul General, wrote:

Mr. Stanley personally attended at the muster of the Zanzibar porters which took place before embarkation; a considerable number of these had served under him on former occasions and his immediate

177

recognition of them, accompanied in every instance with the recollection of their names, and generally of some little incident in connection with their former service, evidently afforded especial gratification; indeed this trait or gift which he eminently possesses, together with a practical knowledge of the Swahili language, would alone account for his undoubted popularity and great influence among his native followers.[2]

During his brief stay in Zanzibar, Stanley reached an agreement with Tippu Tip. The Arab trader had been a thorn in the flesh to the Congo Free State authorities, but Stanley now persuaded him to exercise his undoubted influence on behalf of the Free State and become Governor of Stanley Falls. Tippu Tip also agreed to supply Stanley with six hundred of his followers to act as porters for the ammunition being taken to Emin, once the end of navigable waters had been reached.

The expedition sailed on 25 February. Apart from the British officers, there were six hundred and twenty Zanzibaris, and sixty-one Sudanese, thirteen Somalis, two interpreters, and Baruti, a Busoko boy taken to London a few years earlier, who was brought out by Stanley and soon returned to his own people. Tippu Tip was accompanied by ninety-six of his followers including wives. After a journey via the Cape, Banana Point was reached on 18 March. The Africans were placed in companies under British officers—Barttelot had the Sudanese, Dr T. H. Parke, the medical officer, the Somalis and some Zanzibaris, the rest Zanzibaris alone. Towards the end of March, Herbert Ward, who was anxious to volunteer to join the expedition, met the long caravan, headed by a tall Sudanese soldier carrying Gordon Bennett's yacht flag.

Behind him and astride of a fine henna-stained mule, whose silver-plated trappings shone in the bright morning sun, was Mr. Henry M. Stanley, attired in his famous African costume. Following immediately in his rear were his personal servants, Somalis with their curious braided waistcoats and white robes; then came Zanzibaris with their blankets, water-bottles, ammunition belts and guns; stalwart Soudanese soldiery with dark hooded coats, their rifles on their backs, and innumerable straps and leather belts around their bodies. Zanzibari porters bearing iron-bound boxes of ammunition, to which were fastened axes and shovels, as well as their little bundles of clothing, which were rolled up in coarse sandy-colored blankets.

Working in relays and coping with various problems, including the varied availability and quality of boats, the expedition advanced eastward. By the end of June Stanley had reached the head of navigation

178

and decided to establish a rear camp at Yambuya, where two hundred and fifty-five men, including the sick, were to remain until Tippu Tip arrived with his porters. Most of the Sudanese and Somalis were left, and Barttelot was placed in command, with four other white men. Fifty-seven men had already been lost—at least twenty-two had died, others had been left sick or had deserted. Stanley went on to seek Emin with three hundred and eighty-three Africans and the rest of his British followers.

The advance party set off in good spirits—A. J. Mounteney Jephson, who was in charge of the steel boat, *Advance*, made in twelve sections, noted that his men were gaily dressed and were cheering and dancing, but this soon altered with the burden of carrying loads, and an attack by natives. The *Advance* and some canoes were used when water was available. More attacks with poisoned arrows resulted in casualties, and by 22 August sixteen men were dead and fifty-seven sick; another sixteen were killed and fourteen deserted between that time and 12 September. Though Stanley maintained his advance, this was only possible by leaving small depots of sick men under the somewhat uncertain care of the Arab rulers of the area, or in some cases under his own officers. As conditions allowed, the survivors of these batches were brought back to the main body. At the end of November Stanley and Jephson, with a force reduced to one hundred and seventy-five, emerged into open country after five months in the tropical forest. On 13 December they reached Lake Albert, but there was no news of Emin. There were no boats and little food, so Stanley turned back and established a base at Fort Bodo in which to collect his scattered men. He then returned to Lake Albert, and sent Jephson in the *Advance* to find Emin; he did so successfully, and Stanley and Emin met on 29 April 1888.

Emin proved to be not the soldier-administrator of popular legend, but a scientist whose administration had been kept together by his somewhat oriental skills. There seemed no prospect of his maintaining a strong military command even if the ammunition was brought up, and Stanley therefore assigned Jephson to him to travel round the province and ascertain the views of his Sudanese officers on the question of evacuation; meanwhile Stanley went back to Fort Bodo and thence to discover the fate of the rear-guard, from which no news had been received. He finally reached them at Banalya on 17 August, to discover that only William Bonny, a former medical orderly, was left of the officers; Barttelot was dead; and the other three had gone home—one, it was later learned, died on the way. Death and desertion had reduced the rearguard from two hundred and fifty to one hundred, and many of the survivors were very ill.

Gathering the pathetic remnant, Stanley again headed east; it was a nightmare journey with attacks, illness and demoralisation, and by the time he reached Fort Bodo on 17 December he had lost one hundred and six men by death, including Madi and Manyema carriers, and thirty-eight of the Rear Column survivors. In January he resumed his march, and rejoined Jephson and Emin in February only to learn that the Pasha's authority had collapsed, and he and Jephson had for a time been imprisoned by mutineers. The *Advance* had been abandoned.

Despite this, Emin still vacillated about evacuating Equatoria, and it was May before the march to the coast began. It was a straggling, ill-organised column, with 600 of Emin Pasha's men, women, children and servants; 230 of the expedition; and 680 carriers of various races. Many left in the course of the journey; there was much illness, but the remainder reached Bagamoyo on 4 December, among them 210 of the 708 who left Zanzibar nearly three years before. Stanley crossed to Zanzibar two days later and before going to Cairo paid off the survivors, with a bonus of 40 to 60 rupees each, and a banquet was given for them by General Lloyd Mathews. A special fund was set up for the widows and orphans of those who had perished.

The whole expedition was a hollow triumph for Stanley. Emin, a brilliant and dedicated scientist, had been temperamentally his opposite, they could not work together, and in the end Emin entered the service of the German government. Fierce controversy arose over the rear-guard, and Stanley was attacked for bad leadership, for cruelty, and for endeavouring to place the blame for what went wrong on men who were dead and could not defend themselves.

There seems no doubt, however, as to the qualities of courage and determination with which he encountered the hazards of the journey, and he in his turn paid tribute to his followers, not only the European officers but the Africans, especially the Zanzibaris. The Somalis were the smallest element, numerically and physically, brisker and more intelligent than the Sudanese. The Sudanese were tall and strong, but were generally regarded as sulky and bad tempered, refusing to carry more than their rifles, clothing and rations. They were devout Muslims. Both they and the Somalis suffered from ill-health on the Congo, and the majority of them were left with the rear-guard. In the later stages, therefore, there were only a few with the expedition; these included Sergeant Omar, who, though temporarily disrated for brawling with the Zanzibaris when drunk, was an excellent soldier and officer. Three accompanied Jephson on his mission with Emin—Abdullah, a young man who, though found stealing on one occasion, was very valuable to Jephson and the Pasha, and was promoted Sergeant; Bachit and Moorajan. Five of them rendered good service when crossing the Semliki against hostile natives, but Jephson thought them cowardly on the whole—'On every occasion our Soudanese have failed us.' Disputes between Sudanese and Zanzibaris began on board ship on the outward journey and continued, particularly in times of idleness, throughout the expedition. The Zanzibaris consisted of Rashid bin Omar, the sagacious and experienced 'father of the people', and twelve other headmen, paid from 6 to 14 dollars each, five hundred and eighty-seven men at 5 dollars including two stewards and three donkey boys, and twenty boys at 4 dollars. The nominal roll indicates that, in addition to a few well-known veterans, there were several experienced men. Kalfan Stanley and Kibza wadi Mazuk Stanley had obviously been with Stanley before. Songoro Storms bore the name of a Belgian IAA officer, and at least twenty had 'Balozi' (Consul) added to their names, indicating service with some European.[3] However, Stanley himself had not selected them, and he later considered that only about one hundred and fifty were free men, the rest being convicts or slaves. Slaves would receive, at most, half their wages, and suffered considerable deductions from their advance pay. As a result they lacked incentive and discipline, and indulged in looting early in the journey. They were a great contrast to the selected men who had accompanied Stanley in 1879, but though he admitted their faults, he resented criticisms from his own officers or from local missionaries, and Parke commented 'our chief is invariably predisposed to the black man'.

One great merit of the Zanzibaris was their adaptability. They had a knack of picking up languages and could turn their hands to needlework, tree felling, canoeing, or fighting, though they were poor shots. Dr Parke was very critical of their inadequacy as cooks, their lack of hygiene, and the demoralising effect that illness had upon them. They could be callous, but their discipline improved as the expedition continued, despite some lapses.

Mounteney Jephson modified his earlier criticisms, particularly in contrasting them with Emin's followers. In words recalling those of the UMCA missionaries about the Makololo, he wrote, 'The Zanzibaris are thieves & liars but they are hardworking & have that joyousness & childlike simplicity of character which redeems their bad qualities & one is forced to like them, though one swears at them often . . . a noisey, rollicking lot, excellent fellows . . .' They welcomed him warmly on his return from Emin and he wrote, 'hearing their nonsense & laughter all round the camp one felt what a satisfaction & pleasure it was to be again surrounded by faithful friends.' When one of the Sudanese officers threatened a Zanzibari Jephson declared they 'were not our slaves but out friends'. He learned with regret of some who had died in his absence and on his return to England paid tribute to them in *The Times*.[4]

Among the many accounts of the expedition references to some three hundred and twenty of the men can be found, but a few merit special

G

note. The outstanding man was Stanley's old coxswain, Uledi, who was normally one of Parke's chiefs and remained with him at Fort Bodo, but who was also detached for special duties. Apart from an early quarrel with Barttelot, he appears to have found favour with everyone for his determination and energy, his courage in fighting, and his scouting skill. He was of course excellent in canoeing and Jephson was gratified to have him in the *Advance* to meet Emin in April 1888. Emin had read of his earlier exploits and warmly welcomed him. Uledi also met Jephson when he returned from his journey with the Pasha and went with him on a diplomatic visit to the king of Karagwe.

In Karagwe Uledi was accompanied by Rashid and Murabo. The latter was another veteran of Stanley's trans-African journey (see pp. 117, 129), a somewhat flamboyant member of the *Advance* crew; on the journey to Emin he 'struck up one of the crooning but not inharmonious songs which the Zanzibar boatmen usually sing when rowing, and to which they keep time with their oars. He sang of the forest and the troubles we had gone through, of praise of our great chief, Bula Matari, of the miles we had marched . . .' He told Jephson that Stanley was 'half a white man & half an Arab', a description of the contrasting aspects of his character which Jephson thought very apt.

Another valuable man was Saat Tato, or 'Three o'clock', who had been a soldier in Madagascar and a Sergeant in the Zanzibar forces, but from his habit of being drunk by the hour of his nick-name, was discharged. He was 'faithful, strong, obedient, and an unerring shot', and was chiefly employed as a hunter, but also proved a valuable scout and an expert canoeist as well as something of a philosopher about the varying fortunes of caravan life. Towards the close of the expedition, he and Uledi swam the Semliki to obtain a canoe under arrow fire; Saat Tato was wounded, but recovered.

Two valuable personal servants were Sali and Binza. Sali, Stanley's servant, a Zanzibari, was most resourceful in obtaining information, an important quality in the closing stages, when intrigues among Emin's followers were widespread. He later accompanied Stanley to Cairo and London as a servant.[5] Binza, though engaged in Zanzibar, was a Niam-niam from the southern Sudan, formerly with Junker, the German explorer who had visited Emin, and accompanied Jephson to the Pasha. He was 'without any more profile than a currant bun has, his face however shows plainly he possesses the most humanizing of all influences—the capacity of laughter.'

Some men had varied experiences. Khamis Parry, a headman, had been with Livingstone and had travelled widely elsewhere, but not a great deal is recorded of him, and Mounteney Jephson wrote that he was 'a horrid fellow & is worse than useless for he is a bad example to the men'. Ward met a headman named Muni Hamese, or Uledi Pangana, who by his own account had been with his Arab master to Masai land, with Stanley to find Livingstone, on Livingstone's last journey, with Stanley across Africa and on the Congo, with the White Fathers, Carter's elephant expedition and on other journeys. He can be identified as one of Stanley's porters 1874–77, but one wonders if he was not regaling Ward with a selection of stories gathered from camp-fire yarns with other porters. A Sudanese sergeant with the rear-guard, Mousel Ali, had been with Baker and Gordon.[6]

Links with the past were also found in Ugarrowa, one of the powerful chiefs of the central African forests, whose savage rule brought suffering and destruction to the area. He was formerly known as Uledi Balyuz or the Consul's Uledi, and had deserted from Speke and Grant's expedition on 1 September 1862 (see p. 35). Stanley met him in September 1887 and somewhat reluctantly obtained his cooperation in looking after sick men and helping the expedition's progress.

Another survivor from the same expedition was Kyengo, the Nyamwezi 'doctor' who had met Speke and Grant in Usui in October 1861 and accompanied Grant from Karagwe to Buganda (see pp. 31, 33).[7] Now, a very old man, he had settled as a local chief in Karagwe. The expedition reached his village in August 1889; he was gratified to meet white men again and, wrote Jephson, 'he sat on & on in Stanleys tent talking of Speke & Grant & of his former friends among the white men, he was perfectly senile but he showed such pleasure in seeing us & talking about his former life that Stanley was loth to turn him out but let him run on repeating the same things again & again'—an interesting example of the gentle streak in Stanley's complex nature.

He could be a stern disciplinarian; on two occasions he hanged men for deserting with rifles, and he kept a firm hand on looting in the last stages; but he preferred to rule by consent and reproved his officers when they showed intolerance of the African viewpoint. Mounteney Jephson was cynical about the *shauris* or consultations he held with his chiefs—'another rubbishing Shauri', he wrote, and on another occasion, 'the "shauri" ended, as all "shauris" do, by everyone being brought round to Stanley's way of thinking', but the Zanzibaris undoubtedly gave loyal service under extremely hard conditions.

The Royal Geographical Society decided to make an award to the survivors of the expedition, and the issue of what were at first called 'silver crosses', and later 'stars', at seven shillings each was agreed in April 1890. Stairs supplied a list of those 'entitled to the name chief'— Raschid, Uledi, Murabo, Muini Pembe, Abdallah bin Juma, Saat Tato, Umari, Hatibu wadi Khamis, and Heri—and these were to have their names engraved on the star. A decision on other names was deferred for Stanley's views. It was a five-pointed star, about two inches across, with 'Emin Relief Expedition 1887–9' in a circle round a central design.

Stanley wrote to the RGS in Sali's name expressing 'his best thanks to the Royal Geographical Society for sending to him the high distinction of a silver star as a decoration for his fidelity . . .', and signed also 'Saleh bin Osman'.[8]

While Stanley was in the middle of Africa, a second Emin Pasha Relief Expedition, organised by a German Committee, and led by Dr Carl Peters, a zealous advocate of colonial expansion was making its way inland from the east coast. He set off from Shimbye, in the Sultanate of Witu, in June 1889 with sixteen camels, all of which died within six months, eight donkeys, eighty-five porters (numbers fluctuated), twelve Somali soldiers and four camel drivers, eight servants and Hamiri, a resourceful Lamu man as guide. His journey took him through Kikuyu and Masai country, across to Lake Victoria and thence to Buganda. In Buganda, Peters learned that Emin had left Equatoria with Stanley; he therefore turned his attention to attempting to secure German influence in Buganda, and in February signed a treaty with Mwanga. He travelled back to Bagamoyo, which he reached in July 1890; on the way he met Emin Pasha, who had entered German service and was returning to the interior of Africa—where, two years later, he was murdered.[9]

Peters, a courageous but ruthless man, had no time for conciliation, either with his followers or with the Africans he encountered. He criticised Stanley as weak and inefficient, and Thomson's conciliatory approach as 'clowning'. 'It is quite a mistaken motto of travellers, that in Africa one must learn patience,' he wrote. His policy in the face of any signs of hostility is summed up by his remarks about the Masai: 'I have found, after all, that the one thing that would make an impression on these wild sons of the steppe was a bullet from the repeater or the double-barrelled rifle.' This was exemplified in numerous skirmishes throughout his journey.

His own followers, too, were harshly treated. Porters who deserted were flogged or, on more than one occasion, indiscriminately shot, and those he thought might do so were chained. He scornfully rejected *shauris* apart from a preliminary one in which he laid down the law though he did have one conference with the Somalis. Nevertheless, his followers as a whole gave him good support; in spite of his superior fire-power, he was usually heavily outnumbered in fighting, and depended on the loyalty and cohesion of his small force. His main reliance was on the Somalis, led by Hussein Fara, both for fighting and for maintaining his authority over the porters (whom the Somalis despised).

Peters' activities, diplomatic and military alike, were fruitless, however, for in July 1890 Germany recognised that Buganda was within the British sphere of influence.

16

THE END OF AN ERA

By the early 1890s great changes had come to east Africa. A series of European diplomatic agreements, notably the Berlin Conference of 1884–85 and the Anglo-German agreement of 1890, had defined spheres of influence on the mainland, with Zanzibar's suzerainty limited to a ten-mile coastal strip; and in any case Zanzibar became a British Protectorate in 1890.

On the mainland, the British sphere in the north, extending to the Juba River, where the Italian sphere began, was at first administered by the Imperial British East Africa Company, which received its charter in 1888, but owing to financial difficulties it relinquished this responsibility to the British Protectorates which were proclaimed over Uganda and British East Africa in 1894 and 1895. A German East Africa Company, with Carl Peters as a prime mover, had begun work in the southern area, but after German imperial troops had to be brought in to crush the rising by Bushiri in 1888 (see p. 162), the German Government took direct responsibility for the territory in 1890.

Thus, during the late 1880s and throughout the 1890s there was an influx of Europeans other than explorers and missionaries—administrators, soldiers, traders. One major problem was that of transport; administration was difficult without some form of reliable communication, and an estimated cost of £250 a ton for goods brought to the coast made most commerce with the interior uneconomical. The IBEA Co had tried donkeys and camels as pack animals, ox-carts, a steamer for the Tana and Juba rivers, and even a tramway—'the Central African Railway'—but all these proved ineffective and strengthened the growing demand for a railway. In 1891–92 a survey was carried out by a team of RE officers, but construction did not begin until 1895 and it was the end of 1901 before the permanent way reached Lake Victoria. In the mid 1890s the Germans carried out a substantial roadbuilding programme, and in 1893 began a railway.

Meanwhile existing routes to the interior were followed, the main one for the IBEA Co being from Mombasa via Tsavo, Machakos (which

185

rapidly grew in importance), Fort Smith, and thence by Mumia's, which also developed as a staging centre to Uganda. However, in September 1891 Sir Gerald Portal, the British Diplomatic Agent and Consul-General in Zanzibar, noted with concern that since 1 June the Company had engaged 1,300 Zanzibari porters, over 500 more had gone on other expeditions, there was a continuing demand from the Congo, and even possible recruitment for south Africa. As a result, Zanzibar was suffering from a shortage of man-power, and on 11 September the Sultan issued a decree forbidding 'all recruitment or enlistment of soldiers, coolies, and porters for service beyond His Highness' dominions'. The main source of porterage in the British sphere then became Mombasa, but more than half of the 1,100 men belonging there were habitually employed in the stations of the interior of the protectorates. Rabai had some 1,000 men, but being partly engaged in agriculture, they were not always available, and in any case would not engage for service in the interior, or travel beyond Kikuyu. Taita porters were used to take goods from the neighbourhood of Ndi to the coast, but they too were seasonal owing to the agricultural needs of their community. Much material was therefore carried through the German sphere, where the experienced Nyamwezi were to be found. Regulations regarding the employment conditions, wages, punishments, and welfare of the porters were drawn up in October 1894 by Sir Lloyd Mathews, who had become the Sultan's First Minister in 1891, and new regulations introduced in May 1896 were made more comprehensive six years later.[1]

Even after the construction of railways, human porterage continued to be essential. The demand for men reached its climax in the Great War of 1914–18, when hundreds of thousands of porters were used on both sides during the protracted campaign between Allied and German troops, and in which very heavy casualties were incurred.[2] It was not until the 1920s that mechanical transport and improved roads rendered large-scale porterage obsolete.

In the expansion of activities from the late 1880s experienced traders such as Charles Stokes, with his reputation for fair dealing with all races and his team of trusted African headmen; caravan leaders like James Martin; and veteran Arab and Swahili travellers including Jumbe Kimameta, played a very important part. European newcomers competed for the services of experienced men since reliable headmen could be a great source of strength, though on occasions they proved to be unscrupulous agents. The earlier generation of leaders had died or retired, but there were still many with a well-earned reputation. On the Uganda Railway survey, for instance, Stanley's boy Sali was engaged as interpreter, and another boy from the Emin Pasha relief expedition was employed as a servant. When Captain Stairs led an expedition to

186

Katanga in 1891–92 with two hundred and twenty Zanzibaris and one hundred and sixteen from Mombasa, his followers included Bedue—who was not very satisfactory—and the reliable Hamadi bin Mallum, a Stanley veteran. F. J. Jackson, leading the first IBEA caravan to Uganda in 1889 had as his headman Makatubu, who had also been with him on an earlier hunting trip to Africa. He also had the veteran Tom Charles, as well as others who had been with Teleki. The Germans, too, were glad of experienced men; Oscar Baumann, in his journeys in 1891–93 had some two hundred men from Bagamoyo, Tanga, Sadani and elsewhere, as well as some Sudanese soldiers, and particularly noted the eleven men with previous experience of travel with Europeans.[3]

An interesting episode relates to Kadu, the Ganda who, as a youth, had beaten his drum at the head of Stanley's expedition in 1875 (see pp. 155, 170). As a man, he worked for a time for the Germans at Unyanyembe, and on his return to the coast in 1892 wrote indignantly to the British Consul General in Zanzibar complaining that Africans under British protection were keeping slaves '. . . and their behaviour to them is shameful even to describe here'. The German authorities professed themselves unable to act without British approval, and he urged that this be given: 'I do hope and pray that by your means and power the slaves of British protected persons there will be relieved from bondage.'[4]

One of the most important men of this period was Dualla Idris. He was engaged by Captain Frederick Lugard in the summer of 1890, when he was appointed as administrator for the IBEA Co in Uganda. Lugard had about 350 men, including three or four who had been with Teleki; Shukri Aga, one of Emin Pasha's former officers, and a number of Somalis whom Lugard would not allow to enjoy the superior status they had been granted and came to expect as a right. Lugard found Dualla who remained with him for two eventful years, 'invaluable'. His short-comings became apparent early; he had 'a detestable manner with the men and is hated by them'. Lugard had strong views about humanity in caravan leadership and endeavoured to avoid flogging. Dualla had been given too free a hand by previous employers, who in any case had different standards, but Lugard made it clear that his methods must change.

Dualla, though courageous, did not always keep his head in a crisis, and other faults were also to appear, but his merits far outweighed these shortcomings. His knowledge of English, Arabic, Somali, Swahili, Masai and other tongues made him a valuable interpreter and his wide experience enabled him to conduct negotiations with Kabaka Mwanga, his Muslim uncle Mbogo and others. He showed courage in the fighting of January 1892 and was promoted to 'sole superintendent of all outdoor work' in March. Not only was he efficient but Lugard found him an interesting companion, talking of his past career over the cups of tea and coffee they took together, or giving his opinions on current matters. Indeed, Lugard would have left him in a position of authority in Buganda, but illness and bad news from home, persuaded him to accompany Lugard to the coast in summer 1892.[5]

Valuable service was given to Harry Johnston by a former employee. In 1889 he was appointed Consul to Portuguese East Africa, with the special task of travelling into the interior and making treaties of friendship with rulers outside the existing spheres of European influence—a task that resulted in the foundation of the British Central African Protectorate, of which he became Commissioner in 1891. On his outward journey, at Zanzibar, he re-engaged Ali Kiongwe who remained with him until 1896. He proved 'really invaluable' for gaining information; acted as envoy to the Jumbe of Kotakota; was sent with a caravan to join A. J. Swann in 1890 when he made treaties at the north end of Lake Tanganyika; and became a Sergeant-Major in the Central African Rifles. When Johnston went to Uganda as Special Commissioner in 1899 he again took Ali Kiongwe. He received a pension for his military service and drew it until 1928, when presumably he died.[6]

A secure old age was also enjoyed by some others. The Livingstone veteran Tom Peter Sudi, after his experience of enslavement on the mainland (see pp. 135-36), probably decided to stay in the security of Zanzibar. In December 1907, the fiftieth anniversary of Livingstone's address at Cambridge calling for missionary work in Africa was celebrated. An 'At Home' was held at Kiungani and, 'After tea the Bishop brought forward Tom Peter Sudi, the Kiungani gardener, and said, "Here is one of the men who saw Livingstone die and helped to embalm the body and brought it down to the coast." There was an enormous sensation.' The Bishop also introduced Robert Feruzi, then working on a Government plantation in Pemba, as one of the two survivors of the original five boys baptised by Bishop Tozer. Tom helped Miss Thackeray to plant a commemorative coconut tree in the Bishop's garden. Robert Feruzi died in 1910.[7]

Not all former porters were so fortunate, and indeed memories were fading. After the death of Carus Farrar, his son sold his medal, in 1906, to a government official, but when, seven years later, the purchaser wrote to the Royal Geographical Society asking about the award, the Secretary was unable to find any significant information on it.

The welfare of those who were past work and—perhaps through their own improvidence—ended their days in poverty, caused concern to some. Sir Lloyd Mathews had tried to establish a fund to purchase shambas to which they could retire, but no permanent plan had been made by the time of his death in 1901. At his suggestion, however,

F. G. Hall established a small colony at Fort Smith, where Billali Stanley, among others, ended his days; but there were many, such as Tom Charles, who died penniless. Sir Frederick Jackson tried to help, and when Jumbe Kimameta was old and destitute, he found ways of assisting him.[8]

The last survivor of the Livingstone era was Matthew Wellington, one of the Nasik boys who had gone up from the coast in 1872. He entered the service of the IBEA Company, and later was employed in the Public Works Department of the Protectorate. When he retired in 1911, after sixteen years, Governor Girouard suggested that he should be given a pension of 20 rupees a month in recognition of his link with Livingstone. The Treasury refused because this took place before he entered Government service, and he was entitled only to a £16 gratuity. The Colonial Office tried to find a precedent to justify payment, but without success, and one official minuted 'Frankly disgusting'.

From time to time well-wishers raised small sums to aid him, and in 1929 the British press raised the question of a pension, without result. His reminiscences were edited by W. J. Rampley and published as *Matthew Wellington: Sole surviving link with Dr. Livingstone* (1930). He died on 6 June 1935, aged nearly ninety. Towards the end of his life he was taken to see a film on Livingstone at a cinema in Mombasa. He appeared unmoved by it until the close, but when Livingstone knelt by his bed in the hut in which he died, Matthew rose to his feet and cried out 'Bwana! Bwana!'[9]

Matthew was the last link with Livingstone, and also with the generation of Africans without whom the exploration of east Africa would have been impossible. Those who gathered round the camp fires on the evening of the day in October 1873 when Livingstone's body was carried into Unyanyembe included men who had been on every significant expedition of the previous fifteen years, and many who had major journeys still ahead of them.

Bombay saw the great lakes of east Africa, went with Stanley to find Livingstone, and crossed the continent from east to west, in journeys that must have totalled more than 12,000 miles. His stolid comrade Mabruki Speke accompanied him on his first two journeys, saw von der Decken murdered, assisted Stanley quell a mutiny, and helped bring Livingstone's body to the coast, before dying on the shores of Lake Victoria. Susi, who had crossed the Indian Ocean with Livingstone, carried the dying missionary through the swamps of Lake Bangweolo. He knew praise and rejection, and chose the site of an African capital, now Kinshasha, before ending his days as an honoured stalwart of the Universities' Mission. Chuma, in his short life, gave Livingstone a sometimes erratic loyalty, but his lively extrovert personality and powers of leadership provided staunch support to the missionaries and to Joseph Thomson. Resourceful Manua Sera, with a keen eye to his own advantage, nevertheless proved a courageous if sometimes exasperating caravan leader and guide for nearly thirty years.

The skill, endurance, and resourcefulness of these men and their comrades was essential to the success of the expeditions that penetrated the continent; and, at its best, the cooperation between European and African on these journeys marked the beginning of a transition from the age of slavery to the age of partnership.

WHO'S WHO OF AFRICANS

This list includes the names of the eighteen men who were awarded medals by the Royal Geographical Society for Speke's expedition 1860–63, shown by +, and the sixty for whom medals were issued for Livingstone's last journey, shown by *. Many of the latter never received the award but those who did are indicated by M followed by the date. There are also entries for all the Nasik boys on Livingstone's last journey, and for a number of other Africans who played a significant part in exploration, especially those who served on more than one expedition.

The order is alphabetical by the most frequently used form of name, with a few cross references. Spellings vary from one account to another, and there must be an occasional doubt as to the correctness of some identifications, but most of the names included are well authenticated. Some variant or alternative names are given in brackets. Dates of birth are very approximate, and based on estimates of age given by explorers.

Sources include nominal rolls of Cameron and Keith Johnston in the Royal Geographical Society, of Stanley's Emin Pasha Expedition in the Royal Commonwealth Society, and published lists in Speke's *Journal of the Discovery of the Source of the Nile*, 614–16, and Stanley's *Through the Dark Continent*, 510–15, as well as a great many scattered references. The details of Speke's followers in 1871 come from Stanley's *How I found Livingstone*, 27–29. The Livingstone medal recipients are set out in the 1874 Pay Roll T1/7426A, PRO, and in a list prepared by C. B. Euan Smith, 20 August 1875, in the Royal Geographical Society. There are some corrupt spellings, and a few minor ambiguities in these. There is no authoritative nominal roll of the Nasik boys who accompanied Livingstone in 1866, and they have therefore been listed under the name normally used by him.

ABRAHAM (PEREIRA?) Nasik school. Livingstone 1866–70. Deserted 1870. At Unyanyembe 1872.

*ALI BIN FALUMI 1870 relief expedition to Livingstone; last journey. Stanley 1874–75. Killed in battle Vinyata 25 Jan. 1875.

*AMODA (HAMOYDAH) From Shupanga. Livingstone 1863–64; to India on *Lady Nyassa*. India 1864–65. Livingstone 1866–74. Stanley 1874–76

191

(chief; crew of *Lady Alice*, Lake Victoria). m. Halima. d. 29 Jan. 1876, Bwera, Buganda.

*ANAMURI (BWANA AMURI)   To Livingstone 1872; last journey. Stanley 1874–76. Deserted Feb. 1876.

ANDREW MNUBI   Nyamwezi. b. c1855. UMCA pupil Zan. Stanley 1874–76. CMS Unyanyembe & Mpwapwa, and with Wakefield, 1877–79. Thomson 1879–80. CMS Frere Town 1888.

ANDREW (POWELL?)   Nasik school. Livingstone 1866. Deserted at Mataka's 4 Sep. 1866.

ASMANI   Guide from Unyanyembe. Stanley 1871–72 (carried flag). Livingstone 1872–73. Cameron 1873–74.

BARAKA   Freed slave. Served in RN, Multan 1849. British Consul's boat crew, Zan. Speke 1860–62 (commander-in-chief). To Bunyoro 1862. Imprisoned Zan. for inciting desertion 1864.

BARAKA (ALBERT?)   Nasik school. Livingstone 1866–67. Deserted 1 May 1867.

*BARAKA WADI AMBARI   Stanley 1871–72. To Livingstone 1872; last journey. Stanley 1874–75. Killed in battle Vinyata 25 Jan. 1875.

+BARUTI   Yao. Gardener of Majid; Speke 1860–63. Stanley 1871. d. 5 Sep. 1871 of smallpox, Unyanyembe.

BEDUE BIN AMBARI   From Zan. Thomson 1879–80. Thomson 1883–84 (captain of askari). Hannington 1885. Teleki & Hohnel 1887–88 (guide). Stairs 1891–92.

*BILLALI   Stanley 1871–72. To Livingstone 1872; last journey. At Kilwa 1875.

BILLALI STANLEY   Stanley 1874–77 (gunbearer). Sparhawk's servant, Zan. 1878. Macdonald's gunbearer 1892. Later with Jackson. d. at Fort Smith.

*BIN KHAMEES   Recruited by Livingstone, Unyanyembe Aug. 1872; last journey. Whereabouts unknown Aug. 1875.

+BOMBAY   Yao. b. c1820. Seized as slave; sold at Kilwa. Taken to India by master and released on his death. In Baluchi guard of Sultan of Zan. Burton 1857–59. Speke 1860–63 (caravan leader). Stanley 1871–72. Cameron 1873–76. CMS 1876. Awarded RGS pension 1876. Numerous wives. d. 12 Oct. 1885.

BRAHIM (ALI NGOMBE)   Yao. Thomson 1879–80. Hannington 1882. Thomson 1883–84 (headman). Hannington 1885 (headman). Captured but later escaped.

*BUKHET   To Livingstone 1872; last journey. Stanley 1874–77. M 3 Dec. 1877.

*CHANDA   From Maroro. Stanley 1871–72. To Livingstone 1872; last journey. At Unyanyembe 1875.

*CHANGETTI   Recruited by Livingstone, Unyanyembe Aug. 1872; last journey. Stanley 1874–77. d. Oct. 1877, HMS *Industry*.

CHARLES, TOM   Jackson 1885–86. Teleki 1887–88. Jackson 1889 onwards. In charge of *Ngambo* quarter, Zan. d. 1910, Mombasa.

*CHOWPEREH   b. c1840. From Bagamoyo. Stanley 1871–72. To Livingstone 1872; last journey (head of department: name on Livingstone tree).

192

Stanley 1874–77. M 3 Dec. 1877. Stanley 1882 onwards. m. (2nd time) 12 Nov. 1875.

*CHUMA, JAMES Yao. b. c1850. Slave released 17 July 1861. UMCA 1861–64; to India on *Lady Nyassa*. Dr Wilson's school Bombay 1864–65. Baptised 10 Dec. 1865. Livingstone 1865–74. M 17 Aug. 1875. UMCA 1875–78. Thomson 1879–80. Phipson-Wybrants 1880. Thomson, Rovuma 1881. m. Ntaoeka 3 June 1872 (d. 1880); m. Salima binti Sitakishauri. d. 1882 Zan. (will 25 Sep.).

DALLINGTON SCOPION MAFTAA b. c1860. Released from slavery 1868. UMCA Zan. Stanley 1874–75. Scripture Reader and scribe to Mutesa 1875–81. *Kitongole* chieftainship of Mutezi Nov. 1881.

DUALLA IDRIS Somali from Habr-Anwal; son of police chief. Visited America as boy. Stanley 1879–84. James' Somaliland journey 1884–85 (headman). Teleki 1886–88 (headman). With American sportsmen 1889. Lugard 1890–92 (interpreter & confidential assistant). Drowned off Somaliland (according to H. H. Johnston).

†FARHAN From L. Tanganyika. Slave of Sirboko, released at Speke's request. Speke 1861–63. At Ujiji 1871.

*FARHAN (FEREHAN) WADI BARAKA To Livingstone 1872; last journey. Stanley 1874–77. M 3 Dec. 1877.

*FARJALLAH CHRISTIE Servant to Dr Christie, Zan. To Livingstone 1872; last journey (removed Livingstone's heart). New 1874. Stanley 1874–75. Killed in battle, Vinyata, 24 Jan. 1875.

*FARRAR, CARUS Yao. Nasik school. To Livingstone 1872; last journey (wrote account). India 1874–75. CMS Mombasa 1875. M 24 Sep. 1875. Frere Town 1876 (general shop). Kisulutini 1881 (elder). Shimba (i/c CMS settlement) in 1888. Dead by 1906.

FERRAJJI (MHOGO CHUNGO) Said by Stanley to be 'a runaway of Speke's' but not clearly identified. Stanley 1871–72. Cameron 1873–76. Johnston 1884. Teleki 1887–88. Lugard 1890–91. (Cook in all save Cameron's expedition).

FERUZI, ROBERT From Nyasa. b. c1850. Freed slave at UMCA, Zan., 1864. UMCA journeys 1868–70. Cameron 1873. Stanley 1874–77. UMCA 1878–79. Stanley 1879–82. UMCA caravan leader 1884–1910. m. Caroline Hasina—after her death, m. again in 1886. d. 1910.

†FRIJ Freed slave. Former sailor, widely travelled. Speke 1860–63 (Grant's head servant). Dead by 1871 (but may be identifiable with Ferrajji, q.v.).

*GARDNER, EDWARD Nasik school. Livingstone 1866–74. Stanley 1874–75. d. 14 Feb. 1875, Camp Gardner, of typhoid.

*HAMADI From Unyamwezi. Stanley 1871–72. To Livingstone 1872; last journey. Stanley 1874–77; seized by villagers at Kibonda for theft July 1877, but escaped. Stanley 1879 onwards.

*HAMADI WADI ALI To Livingstone 1872; last journey. Stanley 1874–77. M 3 Dec. 1877.

*HAMEES *See* Shumari and Thomas.

*HASSAN WADI SAFENI. With Muhammad bin Gharib, Manyema, c1868. Engaged by Livingstone 24 July 1872; last journey. Stanley 1874–77

193

(chief; coxswain of *Lady Alice*); lost, insane July 1877. m. Muscati (d. 26 Nov. 1877, Zan.).

*HASSANI To Livingstone 1872; last journey. M 17 Aug. 1875.

+ILMAS Freed slave. Speke 1860–63 (cook to Speke). Dead by 1871.

ISENBERG, RICHARD Nasik school. Livingstone 1866. d. June 1866, Liponde.

JONES, WILLIAM HENRY (FUNDI) Freed slave. In Bombay 1854; to Nasik 1861; trained as blacksmith. To Rebmann at Mombasa 1864. With wife, Jemima, with UMCA Zan. 1867–69. CMS, including visits to India to bring Africans to Frere Town 1869–78. India 1878–81. E. Africa 1881–1904. Deacon (Bp Hannington) 31 May 1885. Hannington 1885. Priest (Bp Tucker) 20 Jan. 1895. d. 4 July 1904, Mombasa.

JUMA WADI NASIB (JUMA BIN NASIBU) In British Consular service Zan. Cameron 1873–76 (personal servant). LMS Mission 1876–85 onwards ('factotum' to Roger Price; journeys to and from Ujiji; sole charge of mission there 1881–83).

*JUMAH Freed slave. Stanley 1871–72. To Livingstone 1872; last journey. M 17 Aug. 1875.

JUMBE KIMAMETA Swahili trader, particularly in Masai country. With Thomson 1883–84. Teleki 1887–88.

*KABUREYA Recruited by Livingstone 1872; last journey. At Unyanyembe, Aug. 1875.

KACHECHE *See* Sarmean.

KADU STANLEY Ganda, former page of Mutesa. Stanley 1875–77 (drummer). Stanley 1879–82. Johnston 1884 (gardener). In German service, Unyanyembe 1892.

*KAIF HALLECK (SUEDI KEF HALEK in medal roll) Letter carrier in relief party sent to Livingstone by Churchill, Nov. 1870. Reached him with Stanley 1871; last journey. Stanley 1874–75. Ambushed and murdered 21 Jan. 1875, Isanjeh.

KALULU (NDUGU M'HALI) Boy slave from Londa, presented to Stanley Unyanyembe 7 Sep. 1871. Stanley 1871–72 and to England and USA with him. School at Wandsworth 1873–74. Stanley 1874–77. Drowned Kalulu Falls, 28 Mar. 1877.

KHAMIS PARRI Said to have been with Livingstone; is perhaps Khamisi, q.v. Stanley 1887–89.

*KHAMISI Stanley 1871–72. To Livingstone 1872; last journey. Stanley 1874 onwards, but fate unknown.

*KHAMSEEN To Livingstone 1872; last journey. Stanley 1874–76; sent to Unyanyembe 1876. Reached Zan. & M 4 Nov. 1879.

+KHAMSIN Slave of Majid. Speke 1860–63. In Kilwa 1871.

*KHATIBU WADI REHANI To Livingstone 1872; last journey. Stanley 1874–77 (storekeeper). M 3 Dec. 1877. Stanley 1879–82 (quartermaster). m. Nampa.

KIONGWE (SCHAONGWE), ALI Swahili. b. c1854. Stanley 1874–77. Mission service. Johnston 1884. With Johnston in British Central Africa 1889–96 (Sgt, BCA Rifles). With Johnston in Uganda 1899–1901. d. c1928.

*KIRANGO (ROJAB) Stanley 1871–72. To Livingstone 1872; last journey. Stanley 1874–77. M 3 Dec. 1877. m. Binti Sumari.

KYENGO Nyamwezi 'doctor'. Travelled with Speke and Grant 1861–62. Chief in Kafurro, Karagwe in 1889.

*MABRUKI Nasik school; possibly known as Nathaniel Cumba. Livingstone 1866–74. M 17 Aug. 1875.

MABRUKI MAJERA Makua from Mzomba enslaved as boy. Served on a man-of-war. Thomson 1883–84. Johnston 1884. With Henry & Foljambe, hunting 1885. Jackson's service 1885–99. Later government storekeeper.

*+MABRUKI SPEKE Slave in Zan., protégé of Bombay. Burton 1857–59. Speke 1860–63. Von der Decken 1865. Commanded coasting vessel for Capt. Fraser, Zan. Stanley 1871–72. To Livingstone 1872; last journey. New 1874. Stanley 1874–5. m. Hadeeya. d. cApr. 1875, Kageyi.

*MABRUKI UNYANYEMBE Stanley 1871–72. To Livingstone 1872; last journey. Stanley 1874 onwards (chief). Deserted.

*MAFTA Recruited by Livingstone 1872; last journey. At Unyanyembe Aug. 1875.

*MAGANGA Stanley 1871–72. To Livingstone 1872; last journey. With Arab traders Aug. 1875. (Probably not the laggard caravan leader whom Stanley met in the interior in May 1876.)

*MAGOWA To Livingstone 1872; last journey. Stanley 1874 onwards. Deserted.

*MAJWARA b. c1857; son of Namujulirwa Pokino. Stanley 1871–72. To Livingstone 1872; last journey (personal servant who found Livingstone dead). Stanley 1874–77. M 3 Dec. 1877. Servant to Sparhawk, Zan. 1878. CMS Mpwapwa 1878–81. m. Tuma-leo. LMS Urambo; drowned in Lake Tanganyika Oct. 1886.

MAKATUBU WADI SONGARO From Nyasa. Thomson 1879–80 (storekeeper; given sword by RGS). Phipson-Wybrants, Sabi River 1880. Thomson, Rovuma, 1881. Thomson 1883–84 (second-in-command). Harvey & Foljambe, hunting, 1885. F. Jackson 1885. Teleki 1887–88. Jackson to Buganda 1889 and with Jackson to 1902. d. 1906, sleeping sickness.

+MANUA Nyamwezi. A twin, widely travelled. Speke 1861–63. Probably returned to trade in Unyamwezi. Reported dead by 1871.

*MANUA SERA (ULEDI) Probably Uledi, freed slave, with Speke 1860–62, sent to Bunyoro 1862. Stanley 1871–72 (caravan leader). To Livingstone 1872 (headman); last journey (head of department; name on Livingstone tree). Stanley 1874–77 (chief captain). M 3 Dec. 1877. CMS 1881. Thomson 1883–84. Jackson 1885–86. Teleki 1887–88. m. Bibi Mse. d. cJan. 1888 of tuberculosis, Lake Baringo.

*MARIKO To Livingstone 1872; last journey. With Arab traders Aug. 1875.

*MASANJI Recruited by Livingstone 1872; last journey. At Unyanyembe Aug. 1875.

+MATAGIRI Recruited on mainland; Speke 1861–63. Possibly enlisted in Egyptian Army as Selim, and in Sudan and Buganda with Baker and Long 1873–74.

+MEKTUB   Slave of Majid. Speke 1860–63. Dead by 1871.

*MGUIZI   Recruited by Livingstone 1872; last journey. M 17 Aug. 1875.

MHOGO CHUNGO   *See* Ferrajji.

+MKATE   Slave of Majid. Speke 1860–63 (potboy). Dead by 1871.

+MTAMANI   Recruited on mainland; Speke 1861–63. In Unyanyembe 1871.

*MTARU   Recruited by Livingstone 1872; last journey. Stanley 1874 onwards. Deserted.

*MUCCADUM or MANA KOKO   From Unyanyembe. Stanley 1871–72. To Livingstone 1872; last journey. Stanley 1874–77. M (Makhadan) 3 Dec. 1877. m. Binti Zawangi.

MUHINNA   From Pangani. Experienced trader in Masai country. With Thomson 1883–84 as guide. Influence at Machakos hostile to IBEA Co 1889.

MUINI HAMESE (ULEDI PANGANA)   Stanley 1874–77. Stanley 1886 onwards. According to his own account, also with Stanley 1871–72, Livingstone 1872–74 and numerous other journeys.

MUINI PEMBE   Stanley 1874–77 (chief). Stanley 1886–89. m. Bint Salam.

*MUSA   To Livingstone 1872; last journey. Stanley 1874–77. M 3 Dec. 1877. (To be distinguished from Musa from Johanna, who deserted Livingstone in Sep. 1866.)

*MWINYA M'FAUMI (MOENI FALUMI)   To Livingstone 1872; last journey. Stanley 1874 onwards. Deserted.

PRICE, SIMON   Nasik School. Livingstone 1866–70. Deserted. Trading in interior 1872.

RAHAN   Served with RN at Rangoon 1852. Speke 1860–61 (Speke's servant). Sent back with despatches & specimens Oct. 1861.

*RAMADHAN   To Livingstone 1872; last journey. Stanley 1874–75. Killed in battle Vinyata 25 Jan. 1875.

*RASASE   To Livingstone 1872; last journey. Stanley 1874–76. Honourably discharged Ujiji May–Aug. 1876.

REUBEN (SMITH?)   Nasik school. Livingstone 1866. Stayed at Mataka's July 1866.

ROJAB   *See* Kirango.

*ROJABU   From Bagamoyo. Stanley 1871–72. To Livingstone 1872; last journey. Stanley 1874 onwards, but fate unknown.

*RUTTON, BENJAMIN   Nasik school. To Livingstone 1872; last journey. M 24 Sep. 1875 Frere Town.

RUTTON, JAMES   Nasik school. Livingstone 1866–71. Killed at Bambarre 4 Feb. 1871.

*RUTTON, RICHARD   Nasik school. To Livingstone 1872; last journey. Servant to J. T. Last, CMS Mombasa 1875. M 24 Sep. 1875 Frere Town. m. Janet 30 Mar. 1875 (d. 17 Feb. 1880).

*SABURI   Stanley 1871–72. To Livingstone 1872; last journey. Stanley 1874–77. M 3 Dec. 1877.

SADI BEN AHEDI   Trader in Masai country. Von der Decken 1862. New 1871. Thomson 1883–84. Exaggerated hazards of route to discourage competition.

+SADIKI Recruited on mainland; Speke 1861–63. Dead by 1871.

SAID BIN SALIM AL LAMKI b. Kilwa c1815 (son of Governor). Governor of Saadani. Burton 1857–59 (caravan leader). Speke 1860–61 (caravan leader but discharged sick). Governor of Unyanyembe until deposed 1878. d. cNov. 1879, Uyui.

*SARMEAN (KACHECHE 'The Weasel') Stanley 1871–72. To Livingstone 1872; last journey. Stanley 1874–77 (chief detective). M (Farmeen) 3 Dec. 1877. Transport to Buganda for Smith Mackenzie 1878–80. Thomson 1883–84 (commissariat). Harvey's hunting journey 1886–87. m. Amina (d. 24 Feb. 1877).

+SANGORO (MAHOKA) Recruited on mainland; Speke 1861–63 (Bombay's servant). Dead by 1871.

SCHAONGWE See Kiongwe.

*SHABA To Livingstone 1872; last journey. M 17 Aug. 1875. LMS Urambo; in charge of boat. d. 1883, Urambo, of smallpox.

*SHUMARI KHAMEES To Livingstone 1872; last journey. M 17 Aug. 1875.

SUDI, PETER See Tom.

*SUEDI (HAMADI SWADI) To Livingstone 1872; last journey. M 17 Aug. 1875.

*SUSI, ABDULLAH (DAVID) From Shupanga. Livingstone 1863–64; to India on *Lady Nyassa*. India 1864–65. Livingstone 1866–74 (head of department 1872–73; name on Livingstone tree). In England 1874. UMCA caravan leader 1875 onwards. CMS on mainland 1877. Stanley 1879–82. UMCA caravan leader 1883–91. Baptised David 23 Aug. 1886. m. Mochosi. d. 5 May 1891, Zan.

*THOMAS (KHAMEES) To Livingstone 1872; last journey. M 17 Aug. 1875.

*TOM SNOWBALL (PETER SUDI) To Livingstone 1872; last journey. M 17 Aug. 1875. UMCA service 1875–1907 onwards. Baptised Aug. 1878. m. Mary Hatosha 1878. With wife seized by slavers Aug. 1881; Peter released Dec., wife 1882. Gardener for UMCA Kiungani in 1907.

*TOWFIKA 1870 relief expedition to Livingstone; last journey. Stanley 1874–77. M 3 Dec. 1877.

*TWAKALI To Livingstone 1872; last journey. M (Juakali) 17 Aug. 1875.

+ULEDI b. c1850. Stanley 1874–77 (coxswain of *Lady Alice*; saved at least thirteen men from drowning). On mainland 1879. Stanley 1879–82. Stanley 1886–89.

ULEDI (ADEMASAKO) Yao. Freed slave. Speke 1860–63 (Grant's head servant). Stanley 1871 (sergeant, but demoted). Killed in battle 6 Aug. 1871.

ULEDI MANUA SERA See Manua Sera.

+ULEDI MAPENGO Slave of Majid. Speke 1860–63. In Unyanyembe 1871.

+*ULIMENGO b. c1841. Slave of Majid. Speke 1860–63 (goatherd). Stanley 1871–72. To Livingstone 1872; last journey. Stanley 1874–75. Killed in battle, Vinyata, 25 Jan. 1875. (Also known as Farjallah Chalinda.)

+UMBARI (AMBARI) Slave of Majid. Speke 1860–63. Stanley 1871–72. Cameron 1873–74; dismissed for theft.

197

WADI REHANI *See* Khatibu.

WADI SAFENI *See* Hassan Wadi Safeni.

*WAINWRIGHT, JACOB Yao. Nasik school. To Livingstone 1872; last journey (cut inscription on tree). England 1874. CMS Mombasa area 1875–77. M 24 Sep. 1875, Frere Town. Zan. 1879. CMS to Buganda 1880–81. Interpreter to Mutesa 1881 onwards. With LMS Urambo in 1891. d. April 1892, Urambo.

WAINWRIGHT, JOHN Yao. Nasik school. To Livingstone 1872; last journey 1872–73. Lost in interior 1873.

WEKOTANI Slave released July 1861. UMCA 1861–64; to India on *Lady Nyassa*. Dr Wilson's school Bombay 1864–65. Baptised John 10 Dec. 1865. Livingstone 1865–66. Stayed at Mponda's Sep. 1866. Assisted Livingstonia mission 1875–76.

*WELLINGTON, MATTHEW b. c1847. Yao, originally named Chengwimbe. Nasik school. To Livingstone 1872; last journey. CMS Frere Town 1875 onwards. M 24 Sep. 1875, Frere Town. IBEA Co 1890 onwards. PWD Kenya 1895–1911. d. 6 June 1935.

*ZAIDI Stanley 1871–72. To Livingstone 1872; last journey. Stanley 1874–77. M 3 Dec. 1877. With 3rd IAA expedition 1880.

GLOSSARY

The following are the principal African words—in most cases Swahili—to be found in this book. Where there are varied definitions, that chosen corresponds to the meaning in which it is used here. Some variant spellings are also given. The prefixes *Ki-* (for a language), *Wa-* (plural), *M-* (singular), and *Lu-*, *Ba-*, *Mu-* respectively in Buganda, are used with ethnic roots in many works on Africa. In the text the root alone, e.g. Ganda, Nyamwezi, is used, but quotations of course retain their original form.

abban	protector accompanying a traveller (Somali)
askari	armed retainer; soldier; used also broadly for the more responsible members of a caravan undertaking special duties
balozi	(*cf. balyuz* in Arabic) consul; envoy; also used loosely of any European
banyan	non-Muslim Indian
bara	the mainland or hinterland
barghumi	antelope horn used as a musical instrument
batela	a type of dhow
bhang, bangi	Indian hemp, cannabis
boma	protected enclosure
Bula Matari	Breaker of Rocks (Stanley's nickname)
bwana	master
dhoti, doti	piece of cloth, 2–4 yards long
diwani	public functionary
frasila	measure of weight, about 35 lb.
fundi	skilled workman or expert (e.g. in hunting)
hongo	road toll
joho	long loose coat or cloak, worn by well-to-do people
jumbe	chief, headman
kabaka	the king of Buganda (Ganda)
kaniki	dark blue calico or cotton cloth, worn by women
kanzu	long-sleeved calico gown worn by men
khambi	mess; group of porters
khoja	Indian of a Muslim sect
kirangozi, kiongozi	guide; leader of a caravan

kitanda	wooden-framed bedstead
kitongole	fief of the Kabaka (Ganda)
liwali	official representing the Sultan of Zanzibar
mbugu	bark-cloth (Ganda)
merikani	unbleached calico sheeting first introduced from USA
mganga	African doctor
mkafiri, kafiri	unbeliever
mzee	an elder
mzungu	a European
nahoda	captain of a vessel
naibere	flowing robe worn from shoulder (Kikuyu)
ndugu	brother; kinsman; fellow tribesman
nyanza	stretch of water (Bantu)
nyapara, mnyapara	headman of a group of porters or askari
pagazi, mpagazi	caravan porter
pombe	beer made from grain or fruit
posho	rations
ruga ruga	irregular troops; bandits
seedi	an African, normally a freed slave (from Hindustani, sidi)
seyyid	prince (title of Sultan of Zanzibar)
shamba	garden; plantation
shauri	discussion; advice
tembe	flat-roofed house
ugali	stiff porridge
wadi	son of
wanguana	free men; normally used of freed ex-slaves from Zanzibar and the coast
zomiri, zumari	wooden pipe with harsh piercing tone

BIBLIOGRAPHY

Manuscript Collections

The principal relevant material consulted is listed in outline, and the abbreviation used for citation in notes appears after the name of each collection.

Church Missionary Society, London (CMS)

Committee Minutes, letter books, and correspondence with missionaries regarding the Nasik School and the establishment of the East African Mission, in the coastal area, and the Nyanza Mission, in Buganda. The manuscript of Carus Farrar's narrative. Accounts from Smith Mackenzie, 1876–81.

Livingstone Memorial, Blantyre (LM)

Original Livingstone letters, notebooks and other sources for his last journey, 1866–73. For convenience, these are usually cited by the number given to the photocopies in the National Library of Scotland, but the originals have been checked to clarify some doubtful readings.

National Library of Scotland, Edinburgh (NLS)

Original letters of Livingstone and his family. Photocopies of material in the Livingstone Memorial, Blantyre.

Public Record Office, London (PRO)

Slave Trade Correspondence, FO 84. Treasury Records T1/7426A have the original pay list of Livingstone's followers, 1874.

Rhodes House Library, Oxford (RH)

Correspondence of Livingstone, Waller and Oswell. Waller's diaries and notebooks, including *Notes, from Chuma and Susi concerning their travels with Dr Livingstone 1865 to 1874* (MSS Afr. $5\frac{16}{4}$, cited as Waller NB). The Pocock Diaries 1874–77, cited as PD.

Royal Commonwealth Society, London (RCS)

Papers of Sir John Gray, including copies of material in the Zanzibar

Archives. Memorandum by E. C. Lanning on the Emin Pasha Relief Expedition star and copy of the nominal roll of the Expedition. Correspondence with Dr A. J. Keevill on Jacob Wainwright. Letters from Livingstone to Admiral Grey. Unpublished typescripts listed below.

Royal Geographical Society, London (RGS)

Correspondence with Burton, Speke, Grant, Livingstone, Stanley, Stairs and Waller. Correspondence with Euan Smith and list of Livingstone Medal recipients. Diaries, Notebooks, and pay list of V. Lovett Cameron. List of Porters engaged by Johnston and Thomson, 1879. Photographs by Grant. Water colours by the Frere sisters.

School of Oriental and African Studies, London (SOAS)

London Missionary Society Archives, including correspondence with the mission at Lake Tanganyika.

Stanley Papers, Furzehill, Pirbright (SP)

Letters of Stanley and Sparhawk, from copies obtained by Richard Hall.

United Society for the Propagation of the Gospel (USPG)

Archives of the UMCA, including Bishop Mackenzie's Diary and correspondence from missionaries. Lovell Procter's Diary.

Zanzibar Archives (ZA)

Numerous extracts and notes from the Zanzibar Archives made by Sir John Gray are now in the Royal Commonwealth Society.

Unpublished Typescripts

Extracts from the Zanzibar Diary of the Universities' Mission to Central Africa 1864–1909. ZD. (From a copy by Sir John Gray, RCS)

MATSON, A. T. The Instructions issued in 1876 & 1878 to the Pioneer CMS Parties. (RCS)

SIMPSON, D. H. The African Members of Bishop Mackenzie's Mission. (RCS)

SIMPSON, D. H. The personnel of Livingstone's last journey. (RCS)

SMITH, E. W. An African Odyssey; the Story of two Porters, Mombai and Mabruki. (RCS)

VISRAM, R. G. David Livingstone and India.(University of Edinburgh thesis)

Newspapers and Journals

Central Africa, UMCA (CA)
Church Missionary Intelligencer (CMI)

Journal of the Royal Geographical Society (JRGS)
The Net cast in many waters
Northern Rhodesia Journal, Livingstone (NRJ)
Occasional Papers of the Central African Mission, 1–19, 1867–82 (OP)
Proceedings of the Royal Geographical Society (PRGS)
Report of the Oxford, Cambridge, Dublin, & Durham Mission to Central Africa (later Universities Mission to Central Africa) 1860–90 (UMCA Report)
Tanganyika (Tanzania) Notes and Records, Dar-es-Salaam (TNR)
The Times
Uganda Journal, Kampala (UJ)

Printed Books and Articles

The place of publication of books is London unless otherwise stated. Articles from periodicals in the preceding list are indicated by the abbreviations shown in brackets.

ANDERSON-MORSHEAD, A. E. M. 1955. *The History of the Universities' Mission to Central Africa.* 3 v.

ANSTEY, R. 1962. *Britain and the Congo in the Nineteenth Century.* Oxford.

ANSTRUTHER, I. 1956. *I presume; Stanley's triumph and disaster.*

BAKER, S. W. 1866. *Albert N'yanza, great basin of the Nile.* 2 v.

    1874. *Ismailia.* 2 v.

BARTON, S. S. 1876. *Memorials of Charles New.*

BARTTELOT, W. G. 1890. *The life of Edmund Musgrave Barttelot.* 3rd ed.

BAUMANN, O. 1894. *Durch Massailand zur Nilquelle.* Berlin.

BECKER, J. 1887. *La Vie en Afrique.* Bruxelles. 2 v.

BENNETT, N. R. 1960. 'Captain Storms in Tanganyika', *TNR*, No. 54, 51–63.

    ed., 1969. *From Zanzibar to Ujiji. The journal of Arthur W. Dodgshun 1877–1879.* Boston.

    1964. 'Stanley and the American Consuls at Zanzibar', *Essex Institute Historical Collections*, v. 100, 41–68.

    ed. 1970. *Stanley's Despatches to the New York Herald.* Boston.

    & YLVISAKER, M., eds. 1971. *The Central African Journal of Lovell J. Procter.* Boston.

BENTLEY, W. H. 1900. *Pioneering on the Congo.* 2 v. Oxford.

BLAIKIE, W. G. 1880. *The Personal Life of David Livingstone.*

BRIDGES, R. C. 1971. 'John Hanning Speke; negotiating a way to the Nile', (Ed.) R. I. Rotberg, *Africa and its explorers*, 95–137. Harvard.

BURTON, I. 1893. *The Life of Captain Sir Richd F. Burton.* 2 v.

BURTON, R. F. 1966. *First Footsteps in East Africa*, (Ed.) Gordon Waterfield.

    1860. *The Lake Regions of Central Africa.* 2 v.

    1859. 'The Lake Regions of Central Equatorial Africa', *JRGS* XXIX, 1–464.

    1872. *Zanzibar; City, Island, and Coast.* 2 v.

CAMERON, V. L. 1877. *Across Africa.* 2 v.

CHADWICK, O. 1959. *Mackenzie's Grave*

CHAMBERLIN, D. 1940. *Some Letters from Livingstone 1840-1872.*

COUPLAND, R. 1945. *Livingstone's Last Journey.*

 1939. *The Exploitation of East Africa 1856-1890.*

CRAWFORD, T. W. W. 1965. 'Account of the life of Matthew Wellington in his own words, and of the death of David Livingstone and the journey to the coast', *NRJ* VI, 99-102 (from typescript dated 1911. See also under Rampley).

CUMMING, R. 1973. 'A note on the history of Caravan Porters in East Africa', *Kenya Historical Review*, I, 109-38.

DAWSON, E. C. 1905. *James Hannington.*

 ed. 1888. *The Last Journals of Bishop Hannington.*

DEBENHAM, F. 1955. *The way to Ilala; David Livingstone's pilgrimage.*

DEVEREUX, W. C. 1869. *A Cruise in the 'Gorgon'.*

FAULKNER, H. 1868. *Elephant haunts.*

FORAN, W. R. 1937. *African Odyssey; the life of Verney Lovett-Cameron.*

FOSKETT, R., ed. 1964. *The Zambesi Doctors; David Livingstone's Letters to John Kirk 1858: 1872.* Edinburgh.

 ed. 1965. *The Zambesi Journal and Letters of Dr John Kirk.* Edinburgh. 2 v.

FRASER, A. Z. 1913. *Livingstone and Newstead.*

GALTON, F. 1856. *The Art of Travel.* 2nd ed.

GIRAUD, V. 1890. *Les Lacs de l'Afrique Equatoriale.* Paris.

GOODWIN, H. 1865. *Memoir of Bishop Mackenzie.* 2nd ed.

GRANT, J. A. 1885. *Khartoom as I saw it.*

 1864. *A walk across Africa; or domestic scenes from my Nile journal.*

GRAY, SIR J. M. 1947. 'Ahmed bin Ibrahim—the first Arab to reach Buganda', *UJ* XI, 80-97.

 1958. 'Albrecht Roscher', *TNR* No. 50, 71-84.

 1966. 'The Correspondence of Dallington Maftaa', *UJ* XXX, 13-24.

 1949. 'Livingstone's Muganda servant', *UJ* XIII, 119-29 (also note by H. B. Thomas, *UJ* XXVIII, 99-100, 1964).

 1953. 'Speke and Grant', *UJ* XVII, 146-60.

 1957. 'Trading expeditions from the coast to Lakes Tanganyika and Victoria before 1857', *TNR* No. 49, 226-46; No. 58, 174, 1962.

GRAY, R. & BIRMINGHAM, D., eds. 1970. *Pre-Colonial African Trade.*

HALL, R. 1974. *Stanley: an adventurer explored.*

HEANLEY, R. M. 1888. *A memoir of Edward Steere.*

HOHNEL, L. von. 1894. *Discovery of Lakes Rudolf and Stefanie.* 2 v.

HOLLINGSWORTH, L. W. 1953. *Zanzibar under the Foreign Office 1890-1913.*

HOLLIS, SIR C. 1958. 'Von der Decken', *TNR* No. 50, 63-67.

HORE, A. B. 1889. *To Lake Tanganyika in a bath chair.*

HORE, E. C. 1892. *Tanganyika: eleven years in Central Africa.*

INSTITUT ROYAL COLONIAL BELGE. 1951. *Biographie Colonial Belge.* v. II. Bruxelles.

 1952. *La Force Publique de sa naissance à 1914.* Bruxelles.

JACKSON, SIR F. 1930. *Early days in East Africa.*

JAMES, F. L. 1888. *The unknown Horn of Africa.*

JAMESON, J. S. 1890. *Story of the Rear Column of the Emin Pasha Relief Expedition.*

JOHNSON, W. P. C1924. *My African reminiscences 1875–1895.*

JOHNSTON, H. H. 1897. *British Central Africa.*

1886. *The Kilima-njaro Expedition.*

1895. *The River Congo.* 4th ed.

1923. *The Story of my life.*

1902. *The Uganda Protectorate.* 2 v.

KERSTEN, O. 1869. *Baron Carl Claus von der Decken's Reisen in Ost-Afrika.* 2 v.

KRAPF, J. L. 1860. *Travels, Researches, and Missionary Labours.*

LAMDEN, S. C. 1963. 'Some Aspects of Porterage in East Africa', *TNR* No. 61, 155–64.

(LEBLOND, G.), ed. 1884. *A l'assaut des Pays Nègres.* Paris.

LIVINGSTONE, D. & C. 1865. *Narrative of an Expedition to the Zambesi and its tributaries* (see also under H. Waller & J. P. R. Wallis).

LONG, C. CHAILLE. 1876. *Central Africa.*

LUGARD, F. D. 1893. *The Rise of our East African Empire.* 2 v.

MAITLAND, A. 1971. *Speke.*

MAPLES, E. 1898. *Chauncy Maples . . . by his sister.* 2nd ed.

MAURICE, A. 1957. *H. M. Stanley: Unpublished letters.*

MIDDLETON, D., ed. 1969. *The Diary of A. J. Mounteney Jephson.*

MOLONEY, J. A. 1893. *With Captain Stairs to Katanga.*

MOUNTENEY-JEPHSON, A. J. 1890. *Emin Pasha and the Rebellion at the Equator.*

NEW, C. 1873. *Life, Wanderings, and Labours in Eastern Africa.*

OLIVER, R. & MATHEW, G., eds. 1963. *History of East Africa,* I. Oxford.

OSWELL, W. E. 1900. *William Cotton Oswell Hunter and Explorer.* 2 v.

PARKE, T. H. 1891. *My personal experiences in Equatorial Africa.*

PERHAM, M. & BULL, M., eds. 1959. *The Diaries of Lord Lugard.* 3 v.

PETERS, C. 1891. *New light on Dark Africa.*

PRICE, R. (?1878). *Private Journal of the Rev. Roger Price.* Privately printed.

PRIDMORE, F. & SIMPSON, D. H. 1970. 'Faithful to the end', *The Numismatic Circular,* LXXVIII, 192–96.

PRINS, A. H. J. 1961. *The Swahili-speaking peoples of Zanzibar and the East African Coast.*

RAMPLEY, W. J. 1930. *Matthew Wellington; sole surviving link with Dr Livingstone.*

RODWELL, E. 1972. *Coast Causerie.* Nairobi.

ROTBERG, R. I. 1971. *Joseph Thomson and the Exploration of Africa.*

ROWLEY, H. 1867. *The Story of the Universities' Mission to Central Africa.* 2nd ed.

RUSSELL, MRS C. E. B. 1935. *General Rigby, Zanzibar and the Slave Trade.*

SEAVER, G. 1957. *David Livingstone: his Life and Letters.*

SHEPPERSON, G., ed. 1965. *David Livingstone and the Rovuma.* Edinburgh.

SILLERY, A. 1940. 'Maizan', *TNR* No. 10, 89–91.

SIMMONS, J. 1941. 'A suppressed passage in Livingstone's Last Journal relating to the death of Baron von der Decken', *Journal of the Royal African Society,* v. 40, 335–46.

SMITH, E. W. 1957. *Great Lion of Bechuanaland; the Life and Times of Roger Price, Missionary.*

1955. 'The earliest ox-waggons in Tanganyika: an experiment which failed', *TNR* No. 40, 1–14; No. 41, 1–15.

SPEKE, J. H. 1863. *Journal of the Discovery of the Source of the Nile.*
    1864. *What led to the Discovery of the Source of the Nile.*
STANLEY, D., ed. 1909. *The Autobiography of Sir Henry Morton Stanley, G.C.B.*
STANLEY, H. M. 1885. *The Congo and the founding of its Free State.* 2 v.
    1872. *How I found Livingstone.*
    1890. *How I found Livingstone.* New and cheaper edition with a memoir of Dr Livingstone.
    1890. *In Darkest Africa.* 2 v.
    1893. *My dark companions and their strange stories.*
    1890. *My Kalulu, Prince, King, and slave; A Story of Central Africa.* New ed. (1873).
    1878. *Through the Dark Continent.* 2 v.
STANLEY, R. & NEAME, A., eds. 1961. *The Exploration diaries of H. M. Stanley.*
STEERE, E. 1876. *A walk to the Nyassa country 1876.* (Central African Mission Occasional Papers No. 5.)
STOCK, E. 1899. *The History of the Church Missionary Society.* 3 v.
TABLER, E. C., ed. 1963. *The Zambezi Papers of Richard Thornton.* 2 v.
THOMAS, H. B. 1950. 'The death of Dr Livingstone: Carus Farrar's Narrative', *UJ* XIV, 115–28.
    1951. 'Jacob Wainwright in Uganda', *UJ* XV, 204–5.
    1962. 'The Logistics of Caravan Travel', (Ed.) M. Posnansky, *The Nile Quest*, 12–15. Kampala.
    1960. 'Mohammed Biri', *UJ* XXIV, 123–26.
THOMSON, J. 1885. *Through Masai Land.*
    1881. *To the Central African Lakes and back.* 2 v.
THOMSON, J. B. 1896. *Joseph Thomson African Explorer.*
TROUP, J. ROSE. 1890. *With Stanley's Rear Column.*
WAKEFIELD, E. S. 1904. *Thomas Wakefield, Missionary and Geographical Explorer in East Equatorial Africa.*
WALLER, H., ed. 1874. *The Last Journals of David Livingstone.* 2 v.
WALLIS, J. P. R., ed. 1956. *The Zambezi Expedition of David Livingstone 1858–1863.* 2 v.
    ed. 1952. *The Zambesi Journal of James Stewart 1862–1863.*
WARD, G. 1927. *Father Woodward of U.M.C.A. A Memoir.*
    ed. 1902. *Letters of Bishop Tozer* . . .
    1898. *The Life of Charles Alan Smythies.*
WARD, H. 1890. *Five years with the Congo Cannibals.* 2nd ed.
    1893. 'Martyrs to a new Crusade', *English Illustrated Magazine*, 1893, 105–9.
    1891. *My life with Stanley's Rear Guard.*
    1910. *A voice from the Congo.*
WILLOUGHBY, J. C. 1889. *East Africa and its Big Game.*
WILSON, C. T. & FELKIN, R. W. 1882. *Uganda and the Egyptian Soudan.* 2 v.
WISSMANN, H. 1891. *My second journey through Equatorial Africa.*
WOLF, J. B., ed. 1970. *Missionary to Tanganyika 1877–1888: the Writings of Edward Coode Hore, Master Mariner.*
YOUNG, E. D. 1877. *Nyassa: a journal of adventures.*
    1868. *The Search after Livingstone.*

Official Publications

Correspondence with British Representatives and Agents abroad and reports from Naval Officers relating to the Slave Trade:
For 1878   C 2422 1879
For 1879   C 2720 1880
For 1880   C 3052 1881
For 1881   C 3160 1882
For 1882   C 3547 1883
For 1883   C 3849 1884.
Cited as STC followed by the year to which the correspondence related.
Despatches addressed by Dr Livingstone, Her Majesty's Consul, Inner Africa, to Her Majesty's Secretary of State for Foreign Affairs, in 1870, 1871 and 1872. C 598 1872.

NOTES

At the beginning of each chapter or portion of a chapter relating to a major expedition, the principal sources are listed, and these are not referred to in detail unless a point needs special explanation. Books and articles are cited by author and date as given in the Bibliography, but a few sources used once only, which have not been included there, are given in full. All unpublished material is listed with the source from which it comes.

CHAPTER 1

1 For the pre-European trade see Oliver & Mathew: 1963; Gray & Birmingham: 1970; Sir John Gray: 1957 & 1965.
2 Burton: 1872, II 406, 418–19.

CHAPTER 2

1 The first part of this chapter is based on Krapf: 1860.
2 Krapf to Hamerton 18–28 June 1849, ZA 1/3.
3 C.M.I., 1851, 42–44.
4 R. Burton to Norton Shaw 16 Nov. 1853, RGS.
5 Material on the Somali expedition is from Burton: 1966; Speke: 1864.
6 Extracts from contemporary reports are in Burton: 1966, 277–84.

CHAPTER 3

1 The main sources are Burton: 1859; Burton: 1860; Burton: 1872; Speke: 1863. For Maizan see Sillery: 1940.
2 Livingstone's notebook XIV, NLS 10729, 83; Burton: 1872, II 179–80; Speke: 1864, 176, 178, 210–12. His name is sometimes Africanised as Mombai.
3 Galton: 1856, 82.
4 Speke: 1864, 251, 261; Burton: 1872, II 315; Livingstone's notebook NLS 10731, 47.
5 Speke: 1864, 269–70. See also Burton: 1860, I 361–62 for this song.
6 For this dispute see Russell: 1935, 244–54, 261; Burton: 1860, II 382–83, 434–39.
7 Burton: 1872, II 388; Burton: 1860, II 171; Speke: 1864, 197. Livingstone's Journal 19 Nov. 1868, NLS 10734; Bennett: 1970, 476; Wilson & Felkin: 1882, I 133.
8 For Roscher see Gray: 1958.

CHAPTER 4

1 The main sources are Speke: 1863 and Grant: 1864.
2 Speke to RGS 25 Jan. 1860; Grant to Blanshard 8 Mar. 1861, RGS.

208

3 Russell: 1935, 87; Speke to RGS 1 Oct. 1860, RGS. Grant's photographs are in the RGS.
4 Speke to Rigby 12 Dec. 1860, RGS.
5 *Ibid.*
6 Speke to Sclater 22 Sep. 1860, RGS.
7 They remained at Unyanyembe for some time, and at least two did not leave Zanzibar for the Cape until January 1863; Devereux: 1869, 372–73.
8 Russell: 1935, 239.
9 Gray: 1853, 146–48; Bridges: 1971, 112–13; Baker: 1866, II 52, records his meeting with three of the deserters at Kamurasi's court in Jan. 1864.
10 *Illustrated London News* XLIII, 1863, 23.
11 Baker: 1866.
12 Grant: 1885, 36.
13 Gray: 1953, 146–47.
14 Engravings based on the photographs, but with considerable variations, are in Speke: 1863, facing 611; *Illustrated London News* XLIII, 1863, 5.
15 Sir A. Anson *About others and myself*: 1920, 264; Foskett: 1965, II 528.
16 Gray: 1953, 148–49. Copies of items in the Zanzibar Archives now in the RCS give further examples of Speke's continued interest in his 'faithfuls'.
17 Gray: 1953, 149; *The Times* 13 & 14 Aug. 1873; Baker: 1874, II 466; Long: 1876, 70, 134, 194; Stanley: 1872, 29, said he was dead by 1871.
18 Gray: 1953, 149–51; Maitland: 1971, 224; Waller: 1874, II 166.

CHAPTER 5

1 This account is based on Livingstone: 1865; Wallis: 1952; Wallis: 1956; Tabler: 1963; Foskett: 1964; Foskett: 1965; Shepperson: 1965.
2 *J.R.G.S.* XXXI, 1861, 273.
3 Devereux: 1869, 223; Bennett & Ylvisaker: 1971, 393.
4 Chamberlin: 1940, 267.
5 Livingstone to Admiral Grey 28 Oct. 1859, RCS.
6 For the UMCA see sources in footnote 1 and Goodwin: 1865; Rowley: 1867; Ward: 1902; Chadwick: 1959; Bennett & Ylvisaker: 1971; UMCA Reports; Anderson-Morshead: 1955.
7 For fuller details see D. H. Simpson *The African Members of Bishop Mackenzie's Mission*, RCS.
8 Rowley: 1867, 12, 17–18.
9 Bishop Mackenzie's Diary 16 July 1861, USPG Al (1) B.
10 Devereux: 1869, 182, 184, 186, 202, 231, 232.
11 Young: 1868, 23–28.
12 Rowley: 1867, 109, 371.
13 Livingstone to Waller 8 Aug. 1863, RH.
14 Livingstone to Waller 28 Nov. 1863, RH. It is not absolutely clear whether there were two or three batches of Johanna men.
15 Waller to Livingstone 3 Dec. 1863 copied by Dorothy Helly from Rhodesian Archives.
16 Waller's Journal 29 Mar. 1864, RH.
17 Seaver: 1957, 440–47, contains extracts from Livingstone's diary of the voyage.
18 Livingstone: 1865, 583.

CHAPTER 6

1 The main source is Waller: 1874, but many quotations are taken direct from Livingstone's journals.

2 Foskett: 1964, 116, 117; Blaikie: 1880, 351; Seaver: 1957, 478; Livingstone to Oswell 6 May 1865, RH.

3 For Livingstone's stay in India see Notebook I NLS 10719; Livingstone to Waller 27 Sep. 1865 & 20 Oct. 1865, RH.

4 Livingstone to Lord Russell 28 Nov. 1865, copied in NLS 10734; Livingstone to Tom Livingstone 2 Dec. 1865, NLS 10701 f 44.

5 Stock: 1899, II 173; Blaikie: 1880, 361; H. Gundert, *Biography of the Rev. Charles Isenberg*, 1885, 53–54, 72–77, 85–86.

6 There is no formal list of the Nasik boys. Livingstone refers to Gardner, Simon Price, Andrew, James Rutton, Reuben, Baraka, Mabruki, Abraham, and Richard Isenberg. Carus Farrar, in Thomas: 1950, 120, 126 gives Edward Gardiner, Simon Price, Abraham Pereira, Andrew Powell, James Brown, Richard Isenberg, Reuben Smith, Albert, and Nathaniel Cumba. Musa mentioned Albert Baraka—Young: 1868, 33. Nathaniel Cumba equals Mabruki by elimination, and by the fact that both remained with Livingstone up to the arrival of the second batch of Nasik boys.

7 Oswell: 1900, II 91; Price to Venn 10 Mar. 1866, CMS C I 3/067–069; Livingstone to John Wilson 24 Jan. 1872, NLS 1792 f 7.

8 Young: 1868, 18–22; Wekotani to Waller 30 Nov. 1865 & Chuma to Waller, 21 Sep. 1865, RH.

9 Livingstone to Waller, Nov. 1871, RH; Young: 1868, 163–64; Bennett & Ylvisaker: 1971, 146–47, 190, 278; *UMCA Report*, 1862, 38.

10 Chuma's story is in Waller's Notebook, RH; Class list in Bishop Mackenzie's Diary, USPG Al (1) B; Young: 1868, 17, 151; Rowley: 1867, 321–33; G. Smith, *The Life of John Wilson*, 1878, 385.

11 Foskett: 1964, 115–16; Livingstone to Thomas Livingstone, 2 Nov. 1865, NLS 10701 f 144.

12 Blaikie: 1880, 366–67.

13 Livingstone's Notebook I, 11 Feb. 1866, NLS 10719, 45—it is not clear who Dungudza was; Young: 1868, 70, 72–73.

14 Agreement copied in NLS 10734; STC 1866A, 96–97; NLS 10721, 9.

15 NLS 10719.

16 Entry for 9 Apr. in NLS 10720, 6.

17 Entry for 20 May, with Ben Ali's signature, NLS 10721, 7.

18 Entry for 17 July, NLS 10722, 16.

19 Diary NLS 10734; Livingstone to John Wilson, 24 Jan. 1872, NLS 7792 f 7.

20 Diary NLS 10734.

21 Entry for 14 June, NLS 10721, 28.

22 Livingstone to Thomas Livingstone, 28 Aug. 1866, NLS 10701 f 150; Diary NLS 10734; Seward to Chief Sec. Bombay, 25 Oct. 1866.

23 PRGS XII, 177.

24 Diary NLS 10734.

25 Livingstone to Waller, 3 Nov. 1866, RH; entries for 1 May 1866 NLS 10720, 34–35; 14 Aug. 1866 NLS 10722, 35–36.

26 Livingstone to Waller, 3 Nov. 1866, RH; Diary NLS 10734; Stanley: 1872, 441–42; Bennett: 1970, 53–54, 103.

27 One Johanna man had died: one deserted at Zanzibar: the rest returned home. Seward to Sunley 17 Dec. 1866; Sunley to Seward 23 Feb. 1867. Copies in NLS.

28 For the expedition see PRGS XI, 111–13, 124–48, 154–55; XII 10–11, 87, 89; Young: 1868; Faulkner: 1868.

29 Bennett & Ylvisaker: 1971, 147.

30 Young was told that he remained because of sore feet but Livingstone wrote to Waller, Nov. 1871, RH, that this was not so.

31 Livingstone to Waller, 3 Nov. 1866, RH.
32 Blaikie: 1880, 395.
33 Entry for 15 Jan. 1867, NLS 10725, 22–23.
34 Notebook, NLS 10725, 29.
35 Coupland: 1945, 66, 261. Note that 'Shortshanks' was not the Gogo chief who met Burton and Speke; he was dead by 1860. Janja may have been Ouled or Wulaydi, one of the 'Sons of Ramji'—STC 1868, 66; *PRGS* XII, 181.
36 Diary 13 Feb. 1867, NLS 10734.
37 Diary NLS 10734.
38 Notebook NLS 10762, 7, 8, 12.
39 Diary NLS 10734; Stanley: 1872, 448.
40 Coupland: 1945, 70–73; Foskett: 1964, 138–39; Livingstone to Barghash, 20 Apr. 1869.
41 Diary NLS 10734.
42 Foskett: 1964, 140–44; Livingstone to Kirk, 26 Nov. 1871, ZA 23.
43 Livingstone to Maclear, Sep. 1870.
44 *PRGS* XII, 206.
45 Livingstone to Kirk 30 Oct. 1871; Thomas: 1950, 120.
46 Entry for 15 Aug. 1871, NLS 10733, 22; Stanley: 1872, 465, 561–62.

CHAPTER 7

1 Kersten: 1869, II 356–57; Simmons: 1941, 335–46; Hollis: 1958, 63–67.
2 Extracts from ZA by Sir John Gray, RCS; Stanley: 1872, 29–30.
3 For this expedition see Stanley: 1872; Bennett: 1970.
4 Stanley's books have a misleading air of precision. The number of caravans is given as five and six in Stanley: 1872, 68; Bennett: 1970, 12. For other discrepancies see Bennett's footnotes.
5 *PRGS* XVI, 433–36, XV, 206–9. There is considerable controversy as to how far Kirk was negligent in this matter, and the extent to which he or Stanley persuaded the laggard expedition to set off.
6 Stanley: 1878, I 56. Manua Sera did not play a major part in this expedition, as he was absent at the coast for some months fetching medicine for Shaw— Stanley: 1872, 292, 604.
7 He is not clearly identifiable with any name in Speke's lists. It is tempting to equate him with Frij, whom Stanley called Ferrajji, Stanley: 1872, 29, but Frij was a 'faithful'.
8 Hall: 1974, 151–53.
9 Stanley: 1909, 256.
10 Livingstone has a circumstantial account of Bombay telling Stanley 'Uledi no come back master' in NLS 10731, 49, derived, presumably, from Stanley.
11 Gray: 1949, 119.
12 Abdul Kader asked for and was given his discharge. Cameron met him in July 1873, going to the coast with a caravan from Unyanyembe, and gave him some cloth—Cameron: 1877, I 124–25.
13 Livingstone's Diary, NLS 10734; Bennett: 1970, 51, 89; this is the simplest version.
14 Stanley: 1909, 266.
15 Notebooks NLS 10727, 16; 10729, 83; 10731, 24–26.
16 Stanley: 1909, 275–77.
17 Foskett: 1964, 155–57; Livingstone to Waller, Nov. 1871, RH; NLS 10727, 22.
18 List of men sent to Livingstone by Stanley, 27 May 1872, LM; W. S. Price, *Nassick Mission of the Church Missionary Society*, n.d., 7; Thomas: 1950, 116; Crawford: 1965, 100–1; Rampley: 1930, 26–29.

19 *PRGS* XVI, 382–83; Barton: 1876, 186. There is no positive evidence that any of New's recruits were included.
20 Stanley: 1872, 662; Stanley to *The Times* 21 Aug. 1872 says 25 of his own men enlisted. Contract of 27 May 1872 in Kirk to Lord Derby, No. 172, 8 Nov. 1877 FO 84/1486, PRO.
21 OP No. 4, 1869, 10.
22 Frere's Memo 1 Feb. 1873.
23 Hall: 1974, 207; Anstruther: 1956, 137, 140, 147, 172, 175, 181; Fraser: 1913, 198–201.

CHAPTER 8

1   The main source for this chapter is Waller: 1874, but many quotations are taken direct from Livingstone's journals or Waller's Notebook.
2   Livingstone to Agnes Livingstone, Sep. 1870.
3   NLS 10731, 43.
4   NLS 10732, 30. Ntaoéka had perhaps come from the coast with Stanley's expedition.
5   Livingstone to Stanley cJan. 1873 in Stanley, *How I found Livingstone*: 1890, lxx.
6   Livingstone to Maclear and Mann cJan. 1873.
7   List of men sent to Livingstone by Stanley, LM; NLS 10727, 43; Thomas: 1950, 117; Stanley, *How I found Livingstone*: 1890, lxx–lxxi.
8   NLS 10727, 43. Waller mistakenly transcribed this as Mabruki Speke. The Nasik Mabruki reached the coast—T1/7426A—so he was presumably picked up again at Unyanyembe in October 1873.
9   NLS 10732, 21; 10729, 27, 87.
10 Livingstone to Maclear and Mann cJan. 1873.
11 Waller NB, RH.
12 Debenham: 1955, 300–27 analyses the route; NLS 10729 23, 35–36, 37, 40; Waller NB, RH.
13 NLS 10728, 45.
14 NLS 10728.
15 Unless otherwise stated, all subsequent quotations are from Waller's Notebook.
16 Thomas: 1950, 119. A letter from Holmwood with some details from Majwara is in *PRGS* XVIII, 244–46, but it adds little to other sources.
17 Crawford: 1965, 100–1; Giraud: 1890, 28. Giraud asserted 'Suzi et Chuma me faisaient quelquefois l'honneur d'une visite' but he did not arrive at Zanzibar until 25 Aug. 1882 and Chuma made his will, presumably because of serious illness, on 25 September. Giraud proved particularly inept in dealing with Africans; his entire caravan deserted.
18 Dr Christie's name does not appear in Waller: 1874, II 315–16, but is in the proof sheets in RH.
19 This simple inscription has been given in varied forms; this version is taken from the earliest copy, E. J. Glave to Alfred Sharpe, 8 Sep. 1894, RGS, from a photograph in LM, and from the portion of the trunk in the RGS. This was sent to England in 1899 by R. Codrington, who cut down the tree because the ravages of insects were already affecting the inscription.
20 Crawford: 1965, 101.
21 Cameron: 1877, I facing 165.
22 See Cameron: 1877, I 167–68.
23 Thomas: 1950, 120.
24 Numerous letters from Prideaux in FO 84/1399, PRO; Waller's complaint of neglect of the Africans (II 345) does not seem to be justified. *PRGS* XVIII, 131, 181–82, 176–77, 222, 408; ZA 310 f 2.

25 *The Times*, 10 Apr. 1874.
26 *The Times*, 11 Apr. 1874; Stock: 1899, III 78; *PRGS* XVIII, 450.
27 *PRGS* XVIII, 254; Stock: 1899, III 78; *The Times* 22 Apr. 1874; Fraser: 1913, 230–31; Waller: 1874, II 230.
28 ZA 310.
29 Fraser: 1913, 211–13, 215.
30 *PRGS* XVIII, 300, 510–11, 495.
31 Fraser: 1913, 233–34; Oswell: 1900, II 133; Waller: 1874, I ix; II 5, 324; Waller Notebook, RH.
32 24 Sep. 1874, NLS 10708; PD E2; Fraser: 1913, 220–28.
33 Pridmore & Simpson: 1970, 192–96, but see also D. H. Simpson: *The personnel of Livingstone's last journey*, RCS for minor modifications; Euan Smith to RGS 1 July 1875, 20 Aug. 1875, RGS; the RGS minutes do not include any decision on his suggestion about Halima's medal.

CHAPTER 9

1 The main source for this chapter is Cameron: 1877. Additional information is in *PRGS* XVII–XX: Cameron's diaries 11 Nov. 1873–28 Feb. 1874 and 3 Mar.–18 May 1874 are in *PRGS* XIX, 136–55, *JRGS* XLV, 197–228, and his original diary 14 Apr.–24 Sep. 1875 is in RGS VLC, 4c. Names have been added from Cameron's pay list in the Kirk correspondence in the RGS.
2 Cameron: 1877, I 35, 39–41, 51, 156, 196, 311, 331; *PRGS* XVII, 335; VLC 4b 3 May, RGS.
3 For the voyage round Lake Tanganyika see *JRGS* XLV, 197–228.
4 VLC 4c, 17–18, RGS.
5 7–8 Sep. 1975, VLC 4c, 102–3.
6 VLC 4b, RGS.
7 VLC 4b, RGS.
8 Foran: 1937, 361, 365.
9 VLC 1c, RGS; fuller copy in Kirk correspondence, RGS.
10 VLC 3c, 16; Pay list.

CHAPTER 10

1 For this expedition see Stanley: 1878; Stanley & Neame: 1961; Bennett: 1970; PD.
2 PD E2.
3 PD 8–11, but he does not record Mabruki Speke's death.
4 PD 27, 42; Stanley: 1878, II 89.
5 Gray: 1966, 18, 23–24; OP 7 1877, 18; Stanley: 1877, I 76, 322; Bennett: 1970, 474; Stanley & Neame: 1961, 101; PD 43–44.
6 The following pages draw extensively on PD.
7 Gray: 1966, 13–24.
8 Hall: 1974, 63; PD 78, 118.
9 The RGS has a group by Catherine, and separate portraits of Uledi, Majwara, Mameshai and Mameumi (women) by Lily. For Hasina and Alice see PD 51 & *The Net* 1878, 154–56.
10 The complex story of the pay claims is to be found in Kirk to Lord Derby, 8 Nov. 1877 and enclosures, FO 84/1486; Kirk to Lord Derby, 3 May 1878, FO 84/1514; Kirk to Lord Salisbury, 4 July 1878, FO 84/1515, PRO; extracts from ZA in Gray collection, RCS. Prideaux's pay list is in the PRO; T1/7426A.
11 A. Sparhawk to Stanley, 4 July 1878, SP; Johnston: 1886, 60–61.
12 Kirk to Lord Derby, 1 May 1878, FO 84/1514.

H   213

13 Bennett: 1964, 56. It is not known what happened to the unpresented medals. Some have appeared in the sale rooms.

CHAPTER 11

1 *CMI* 1881, 376–77; Anderson-Morshead: 1955, I 38–39.
2 Wakefield: 1904, *passim.*
3 Heanley: 1888; *UMCA Report* 1875, 7; Steere: 1876.
4 Maples: 1898, 60–62; Heanley: 1888, 167.
5 Heanley: 1888, 189–92; Johnson: 1924, 18–25, 30; Maples: 1898, 91; ZD 21–22; *UMCA Report* 1877, 5; STC 1878, 157–58.
6 Johnson: 1924, 30; ZD 23; Maples: 1898, 106, 116; Ward: 1927, 14; *The Net* 1878, 154–56; 1881, 159. He was baptised the same day as Caroline Hasina.
7 *UMCA Report* 1878, 10; 1881–82, 17–18; ZD 24, 34–35, 38–39; Heanley: 1888, 229, 340; CA, I 28, 81–83, 91–93, 1888; Maples: 1898, 182.
8 Young: 1877, 39–40, 51, 52, 56, 58, 59, 63–66, 82–83, 147, 164, 183–84, 218–19.
9 *CMI* 1875, 146–48, 159–60, 315–16; 1876, 205, 212, 214; 1877, 57–58; 1881, 33–34, 376–77, 440; Price's diary 6 Dec. 1874, 22 Jan. 1875, 25 July 1875, CMS CA5/023; ZD 9, 12.
10 *CMI* 1879, 537–38.
11 Nyanza Sub-Committee 10 Mar. 1876; CMS to Kirk 7 Apr. 1876, CA 6/L 1; Price's diary 5, 6, 8 May 1876, CA 5/023. All CMS.
12 CMS to Smith 5 May 1876; Mackay to CMS 27 July 1876, CA 6/022; *CMI* 1876, 571, 573, 574.
13 *PRGS* NS, I 532.
14 *CMI* 1876, 665; A. T. Matson: *The instructions issued . . . to the Pioneer C.M.S. Parties*, 14, 16, 42, 35, 44.
15 Wilson & Felkin: 1882, I 27–97, 108, 349–50; Gray: 1966, 20–21; *CMI* 1878, 119–20.
16 *CMI* 1877, 647, 649; 1879, 89; Price: 1878, 122.
17 STC 1879, 263–64; 1880, 280–81, 301–2; ZA 310 f 28. See F/Y A6/1 CMS for details of Smith Mackenzie's activities.
18 *CMI* 1879, 606, 711, 719, 725; 1880, 417–18, 421, 422; 1881, 618–19.
19 Thomson: 1881, I 34; *CMI* 1882, 95, 486, 489; Thomas: 1951, 204–5.
20 Leblond: 1884, 1–187.
21 Price: 1878, 24, 28–29, 47, 52, 57, 92, 99, 140; Smith: 1957, 208–55; Smith: 1955; Bennett: 1969, ix–xvii.
22 Hore: 1892, ix, 33, 34, 48, 50, 81, 110, 112, 184–85, 203, 208, 220–21, 248; Wolf: 1970, 27–28, 33–35, 44, 60–62; Bennett: 1969, 12, 57, 58, 62, 64.
23 Hore: 1892, 248–50, 259, 261, 272; Hore: 1889, 54–55, 59, 67, 108, 123, 192, 198–99.
24 E. Muxworthy to Thompson, 30 Oct. 1883, 20 Dec. 1886; W. Draper to Thompson, 9 Dec. 1891, 16 Apr. 1892; T. F. Shaw to Thompson, 16 Apr. 1892; LMS in SOAS.
25 Information from Dr A. J. Keevill and the Moravian Missionary Society, RCS.

CHAPTER 12

1 Anstey: 1962, 59–64.
2 The main source is Thomson: 1881.
3 *PRGS* NS, II 722; OP 12, 6. The list is in the Keith Johnston correspondence, RGS; most of it is reproduced in Rotberg: 1971, 306–14.
4 *PRGS* NS, I 670.
5 For the IAA see Coupland: 1939, 331–32; STC 1878, 163; 1879, 211; 1880,

345; Becker: 1887; Thomas: 1960, 123–26; Bennett: 1960. Becker is very valuable for details of caravan organisation, etc.; see also his reaction to Thomson's criticisms of the IAA, II 116 ff.

6 STC 1878, 237; 1879, 210; 1880, 293.
7 For the elephant expedition see *TNR*, 11, 64–65; 12, 61–63, 1941; STC 1879, 215, 233; Becker: 1887, I 435–37, 442–44; *PRGS* NS, I 382.
8 *PRGS* NS, II 561, 558.
9 STC 1880, 349, 364–65; *TNR* 12, 62.
10 *PRGS* NS, II 562; Rotberg: 1971, 107.
11 *PRGS* NS, II 351, 353, 741–42, 761, I 533; Waller to RGS 2 Feb. 1880, RGS.
12 STC 1879, 251; 1880, 214–15, 365–66; M. A. Pringle, *A Journey in East Africa towards the Mountains of the Moon*, 1886, 43–44; *PRGS* NS, III 238–40, 355–56.
13 *PRGS* NS, IV 66–73; Thomson: 1896, 79–87.

CHAPTER 13

1 Anstey: 1962, 202–3.
2 STC 1879, 214, 226. The main source for the foundation of the Congo Free State is Stanley: 1885; his letters are from Maurice: 1957.
3 Johnston: 1885, 35; Johnston: 1923, 139; Stanley: 1893, 126–27.
4 Stanley to Greffulhe 11 May 1879, SP; STC 1879, 231; Bennett: 1964, 52–54.
5 Bentley: 1900, I 396.
6 STC 1881, 159.
7 Brazza, originally in the service of the IAA French Committee, became the founder of the French Congo.
8 Stanley: 1893; Johnston: 1895, 126; Bentley: 1900, I 302–3, 385–86, 405–6, 417, 426–41 (two episodes involving Susi and Robert Feruzi), 454, 463–65.
9 Stanley: 1909, 347–48.
10 *Biographie Colonial Belge* II, 520. Bruxelles.
11 Bentley: 1900, I 463.
12 *La Force Publique* ... 12, 16, 45, 57, 109, 111, 113, 120, 783; Johnston: 1895, 34, 66, 111, 213–14; Wissmann: 1891, 76, 137–38, 140, 198, 235–38, 300.
13 *Midland Evening News*, 28 Aug. 1895; Chuma's will copied from ZA by Sir John Gray.
14 Stanley to Grant, 14 Jan. 1886, RGS.
15 For Susi's mission service see CA, II 41, 73, III 83, 138, 151–52, IV 2, 26–27, 177, IX 120–21; ZD 46–51; Ward: 1898, 32–38, 41, 47, 64–69, 128–35; *UMCA Report*, 1886–87, 22.

CHAPTER 14

1 For von der Decken see Russell: 1935, 87, 271; Hollis: 1958; *TNR* No. 58–59, 51, 1962; No. 64, 10, 14, 1965; Kersten: 1869, I 141, 151, 171, 229; *JRGS* XXXV, 15.
2 New: 1873, 286–90. Aba Shora was killed by the Masai at the Golbanti Mission in 1886; Wakefield: 1904, 243. Tofiki does not seem to be identifiable with either of the two men of that name with Livingstone on his last journey. Sadi gave Wakefield much information on trade routes in the interior. *JRGS* XL, 303–39.
3 *JRGS* XLV, 414–20; Barton: 1876, 198–214.
4 Rotberg: 1971, 137; for the expedition see Thomson: 1883.
5 STC 1883, 88.
6 Rotberg: 1971, 142–43.
7 For this expedition see Johnston: 1886.

8   Johnston: 1923, 326.
9   Johnston: 1923, 138, 164–69; David Virapan accompanied Johnston to west Africa in 1886, but killed a man in the delirium following fever. After being detained for a time he recovered, went back to Ceylon, married, and became a steward on a liner.
10 Dawson: 1905, 180–251, 295, 297.
11 *CA* IV, 132–34; for Hannington's last journey see Dawson: 1888 and Dawson: 1905.
12 *CMI* 1886, 205. Jones was later ordained priest: he also supervised a settlement for freed slaves. *CMI* 1905, 693–94.
13 UJ, VIII 25, XIII 16, 20, 22, XXIII 29–36.
14 For this expedition see Hohnel: 1894.
15 James: 1888, *passim.*
16 Jackson: 1930, 104.
17 Willoughby: 1889, 38–39, 236–37, 252–53.
18 Perham & Bull: 1959, I 262, 298, II 61; two other veterans of Teleki's journey were still alive in 1954. See *Kenya African Land Development Report Jan–June 1954,* plate 66.

CHAPTER 15

1   The main sources are Stanley: 1890; Jameson: 1890; Middleton: 1969; Mounteney-Jephson: 1890; Parker: 1891; Troup: 1890; Ward: 1890, 1891, 1893, 1910; Barttelot: 1890.
2   Holmwood to S of S, 25 Feb. 1887, FO 84/1851, PRO.
3   Xerox copy of nominal roll of Stanley's expedition (incomplete), in office of Mackenzie Dalgety, Nairobi, RCS.
4   *The Times,* 10 Apr. 1890.
5   E. Marston, *How Stanley wrote 'In Darkest Africa',* 1890, 16, 17, 21.
6   Ward: 1893, 109; Ward: 1910, 171–77.
7   Speke: 1863, 175–76, 425, 473.
8   Minutes of Stanley Reception Committee, 14 & 20 Apr. 1890; Stairs to RGS, 18 Apr. 1890; Stanley to RGS, 10 July 1890, RGS; Memorandum with rubbing of medal by E. C. Lanning, 13 Oct. 1970, RCS.
9   Peters: 1891.

CHAPTER 16

1   Hollingsworth: 1953, 88–90; *Papers relating to Slave Trade and Slavery in Zanzibar,* C 6702, 1892, 4–5; *Zanzibar Gazette* III, 1894, 19 Oct., 9–10; Lamden: 1963; Cumming: 1973; *Report by Sir A. Hardinge on the conditions and progress of the East Africa Protectorate* . . . C 8683, 1897, 51–53; *East Africa Protectorate Orders in Council* . . . (*1876–1902*), 1903, 28, 123–29.
2   A marching song of the Carrier Corps epitomised the diminishing returns of this costly method of transport:

> We are the porters who carry the food
> Of the porters who carry the food . . .

and so *ad absurdum.* Thomas: 1962, 12.
3   H. H. Austin's Diary, RH; Moloney: 1893, 23–24; Jackson: 1930, 33, 53, 55, 147, 158, 187; Perham & Bull: 1959, I 290; Baumann: 1894, 370–77.
4   Letter of 14 June 1892, ZA.
5   Perham & Bull: 1959, I–III *passim*; Lugard: 1893, I 300–2, II 243–44.
6   Johnston: 1897, 82, 90, 96; Johnston: 1923, 249, 260, 266, 268, 277, 326;

216

7 Johnston: 1902, I 248, 250; *B.C.A. and Nyasaland Blue Books.*
   CA XXVI, 32–33, 36.
8 Jackson: 1930, 104–5.
9 CO 533/92 38731; CO 533/112 308; Rodwell: 1972, 84–85; in *CMI* 1906,
   213–14, there is a brief account of Matthew Wellington by Mrs J. A. Bailey;
   Crawford: 1911 tells his story in the first person; Rampley: 1930 elaborates it
   as a third person account with historical background. He was a Yao, named
   Chengwimbe, enslaved as a boy of about 10 (the details in the two accounts
   differ) and then in the service of several masters in the Lake Nyasa area. He was
   later sold at Kilwa to an Arab who took him to Zanzibar and thence north in a
   dhow. He was rescued from this by HMS *Thetis* and landed in Aden; soon after
   he was taken to India and entered the Nasik school in 1865, at the age of about
   18.

INDEX

Personal names are given in the form most frequently used, with contemporary ranks and titles, and with alternatives and additional identifications in brackets where applicable. See also 'Who's Who of Africans' on pp. 191–8. Races and languages appear under the same heading, e.g. Masai.

Aba Shora, 165
Abban, 8, 9, 74
Abbe Gunja, 7, 133, 138
Abdalla ben Pisila, 5
Abdallah, 170, 171
Abdallah bin Juma, 183
Abdio ben Nur, 74
Abdul Kader, 76
Abdullah bin Nasib, 152
Abdullah, Sgt, 180
Abraham (Pereira?), 54, 59, 60, 64, 66, 67–8, 70–1, 72
Abu Ahmed, 37
Aden, 8, 9,23, 37, 170, 176, 177
Advance, 179, 180, 182
Africa: lakes of, 5, 6, 10; maps of, 1, 10; missions in, 5, 39, 88, 131, 133ff., 188; scramble for, 143, 185; trade in, 2–4; transport problems, 1–2
Africans, attitude to: Burton, 18, 20, 23; Cameron, 109; Hore, 151; Livingstone, 40, 57, 82, 88–9, 103; Peters, 184; Speke, 23–4; Stanley, 76–7, 82, 114–15, 159, 177–8, 183, 184; Thomson, 148, 184
Agnes, 146, 147, 150
Ahmed (interpreter), 8
Ahmed bin Ibrahim, 3
Akaheka, 65
Akida, 124
Albert, Lake, 36, 53, 120, 122, 123, 125, 179
Alexanderson, Capt. Carl, 112
Alexandria, 38
Ali, 90
Ali bin Salim, 76
Ali ibn Mshangama, 112
Alice (Robert Feruzi's daughter), 129
Alington, Rev. C., 51, 121
Almass Bischibu, 172, 174
Alvez (African trader), 110–11
Amice Amfalla, 122
Amoda, 52, 54, 56, 57, 64, 68, 70, 71, 84, 85, 89, 93, 96, 97, 115, 118, 123
Andersen, Hans Christian, 103–4

Andrade, Gaetano, 10, 11, 17, 20, 21, 23
Andrew Mnubi, 116, 145
Andrew (Powell?), 54, 61
Anson, Capt. A., 37, 38
Antonie, Joseph, 45, 46
Antonio, 62, 64
April, 25
Arabs: Burton's view of, 18, 20; caravans, 3, 14, 67, 95; conflicts with Africans, 29, 69, 72, 78–9; Livingstone and, 66–73; Speke and, 29, 31; trade in Africa, 3, 13, 18, 19, 24, 29, 71, 152; way of life, 18, 68, 124
Arimasau, 50
Asikari, 145
Asmani (guide), 79, 80, 81, 82, 84, 98, 107, 108, 110
Asmani (Othman), 78, 84
Association International du Congo, 158
Athmani, 170
Awathe, 71

Bachit, 180
Bachoro, 52
Bagamoyo, 3, 15, 16, 26, 75, 76, 86, 87, 89, 99, 100, 105, 115, 118, 133, 138, 141, 152, 180, 184, 187
Bahati, 96
Baines, Thomas, 39, 40, 44
Baker, Samuel W., 36, 38, 53, 183
Bakunu, 126
Baluchis, 11, 12–13, 14, 15–16, 18, 19, 20, 21, 22, 23, 26, 53, 115, 164
Bambarre, 70, 72
Bana Kheri, 5–6, 7
Banalya, 179
Banana Point, 156, 178
Bangweolo, Lake, 67, 68, 90, 92, 93, 124, 189
Baptist Mission in Congo, 157, 158
Baraka, 26, 27, 29, 30, 31, 32, 35, 38, 76, 80
Baraka (Albert?), 54–5, 59, 64, 65, 66
Baraka (Galla), 74
Baraka (with Stanley), 84
Bardera, 74

219